FROM THE HEART
OF THE AMERICAN CHURCH

FROM THE HEART
OF THE AMERICAN CHURCH

Catholic Higher Education
and American Culture

DAVID J. O'BRIEN

ORBIS BOOKS

Maryknoll, New York 10545

The Catholic Foreign Mission Society of America (Maryknoll) recruits and trains people for overseas missionary service. Through Orbis Books, Maryknoll aims to foster the international dialogue that is essential to mission. The books published, however, reflect the opinions of their authors and are not meant to represent the official position of the society.

Copyright © 1994 by David J. O'Brien

Published by Orbis Books, Maryknoll, NY 10545-0308

Manufactured in the United States of America

Library of Congress Cataloging-in-Publication Data

O'Brien, David J.
    From the heart of the American church : Catholic higher education and American culture / David J. O'Brien.
        p.   cm.
    Includes bibliographical references.
    ISBN 0-88344-994-3 (hard) — ISBN 0-88344-985-4 (pbk.)
    1. Catholic universities and colleges — United States — History.
2. Catholic Church — Education — United States — History.   3. United States — Intellectual life — History.   I. Title.
LC501.026   1994
377'.82'73 — dc20   94-28671
                                                              CIP

To

Alice Gallin, O.S.U.

professor, historian, leader

A lifetime witness of faith,
fidelity and friendship

in service to

Catholicism and the intellectual life

Contents

Foreword

Rembert G. Weakland, O.S.B.
Archbishop of Milwaukee

All Catholic institutions are in crisis. When the history of the last quarter of this century is written, it will emphasize how Catholics in the United States struggled with the question of the Catholic identity of the many institutions that were its glory in the early part of the century. The immigrant church made remarkable sacrifices to build such institutions and saw in them a strong force for maintaining the integrity of their faith in a culture that was predominantly Protestant. By the third quarter of this century, however, the culture was no longer seen as Protestant and Catholics had become the largest church in the nation. A new situation demanded a new mission.

Many seemed at first to blame this calling into question of the nature of Catholic institutions on the confusions that arose after Vatican Council II. Such an analysis would be totally unfair to that Council. Whether there had been a Council or not, this crisis would have come. The conciliar documents probably helped Catholics to face the challenge in a more profound way than would have been the case without that Council. That Catholics moved ahead in the American society to take their places in all areas of life had nothing to do with the Council. It was the results of G.I. bills after World War II and the general thrust in the Catholic community for learning and education, seen as the way for advancement in American society. One could argue, in fact, that without the Council the Catholic community in the United States would have become prey to a total secularization and that the Council gave, especially to the Catholic laity, a sense of their special mission and a way of looking again at the values inherent in this world itself.

The question of identity for the Catholic institutions of higher education is also posed for Catholic hospitals and health-care units, for Catholic Charities, and for Catholic Relief Services. Previously the word Catholic in those titles meant something distinctive and set-apart. They were not necessarily meant to serve only Catholics, but they were very much a part of the pride and joy of the Catholic community and seen as the Catholic response, or the response by Catholics, to problems of society. All of these institutions continued to grow and develop because of the free American context in which they were created. The large number of religious men and women who worked in those institutions assured them of their identity. By the decades of the 1980s, however, it became less and less clear what a "Catholic" response really was and should be. The presence of religious men and women had become imperceptible.

No institutions, however, have been more deeply touched by the debate over their new role in the current cultural context than those of higher learning. The question of their catholicity could be formulated in various ways. Some still define Catholic as "over-against," but not against Protestantism. It is now secularism that has become the enemy. For them the Catholic quality must be very visible and identifiable, recognized and assured as such by the hierarchy. It is the task of the hierarchy to see that only orthodox Catholic doctrine is taught in the departments of theology. Others see the identity question in much broader strokes.

Professor David O'Brien lays out for us all these options and their merits. His analysis of the current literature and the major players is most helpful and clear. As one who grew up in the older model and yet lived with and became a major participant in the struggles of the nascent newer models, he is able to articulate well what is happening. He is correct in underlining that the crisis must be seen in terms of the striving of the institutions now to be both American and Catholic. They have come of age in the United States culture and must play a new role in it.

It is helpful to all of us that the larger question of Catholic identity in the field of Catholic higher education is now being asked. There is no area with so many thoughtful people so well prepared to deal with this issue and thus able to enlighten us. At first, it might frighten us that some even pose the question more critically: Because Catholics are now well integrated into the American society, is such a thing as a specifically Catholic institution now anachronistic? Instinctively we might answer no to such a question. But it is good that we are forced to say why.

A similar question then must be posed: Is there something essential about the Catholic tradition and identity that must always be preserved in order to be Catholic? Most of us would instinctively say yes to this last question, but we might be hard put to say what that essential element really is. A second question must also be posed: What should the specific contribution of the Catholic institution be to the Catholic Church and to our American society today? If Catholics are now the largest religious body in the United States, it is important that they think out their place as individuals and the role of their institutions in that society.

Tied into this identity question is the debate over the very role and nature of a university. Some may see it primarily as an evangelizing tool of the larger church. Such a limited view can then give an easy if somewhat simplistic answer to the identity question. Most of us, however, would not be satisfied with such a limited view of the purpose and aims of institutions of higher learning, whether they are Catholic or not.

Most of us feel that the Catholic tradition has much to contribute to the major questions that plague our day. Our tradition has been dealing with most of these questions for centuries now. We also feel that our general view of the human person, how that person should relate to society and this world, and what that society should be all has something important to say to any nation or community. We are proud of that heritage and do not see it as anti-intellectual. One should not deny, however, that at times the church has seemed too reluctant to accept scientific advances and has been a follower and not a leader in intellectual pursuits. But we are eager to bring to bear on the challenges of our day the wisdom of our heritage.

On the other hand, we know that Catholics cannot and do not want to live in a controlled Catholic environment. We are a part of a larger society and must both learn from it and contribute to it. There can be no Catholic isolationism if that Catholicism is to be vibrant and in tune with the challenges of the times. I sense that the Catholic universities and colleges have seen this need for involvement a bit before the rest of us because they are involved in educating leaders for tomorrow. Institutions of higher learning must see themselves as coming out of a larger historical Catholic tradition but not isolated from the ever changing and challenging American society from which they have learned so much and from which they will continue to learn. They must, however, be looking toward the future.

Rather than engage in a discussion over how to maintain a Catholic identity, a discussion that might be very abstract and result in only superficial and purely external safeguards, the Catholic community engaged in higher education must generate a larger debate over that Catholic heritage itself, its intrinsic values and merits, its contributions of the past, and the main threads of its contribution now and in the future. That larger project will not be an easy one. It will be ecumenical and interfaith in nature and will of necessity engage scholars of all hues and ideas. All of these thoughts are well presented by Professor O'Brien. This book will be a must for those engaged in such discussions. The author is keenly aware of the deeper issues at stake and will not settle for simplistic solutions. For my part, I can state that, as a bishop, I am deeply interested in the issue. I am also positive that the Catholic identity question will not be solved by hierarchical control over who teaches theology in such institutions. There is more in question than which theologian is teaching and what religion is being taught. The identity issue touches the whole institution and the principles that guide it. It also involves how one sees its role in the American society. More than anything else, it probably will involve good leadership in how the question is posed and how the discussion is conducted. There is also a Catholic way of discourse, one that must be honest, open, and civil.

Our generation wants our institutions of higher education to be academically excellent, to form leaders in our American society who have vision and values, to work out of the larger and greater Catholic tradition of learning. We want our graduates to know the Catholic tradition, even when they decide to reject it. Most of us are convinced that such a tradition is not just one of private religion but also one that has something to say to this world and to the American society.

Are we asking for too much? Any reader of Professor O'Brien's book will see the complexity of that question and not come up with easy answers or ready-made solutions. Catholic institutions of higher education may now have to change their mission statement from the days when they were founded. But they have, I am convinced, a new mission that is worth the effort to articulate and put into effect. We must all be a part of that struggle.

Perhaps one other factor must be taken into account. What does the Catholic constituency say about this issue? Put more bluntly, what will Catholic parents pay for? It may well be that the market will determine so much of what happens to Catholic higher education in the future. Is the Catholic identity the drawing card for the present generation of those footing the bills? Or is it nostalgia (I went there, so my son or daughter will too)? Is the next generation of Catholics, already so weakly attached to their church, going to be concerned about these issues of identity? In that area we know so little and can only guess, but the answer must be a part of the equation with regard to the future existence of our schools of higher education. It would be my hope that present Catholic institutions of higher education would be educating people to whom such a question is of the utmost concern.

Preface

This is a book about Catholic higher education in the United States, written by a lifelong professor in a Catholic college from the point of view of a Catholic layperson, which is to say it is about the church as much as it is about the college.

Why a book about Catholic higher education? Why did I write it? Why should someone read it? My answers are fairly simple: I wrote it because I felt called to write it, and because I regard it as an important subject. People might want to read it who share my belief that Catholic higher education is important, or at least interesting.

Each of these statements deserves some additional comment before we start.

First, I am an historian, but I did not set out to write a history of U.S. Catholic higher education. Philip Gleason of the University of Notre Dame has been working on such a history for over a decade. This is very good news because, as readers will discover, Professor Gleason has already provided most of the good writing about that history. His articles are indispensable to anyone trying to make sense of this subject.

Gleason plans to end his survey at Vatican II. For the rich period since the Council, the period of near revolutionary change, we now have a superb collection of basic documents, edited by Alice Gallin, O.S.U.[1] From 1981 to 1993, Sister Alice served as executive director of the Association of Catholic Colleges and Universities (ACCU), guiding that body through the treacherous waters created by Vatican interventions in American academic affairs. After her retirement from the ACCU, Sr. Alice began work on a history of U.S. Catholic higher education since the Council. This work, temporarily interrupted by her generous decision to serve as interim president of St. Bonaventure's University, will be tremendously valuable for everyone who cares about these schools.

So I have not written a history. Instead, I have tried to pull together some thoughts on contemporary Catholic higher education. Motivation came from experience. I attended the University of Notre Dame (B.A.'60) as an undergraduate and, after graduate study at the University of Rochester (Ph.D. '65), I have worked at Catholic schools my entire career, first at

Loyola College in Montreal and then, since 1969, at the College of the Holy Cross. Along the way, I taught for a year at Stonehill College, I regularly offered courses for church personnel at Assumption College, and I taught occasional summers at Notre Dame, Loyola University of New Orleans, Marquette University, and Boston College.

In the mid-1970s, inspired by a local Holy Cross controversy, I wrote a few articles about Jesuit higher education. This led to opportunities to visit many campuses. When my friend Sister Alice became involved with the ACCU, I became a member of its Task Force on Justice and Peace Education. A few years later, I accepted the invitation of Father John E. Brooks, S.J., president of Holy Cross, to chair a committee charged with preparing a mission statement for the College. In the midst of that four-year process, I was named to a new National Seminar on Jesuit Higher Education, a remarkable joint initiative of Jesuit provincials and Jesuit college and university presidents. Finally, in January 1992, I received the ACCU's Theodore M. Hesburgh award for contributions to Catholic higher education. Unsure that my contributions were all that numerous, I decided to use my upcoming sabbatical to think about Catholic higher education and put into writing some thoughts that had been evolving for three decades.

My second reason for writing the book is that I believe Catholic higher education is an important subject, suggesting another question: how to make a positive and constructive statement about it. Most of all, I wanted to avoid the abstraction that besets so much discussion of this subject. There are many philosophical and theological texts about Catholic higher education that make great sense, especially if one is a Catholic. But they often seem light years removed from the average American Catholic campus. Any professor who has served on a committee charged with reforming the core curriculum can only wonder at the talk of theological "integration" that always arises in discussion of Catholic higher education. Similarly, emphasis on a Catholic inspiration of the institution, as distinct from individuals, marks almost all the documents, but simply bypasses questions about who receives this inspiration and by what process institutions respond to the inspirations they receive.

Still, I will take what account I can of papal texts and theological and philosophical reflection on the meaning of Catholic higher education. Indeed, that material contains considerable wisdom on matters of importance for the three publics within which Catholic higher education is located: in the Catholic community, the academic community, and the American people as a whole. But I will also try to do something a little different — relate the discussion of large questions of Catholic mission and identity to the concrete realities of contemporary university and college life.

I hope to state these questions in such a way that all faculty and staff, Catholics and non-Catholics alike, can see the discussion as one that relates to their experience, to their work, and to their aspirations. On Catholic campuses, as in so many other places, such as government agencies, urban classrooms, more than a few professional and business offices, and even churches, good people are doing remarkable work, far better than public complaints would suggest. Catholic colleges and universities, and the people who work in them, are well positioned to make a major contribution to the renewal of the church and the reform of our educational enterprise. But their potential will not begin to be realized until we overcome the "culture of complaint" produced by the divisions that have developed in recent years. I hope this book will spark positive discussion about projects people might initiate to bring religion back into public and academic discourse.

I also wanted to relocate the discussion, to move it away from its usual ecclesiastical context — Pope, bishops, religious orders, and presidents — to the wider if more diffused context of Catholic community life in the late twentieth-century United States. Of course, no statement on the subject can ignore the Vatican, the bishops, and the religious orders or neglect issues of institutional relationships as they touch on academic freedom, academic autonomy and self-governance, teaching, and research. But I hope to locate the Catholic dimension of such matters within the church as the people of God and within the specific setting of an American church, which is often misunderstood, especially in Rome but also in many academic settings. Most of all, I want to say something constructive, not about how to "live with" a church affiliation, but about how to see that affiliation as a source of support and encouragement for the works of teaching and research to which Catholic and non-Catholic academics alike are committed.

I have some audiences in mind. First are the trustees, faculty, administrators, professional staffs and graduate and undergraduate students at the 238 Catholic colleges and universities in the United States. I hope this book can be handed to them and to newcomers as a clear statement of what Catholic higher education is and hopes to become.

Then there are American Catholic laypeople and the priests, sisters, brothers, and lay professionals who serve them. They generously support these schools — directly, with their financial donations and the tuition they pay for themselves and their children, and indirectly, through the emotional bonds that tie every one of these schools to specific groups of people who really care. Ordinary Catholics have reason to be worried by accounts of Catholic higher education dominated by images of so-called secularization, declining numbers of priests and religious, lack of purpose, and even integrity, in too much recruitment material, and well-publicized fights about pro-choice groups on campus. Catholics have the right to know whether Catholic colleges and universities wish to continue to serve them and, if they do, how they can share in defining the forms that service will take.

Finally, there is the larger public, which also supports these schools through taxpayer-assisted grants and loans, innumerable benefactions, and obvious respect, often gratitude for the contributions these schools make to their local communities. I would like to offer them a better understanding of Catholic higher education and its unique problems and possibilities. Even more, I would like to persuade them that Catholics and their church, with the help of these colleges and universities, are wrestling with questions of immense public significance. It makes a difference—for everybody—whether Catholic colleges and universities are vital and exciting centers of encounter between religion and culture.

So there is another, far more basic answer to my question of why I should write this book: because I believe that Catholic Christianity has crucially important contributions to make to the human enterprise. After all, the Catholic in the term Catholic higher education refers to a concrete historical reality—the Roman Catholic church. I believe that church to be in some struggling sense the very presence of Christ in our history. And I make that statement aware that, at the end of this tragic century, it is no simple or easy matter to have faith in the church. Many advocates of Catholic higher education think it is self-evident that Catholicism and the Catholic church are good things; that complacency, evident in a thousand broadsides on the need to preserve "The Catholic University," is a major stumbling block to unleashing the potential of these schools. No, Catholics and their church, all of us, are too deeply implicated in the crimes of this century to rest easy with the Catholic affirmation. Still, I believe with so many others that this church, in its concrete human form, can be—and often is—an agent of God's liberating and healing grace. Believing this and believing that colleges and universities can make for a more vital and intelligent Catholicism, I have to conclude that a vigorous Catholic intellectual life and strong Catholic academic institutions are worth working for.

The next question was how to accomplish these awesome objectives. I hope to set out the "state of the question," to describe contemporary U.S. Catholicism and Catholic higher education, and then outline as clearly—and I hope as fairly—as possible, some of the major controversies presently stirring the church and its campuses. I will try to analyze and clarify those questions from the point of view of the American church and American society.

So that is the project. Its construction reflects the support and friendship of many people. I entrust these suggestions to them and to those good people who choose to read this book.

Acknowledgments

This book arises from my years of involvement in Catholic higher education. So the list of people whose generosity and care helped make the author and, therefore, to make this book possible would include almost everyone with whom I have studied and talked about these matters for the last thirty-five years. Thanks to all of you. Here I can only name, with profound appreciation, some of those who played a direct role in bringing this project to completion.

First, there is the College of the Holy Cross and its wise trustees who make available the remarkable gift of sabbatical leaves. Next is Holy Cross President John E. Brooks, S.J., who approves such leaves and who made a few additional and invaluable contributions to this project. Academic Vice President and Dean Frank Vellaccio and Associate Dean James Kee encouraged the project, and me. So did a number of faculty colleagues, most notably the members of the Ad Hoc Committee on the Mission of the College, discussed in chapter 5: Theresa McBride, John A. MacDonnell, S.J., Maurice Geracht (who at several key moments made me feel like I knew what I was doing), David Gill, S.J., and the aforementioned—and always wise—Dean Kee.

I received wise counsel and had good times with the founding members of the National Seminar on Jesuit Higher Education: John Padberg, S.J., Gregory Lucey, S.J., Gerald McKevitt, S.J., Vincent O'Keefe, S.J., Jim Bernauer, S.J., Eileen Poliani, Robert Miola, Ron Walker, Rosaleen Trainor, C.S.J.P., Betsy Linehan, Mary Ann Donnelly, and Allan Service. The seminar was joined from time to time by its backers, Patrick Burns, S.J. of the Jesuit Conference and Paul Tipton, S.J. of the Association of Jesuit Colleges and Universities.

At the Association of Catholic Colleges and Universities, I have learned a lot from David Johnson, one-time associate executive director, and his successor, Paul Gallagher. I worked with both on the Task Force on Justice and Peace Education, among whose members Peter Beisheim of Stonehill College and Don McNeill, C.S.C. and Kathleen Maas Weigert of Notre Dame have been particular friends. The staff at the ACCU, especially Francine Simon, have been invariably helpful and supportive, as has Benito

M. Lopez, Jr., who became executive director in 1992. Frances Freemen joined the ACCU to help with two interesting workshops for trustees of Catholic colleges and universities, at which I also enjoyed working with Barbara Taylor of the Association of Governing Boards and Jim Laughran, S.J., former Dean at Fordham University and president of Loyola-Marymount in Los Angeles. When I cross paths with Father Loughran, as I do every couple of years, I always come away enriched.

On my trips to various campuses, I was assisted by many people. I received help from Mark Schwehn, dean of Christ College, and especially from my historian friend Mel Piehl at Valpariaso. At Notre Dame I had valuable conversations with Nathan Hatch, Michael Hamilton, David Burrell, C.S.C., and Lawrence Cunningham. At Loyola in Chicago, in addition to visiting with my Jesuit seminar friend Ron Walker, executive vice president, I was assisted by Sister Gertrude Patch, director of the Center for Faith and Culture, sociology chair Philip Nyden, theologian John Haughey, S.J., and my old friend Dean Paul Messbarger. At DePaul I benefited from the experience of Bob Ludwig, director of university ministries, and a group he gathered to talk with me, including Jack Lane of the Center for the Study of Values. In Chicago I also gained insight from John Fontana of the Crossroads Center for Faith and Work, Jim Lund and Mary Heidkamp of the Archdiocesan Social Action staff, and my mentors Peggy Roach and Monsignor John Egan. At Seattle University I talked with President William Sullivan and Bernard Steckler of Matteo Ricci College. Joseph Appleyard, rector, and Michael Buckley, director of the Jesuit Institute, both Jesuits at Boston College, were generous with their time.

I spent a week in Minneapolis and St. Paul in November 1992, where I was helped by the staff of the Newman Center at the University of Minnesota, particularly Steve Bossi, C.S.P., by Rev. Dennis Dease, president of the University of St. Thomas, academic dean John Nemo, who died suddenly and tragically the following spring, and Dean Michael P. Murphy and Sister Pat Kowalski of the new downtown Minneapolis campus of St. Thomas. I also met with Peg Michaels of the Public Citizen Program at the University of Minnesota; I later talked with the program's director, Harry Boyte, about citizenship and undergraduate education. I traveled north one day to visit the wonderful Lutheran liberal arts college, St. Olaf's, where I was hosted by and had marvelous conversation with political scientist Don Heffrening.

I was excited when I visited Washington to meet with the staff of the Christian College Coalition; there I received special help from Karen A. Longman. Later I talked with President R. Judson Carlberg of Gordon

College, who graciously asked Ted Englund of the Christian College Consortium to join our discussion. All this was arranged by Harry Durning.

Perhaps the high point of a year of talk about Catholic higher education was a three-day conversation at Notre Dame with five of the people who shook the foundations of Catholic higher education back in the 1960s: Paul Reinert, S.J. of St. Louis University, Theodore M. Hesburgh, C.S.C. of Notre Dame and Ann Ida Gannon, R.C.S.J. of Mundelein College, and the founding chairmen of the first lay boards of trustees, Daniel Schlafly of St. Louis and Edward M. Stepan of Notre Dame. Their recollections of the history of these years of great change were fascinating; they showed a vision, generosity of spirit, and quiet confidence that was inspiring.

A new experience was helping to set up Collegium, a project to encourage young scholars to consider Catholic intellectual life, initiated by Jesuit Thomas Landy and supported by the Lilly Endowment. Working with Tom Landy, his associate, Mary Frances Malone, and his assistant, Mary Beth Pinard, the board, the faculty, and the graduate student and junior faculty participants in the inaugural seminars was a wonderful experience of hope.

When it came time to write, I was assisted by Ellyn McNeil and Jim McCartin at Holy Cross. At Orbis Books Robert Ellsberg was warmly supportive and production coordinator Catherine Costello showed remarkable skill and near infinite patience with my handwriting and my overly casual approach to the technicalities of publication.

I owe an enormous debt of gratitude to several others who have helped shape my ideas about Catholic higher education: Father J. Bryan Hehir, longtime advisor on peace and international relations to the U.S. bishops and now pastor of St. Paul's Church in Cambridge; William Shea, chairman of the department of theological studies at St. Louis University, with whose ideas I almost always agree; and Philip J. Gleason, the Notre Dame historian, with whom I am apt to disagree, but whose friendship and support I cherish.

Still, over the last two decades of meetings and talks and discussion about this subject, one person has come to symbolize for me the rich legacy and enormous potential of American Catholic higher education. Sister Alice Gallin, O.S.U. served for many years as professor of history and administrative jack-of-all-trades at the College of New Rochelle. In 1975, she and I teamed up to help the bishops prepare for the remarkable Call to Action Conference. We were both permanently changed by the experience of directing eight committees of bishops, scholars, and active ministers preparing reports and draft recommendations for the church's first national convention in Detroit in October 1976. The "experience of church" we had convention in Detroit in October 1976. The "experience of church" we had with those committees and with the Call to Action event itself has enriched our faith ever since.

When our work with the bishops was done, I went back to Holy Cross and Alice became Associate Executive Director of the Association of Catholic Colleges and Universities. In 1980, she succeeded Monsignor John Murphy as Executive Director. For twelve years, she guided the ACCU through treacherous waters, helping to negotiate between bishops, Vatican officials, and the presidents of 238 Catholic colleges and universities. Along the way, she found time to complete her second book, *Midwives of Nazism: University Professors in Weimar Germany, 1925–1933* (Mercer, Ga., 1986), a depressing study of universities during the period of the Weimar Republic. She also helped bring greater attention to the enormous contribution that women religious have made to the work of Catholic higher education in the United States. Alice Gallin has been a serious and respected historian of modern Germany, the key person in organizing U.S. participation in international dialogue on Catholic higher education, and a witness to the best parts of this apostolate. In her critical yet totally committed love for the church and her deep commitment to scholarship and teaching, Alice Gallin exemplifies the Catholic intellectual. She has also been, to my great benefit, a wise counselor and generous friend. To Sister Alice this book is gratefully and affectionately dedicated.

CHAPTER 1

Autobiography and
Catholic Higher Education

SHARING

Gordon C. Zahn, who for half a century has been a most distinguished American Catholic pacifist, once snapped: "The worst thing to happen to the Catholic church in my lifetime was the introduction of the word 'sharing.'" Zahn smiled as he said it, but his irritation was genuine. The Catholic church has changed, and so have Catholics. One change, no more dramatic than a dozen others, is a far greater willingness to speak openly about spiritual experiences. Some even measure the quality of parish life by the presence of small communities in which such sharing can take place. A few earnest, prayerful people, sitting in a circle and speaking quietly of the action of the Holy Spirit in their lives—it seems so Protestant. The contrast could not be sharper with the dominant image of American Catholicism for a century: a huge neo-Gothic church on Sunday morning, filled to capacity with hundreds of worshippers kneeling in utter silence before an altar where a brightly vested priest, his back turned to the congregation, offers in mumbled Latin prayers the Holy Sacrifice of the Mass.

The two images of the Catholic church—one a tightly knit, silent, devout people united by the priest in spiritual action, and the other a small, voluntary, perhaps temporary community, its members speaking to one another about God and their own lives—reflect the historic transformation of American Catholicism. Pastoral leaders work very hard, with some success, to blend the two, with small prayer and renewal groups supplementing the weekend liturgies of the parish. But there are tensions, which have appeared often before in Christian history, between charism and office, movement and order, exclusive sect and inclusive church.

Each image—bottom-up renewal groups with their sharing of faith experience, and the gathered diverse church, with its regular routine of

1

liturgical worship—suggests a different way to initiate a discussion of Catholic higher education. The classical form, so dominant in Catholicism after the Reformation and especially after the French Revolution, begins with the idea of the Catholic university, exploring the essence of each of those words, *Catholic* and *university*. Then that idea is located in its various historic embodiments, from the medieval universities to the present, taking note of how the idea has been modified by changing understandings of *Catholic* and *university*. We end up with a modern idea or model of the Catholic university, provided best by John Henry Newman in the middle of the nineteenth century and articulated most recently by Pope John Paul II in his Apostolic Constitution *Ex Corde Ecclesiae*.[1] This abstract, universal model is then used to provide guidelines to measure existing institutions and answer the question: Is this a truly Catholic university? Not surprisingly, as we will see, today's Catholic colleges and universities in the United States do not measure up very well, especially on the Catholic side of the scale.

The second image of the church—as a sharing group based on personal experiences—suggests a very different approach into any subject, including Catholic higher education. This approach begins with autobiography, with experience. At one time, when a couple visited a rectory to ask the priest to preside at their marriage, he asked them to provide evidence that they had been baptized and received first Holy Communion; then they were instructed in Catholic doctrine and law on marriage. Nowadays, they are invited into a discussion about their understanding of faith, church, and sacraments and then are asked to participate in a marriage preparation program in which doctrine and law play only a secondary, supportive role.

This autobiographical, personal emphasis has deep roots in American, if not Catholic, culture. In periods of rapid social and cultural change, when institutions lose their authority to command assent and communicate values and norms that are taken for granted, people naturally look for alternative sources of authority. Thus, during the Reformation era or, in the United States, during the period of rampaging democratization in the early nineteenth century, ordinary Christians turned away from the contending factions of ministers and theologians and looked directly to scripture, the word of God.[2] In the United States, with its religious diversity and constant change, religious experience almost always trumped religious organization and religious knowledge.

Something similar has happened in American culture in the last quarter century, as various groups have challenged dominant cultural norms, producing new and ever more divergent pluralisms, forcing people to rely more and more on their own experience, or, in religious terms, on their "geography of faith."[3] One need not be a romantic to find the bottom-up, autobiographical method attractive, especially if it is not made exclusive or ideological. It is particularly interesting in discussions among and about Catholics because, at least since the Reformation, Catholics have been fascinated by universal and abstract doctrines and top-down forms of administration as opposed to historical and experiential categories and democratic forms of governance.

Yet the two were connected, for lack of interest in popular religious experience went hand in hand with bureaucratic and hierarchical power. Once, in the 1950s, a bishop told a congregation gathered for the opening of a new Catholic grade school that each parish needed three things to be truly Catholic: a school in which the priest, assisted by the sisters, could teach Catholic doctrine; a church in which the priest could offer Catholic worship; and, of course, a priest. He neglected to mention the people, perhaps because, in some sense, they were in fact *not* needed.[4]

Discussion of the Catholic university is often like that: to be truly Catholic and truly a university, according to the top-down model, you need the right ideas embodied in the right programs in an institution accountable to the right officials. People — parishioners or professors, the faithful or the students — can be taken for granted. In contrast, an autobiographical starting point for a discussion of Catholic higher education, like the good pastor's invitation to share experience, makes clear that institutions, and especially Christian institutions, depend on and serve people. As Pope John Paul II said of Christian humanism: not abstract "man in general," but real, concrete historical men and women are "the way of the church."[5]

This suggests another reason to begin a discussion of Catholic higher education with a bit of autobiography. I have always loved basketball; for a few years I even coached a junior high church league team. Once, while trying to understand why certain coaches were successful and others not, I noticed that some coaches had a system and won when they had players who fit that system. Other coaches fit their system to the players, regularly reshaping their offense and defense to take the fullest advantage of the talents of the players in front of them. These coaches, it seemed, were more consistently successful.

One can make an analogy with Catholic higher education (if not the church as a whole). Some Vatican bureaucrats, bishops, and theologians have a powerful picture of what the Catholic university is (they mean *should be*, but they always say *is*) and they work very hard to write documents and construct laws and procedures that will compel existing colleges and universities to fit that image. The many people who decry the loss of identity of Catholic colleges and universities also carry in their heads powerful images of the way the institutions should be organized and what they should do.

People closer to the scene—bishops who engage in campus life, successful administrators, and certainly most faculty and professional staff—usually have few problems nodding their heads when the model is presented to them, but they dig in their heels when efforts are made to make them conform to it. When officials attempt to translate their system into policies and programs without taking into account the talents, hopes, values and beliefs of the people involved, there is conflict, as well there should be.

Conflict does not arise simply because there are now too many non-Catholic professors or because administrators and faculty have sold out to secular gods, trying to be like Harvard or Amherst. Conflict arises because people understand differently their responsibilities as trustees, presidents, deans, teachers, scholars, or professional staff. And they also differ over religion. Even those among them who are Catholic have their own ideas about that. In other words, they are mature professionals and mature adults; they have their own, sometimes hard-won, ideas about universities and equally hard-won religious beliefs. On any program or policy that touches their vocations, they expect to be consulted, to be asked.

Of course, as bishops like to point out, leadership is never simply a matter of taking a poll. It involves a dynamic relationship between overall plans and ideals, often presented from the top down, and the talents and qualities of the people in the organization. The president or dean, like the good coach or pastor, does not simply keep the peace by accommodating the desires of his or her people. The good leader knows that success depends upon the commitment of people to the mission of the institution as well as the competence of the professors and staff. Good pastors and good presidents are like good community organizers: they work with what they have. They try to develop the talents of all their members, and that in turn requires knowledge of the persons with whom they work. Most of all, leadership requires willingness to listen, to engage in dialogue, and, hardest of all, to share responsibility and therefore to be accountable. On campus that means connecting the mission of the school with the vocations of those who participate in its life. And that means attending to their autobiographies.

So, the first step in constructing a good mission statement is to ask people what they are doing and why they are doing it. And here, as I begin to write about the mission of Catholic higher education, I have to ask that question of myself, with apologies for the sharing to my friend Gordon Zahn.[6]

HISTORY'S AMBIGUOUS LIBERATION

The story is told of a recent Ph.D. interviewed for a faculty position at an eastern Catholic college. As he walked down the hall after a public presentation to the faculty, one philosophy professor pulled him into his office and asked in a hushed tone: "Tell me, what do you really think of historical consciousness?" A philosopher's question, not an historian's, was my first thought. But perhaps that is the problem. In any event, historical consciousness, once used by post-Renaissance critics to put Christian believers to rout, has turned (once again?) on its promoters, driving yet another nail into the coffin of enlightenment rationalism. Or at least it has reasonable people on the run. The person who told me this story said that, after his own conversation with the candidate in question, the latter called him a "foundationalist," meaning, I guess, that he thought there was some foundation—faith or reason—on which ideas could be erected and sustained. After spending a decade in generally friendly combat with "religious exclusivists" and "secular exclusivists" and promoting what he calls "inclusive conversationalism," my friend found the new classification amusing.

As for me, I have always gotten extremely nervous when conversations about such subjects move beyond the bantering stage. Like most historians, I dislike, or better distrust, philosophy, especially epistemology. I occasionally teach a historiography course in which we explore some issues of text, context, and interpretation (although definitely not epistemology). But I do realize during such exchanges why I am an historian and not a philosopher.

In 1970 and 1971, when I had a wonderful postdoctoral grant to study theology,[7] I had a similar reaction to systematic theology and large portions of scripture studies. In Catholic theological circles, this was the time of heady post–Vatican II excitement, mostly about discovering history, kept so long at a distance by the systematic repression of scholarship that followed the condemnation of modernism in 1905. Having learned a bit about the ambiguous outcome of earlier Protestant "quests for the historical Jesus," I was worried about the enterprise. It is perhaps a measure of the times that I kept my doubts to myself, because I did not want to be identified with the reactionaries of the period, then struggling to maintain what Michael Novak called, rather contemptuously, "non-historical orthodoxy."[8]

Novak would later change his mind about such things, precisely because he found that history, as the antimodernists always understood, could do a demolition job on all orthodoxies. Pope John XXIII had distinguished between the fundamental truths of faith, which were unchanging, and the manner in which they were expressed, which could and should change to meet the needs of the church and the human family.[9] The Pope's distinction opened the long-closed door to history. Novak eventually slammed the door shut to salvage the Nicene Creed; Pope Paul VI closed it to save "transubstantiation."[10] Both, like prodigal sons, came back to the "foundations" (does one hear echoes of "the fundamentals"?), supposedly exempt from the corrosive acids of historical consciousness.

The journey of modern Catholic historical consciousness has many similarities with that of earlier post-Calvinist American Protestants, whose rebellions in the later nineteenth century produced liberal theology and the social gospel (both new discoveries for many Catholics three generations later). For neither group was this simply a matter of intellectual politics. Harry Emerson Fosdick once tried to explain to an unsympathetic 1920s public that his generation of Protestant liberals would simply not have been able to remain Christian if they had not reinterpreted the faith of their fathers in terms comprehensible to modern intelligence and if some among them had not found in works of mercy and justice what they had trouble finding in faith alone. Liberal theology and the social gospel not only enabled Protestant Christianity to remain connected to the movement of history, but it also enabled serious and sincere men and women to be faithful to their religious heritage and responsible participants in the life of their times.[11]

I suspect that there were more than a few Catholics of my generation who could say the same. As we pushed against the constraints of the Catholic subculture and learned more of its moral shortcomings, could we have kept the faith if we had not had Pope John's distinction and his invitation to historical responsibility? Earlier Protestants could not stay in churches that did not address industrial poverty and injustice and that did not affirm their more personal quests for authenticity and love. Could we Catholics, decades later, have stayed in a church that remained indifferent to racism, the plight of the world's new poor, or nuclear weapons? Could Catholic intellectuals have accepted the responsibility to engage modern culture assigned them by Vatican II's "Pastoral Constitution on the Church and the Modern World" if they had not embraced that historical consciousness that is such a distinguishing feature of the men and women of our age and place in history? Whether it was the charismatic young Swiss theologian Hans Küng touring the United States early in the Council years, speaking to overflowing audiences about a Catholic *"eccelesia semper reformanda"* and "truthfulness in the church" or the Canadian Jesuit Bernard Lonergan's explanation of the passage from classical to historical consciousness, there was an earthquake that shook foundations that badly needed shaking. But it also opened chasms, for awhile unnoticed, into which people like us could, and sometimes did, fall.[12]

My outline of recent Catholic modernization is phrased in liberal language, language that gave form to my experience of those changes. There were many Catholics who did not hear the same questions and whose response to the challenges of modernity were, and are, quite different. Like Fosdick's beleaguered liberals, Catholic liberals like me became historically conscious believers; we came to know that the fact and the content of belief were always in part culturally determined; doubt was a fact, not an option, and yet we still believed. So ours was a balancing act between faith and history, between Christian commitment and awareness of our own historical limitations, and thus filled with ambiguity and uncertainty. It was, for Catholic Christians and their church, a "precarious posture," to use a phrase coined in another context by Joseph Cardinal Bernardin.[13]

And at some point it became a fairly lonely posture as well. Less anxious advocates of historical consciousness and responsibility—my friend's "secular exclusivists"—confidently awaited our surrender of outdated religious preoccupations. Within the house of Catholics, liberalism's desire for dialogue, its yearning to see things as others saw them, produced for a bright moment Vatican II and our reading of it—my friend's "inclusive conversationalism." But the moment passed, at least in the United States, and boundaries between Catholics and others—"religious exclusivism"—reappeared. One form was a Catholic but almost evangelical fideism—a commitment to Jesus and to "Gospel values" deeply grounded in American religious culture. Another was a peculiarly Catholic form of fundamentalism, believing that what the church teaches is what Vatican officials say it teaches. A third, more sophisticated and tempting form was a Niebuhrian neoorthodox conservatism, complete with the worldly shrug of the shoulders at the passing of yet a few more idealisms.

For the remaining liberals among us, still seeking inclusive conversations, whose results are not known ahead of time, with Catholics and with everyone else, things are not so clear on either the sacred or secular side. "Life is a test," says the preacher in the comic strip *Kudzu*. "Yes," responds the gangly teenager, "but I prepared for true or false and it turned out to be multiple choice." So it did. It left us with an ambivalence we have never lost, and probably never will.

A CATHOLIC AT SCHOOL

I made my discovery of the liberating utility, and the hidden dangers, of historical consciousness in graduate school at the University of Rochester, where I went after four years at Notre Dame. I was introduced to philosophy of history in a wonderful seminar with Wilson Coates, but the dominant figure in the department was a young European intellectual historian, Hayden V. White. As a U.S. historian, I did not take White's courses, but I did work as a teaching assistant in his survey course. A paper I wrote (on Christopher Dawson), once caught his attention, and I often listened intently at the edge of a crowd to his cocktail party conversations. What I got from it all was that history had a history. Like everything else, historical consciousness was itself historically conditioned. Nowadays that may be second nature to all postmodernist graduate students, but then it was for me, just out of fifteen years of Catholic education, what illicit sex must have been for the Puritans: forbidden but so very interesting. Everything was open, this rather uptight Catholic discovered. (Notice the dates of all this: 1960–1964.)

Now I can't explain, in post-sixties America, how liberating I found that idea. On the one hand, history could free us from the dead hand of the Roman Catholicism constructed in the period between the French Revolution and World War II. Oddly enough, Wilson Coates and Hayden White, both a bit anticlerical, prepared me for Vatican II. I almost jumped with delight when I read Küng's *The Council and Reunion*, which used historical consciousness to reconstruct a Catholicism becoming half (at least) Protestant. The items in need of reform ranged from birth control and the emotion-charged problem of religious liberty to more abstract, less interesting issues of doctrine, scripture, and hierarchical authority. In place of my once taken-for-granted orthodoxies was a new skepticism, but one that was not at all pessimistic. Like Pope John, I had no doubt that renewal based on historical reconstruction would strengthen the church and enable it, and me, to take a more responsible place at the center of our times.

The same skepticism about language and muckraking conviction that the truth would indeed set us free informed my politics. I found the key to American arrogance in the famous "Mr. X" essay of George Kennan, which laid the basis for the containment approach that dominated American foreign policy in the Cold War era. Kennan concluded his supposedly realistic critique of American idealism with the shocking claim that "the thoughtful observer of Russian-American relations" would "find no cause for complaint in the Kremlin's challenge to American society" because it made the American people's "security as a nation dependant on their pulling themselves together and accepting the responsibilities of moral and political leadership that history plainly intended they should bear."[14] That dangerous linking of power and historical destiny had to be replaced, I believed, by the same humbling awareness of our own historicity that was reforming the church.

I, and I think most of my Catholic contemporaries, were innocents still, with few doubts that we could build a more reasonable society—one even more dedicated to liberty and justice for all—and a more reasonable church—no less Christian and surely no less Catholic—by exposing the illusions of the past while holding fast to Pope John's essential truths.

What I did not hear from White then (probably because I did not want to hear it) was the flip side of the message. Historical arguments about divine mission, like Kennan's, had long endorsed American as well as Catholic pretensions. We could use critical historical tools to destroy that arrogant exemption from history, but the same technique could be turned on us. For those burdened by history as experience, historical consciousness becomes a tool for liberation. Yet once their own historically conditioned character is recognized, the moral leverage is lost. It is one thing to hold racial segregation under the spotlight, assuming it will be judged by the standard that "all men are created equal," but quite another when that standard, like so many others, loses its quasi-religious authority. If all ideals are culturally conditioned, products of one or another form of self-interest, where is the ground on which to stand to challenge the powers and principalities?

In the end, my generation did succeed in opening up the church and eroding the foundations of American civil religion, or, as it is better called, the American democratic faith. Surely the disintegration of the Catholic subculture, here and in other parts of the world, has been in many ways liberating. But it has also meant the loss of a Catholic identity that could bind diverse communities together. So we are left wondering, at times, who we are. In the nation, a similar experience has taken place. Destiny, manifest or not, is gone, and with it any common ground that might allow us to deal with issues of significance for us as a people, if we are in fact one people.

So my discovery of historical consciousness relied upon an unspoken confidence that the claims of faith and reason could be rather easily reconciled. Hard times came not only when I, like so many Catholics, had to ask whether faith could be sustained without the supportive subculture with which it had come to be identified, but also when I realized that reason supplied no firmer foundation, for it too arose from communities sustained by faith and subcultural supports. Religion had of course influenced my approach to history, but it became increasingly clear that this was true for everybody. To paraphrase Jesse Jackson, "religious exclusivists" and "secular exclusivists" may have come to this moment in different ships, but we're all in the same boat now.

So the professor's worried question: what, after all, do we think of historical consciousness? We no longer have the modernist option: we cannot place our complete trust in science, or, more generally, in human intelligence, or in the process of history. This is not to say that we have become anti-intellectual, but only to confess that all knowledge is culturally conditioned, tentative, hypothetical, and metaphorical and that the old lines between art and science, faith and reason, are blurred.

And what of the alternative to modernism? Some among us may find a resolution in one or another form of fundamentalism, be it the scriptural fundamentalism of a variety of evangelicals, the doctrinal or papal fundamentalism of some Catholics, or the simple reassertion of enlightenment pieties of objectivity, detachment, and knowledge for its own sake among those that Page Smith terms "academic fundamentalists."[15] But modernisms and fundamentalisms alike require us, for the sake of certitude, to purge ourselves of, or at least set sharp limits to, historical consciousness. For some of us, that acid has eaten too deeply to be easily purged, and we are led to ask whether purging it is what the Lord and the times require of us.

There is another option of course, one that all of us take some of the time, an option we share with our neighbors and friends, which is to make a radical but altogether understandable distinction between private and public life, faith and work. One or another simple faith may guide our private and personal lives, while we simply cease to wonder about the meaning of the larger social and cultural worlds we inhabit. It is the way in which we Americans are religious — and we are very religious, most of the time. We still believe, we pray far more than most people, and we find church important, especially when we have families. But more and more of us are unsure about the meaning, much less the morality, of our work, our culture, and our politics. So we get along as best we can, increasingly detached from economy and politics, and pour our hearts into relationships and families and communities if we are lucky, or into consumption of various kinds, if we are not.

In theory we all reject these options and yearn for integration. We would like to avoid the righteousness and exclusivism of the subcultural voices contending for our allegiance and the soft hypocrisy that haunts so much of American life. Independent now, we can critique all voices, but can we find our own? Clinging still to the twin poles of faith and reason, we search for a middle ground, but one with enough power and moral force to enable us to play a significant role on the historical stage. For Catholics, it is the ground that was once occupied with such grace and dignity by John Henry Newman. But it is a ground hard to locate today.

My choice has been to find that ground by commitment to the life of my church, to stand within my tradition, to identify as best I can with my people, to accept the identity given me by my parents and those who have cared for me, and to see the world and Catholic higher education from there.

BEING CATHOLIC

When I think about my own experience of being a Catholic, I am reminded of an essay by Daniel Callahan written in the midst of post-Vatican II Catholic enthusiasm, when all kinds of previously reticent persons were telling the world about their experiences of God. Callahan thought that people who had such interesting encounters with the divine occupied the penthouses, high atop the skyscrapers. Sadly, Callahan located himself among the "religious slum dwellers" who had never risen to such heights.[16] Like Callahan, I would like to avoid description of the "mean streets" of my quite conventional and uneventful religious experience. What is important to our discussion is the relationship that might exist between my Catholicism, of which I will say more presently, and my work as a professor.

At some point along the way I made a more or less conscious decision to locate my work in the context of the Roman Catholic community in the United States. In particular, I chose to look at my work within that segment of the community that was working for renewal in the context of a commitment to peace, social justice, and human liberation. The former choice—to reaffirm my Catholicism—derived, I think, from loyalty and gratitude to the family, friends, and institutions that had formed me. The other choice—for the social action segment of the community—derived from my troubled but unapologetic appropriation of a form of American civil religion and from a series of "little Providences." In any event, in a peculiarly Catholic, and therefore institutional, way, I came to see myself as historian, writer, and college professor in the setting of the Catholic social movement.

This was no abstract commitment, but one made in relationship to specific people and specific organizations. When I arrived in Rochester to attend its university in the fall of 1960, a graduate student fresh from Notre Dame, I was guided by the local newspaper to a home near campus where a room was available. My "landparents," as they soon called themselves, were long-time Catholic Workers, associated with the Rochester House of Hospitality, the nation's second oldest. They took great joy in introducing me to Dorothy Day and the Catholic Worker movement and to other lay and social action elements of the Catholic tradition that I had somehow overlooked during my fifteen years of Catholic education. The *Catholic*

Worker paper pointed me to an engaged Catholic intellectual life and with the help of my activist Jewish graduate school friends, transformed my politics. Although trained in American political and social history, I decided to write my thesis on American Catholic social thought in the 1930s; thus I became a "Catholic historian."[17] Strangely, then, I found the church more interesting and discovered its intellectual tradition while attending a very secular graduate school.

During graduate school and the five years that followed at Loyola College in Montreal, my political and ecclesiastical engagement was largely confined to teaching and writing. Then, in 1970, a year after I came to Holy Cross, I attended an annual meeting of the Catholic Committee on Urban Ministry (CCUM), a national network of priests, sisters, and laypeople working for social justice in pastoral and social ministry. CCUM's guiding spirit, Monsignor John Egan, asked me to join its board, and, for the next eight years, I happily helped organize conferences, taught in a summer training program, and traveled around the country giving talks and workshops. Egan led me into other work, including service on committees of the national bishops' conference, on the Faith and Order Commission of the National Council of Churches, and, later, on the Board of Directors of the *National Catholic Reporter*. This work built friendships and gave me experiences of authentic community: people united by a common vision, sharing common language and meaning, working for common ends, and praying and celebrating together.

The experience also transformed my understanding of the intellectual life. I had enormous respect for the shock troops working in the church's most difficult ministries. I continually learned from them about faith, culture, and politics, about power and its uses, and about the tough work of building democracy among real people. I was awed by the experience of being told that they found my work useful and affirming, that they appreciated the critical lens I tried to hold up to their language and symbols as I tried with them to understand how to translate religious meanings and moral values into public practice. Abstract ideas of theory and practice and action and reflection were made real by dialogue with experienced, mature adults, mediated by communities of faith and moderated by the healthy, unromantic Catholic realism of the older generation, led by people like Egan and Monsignor George Higgins, the nation's foremost "labor priest."

For me it gave rise to a vision of academic intellectuals and colleges and universities enriched and empowered by serving the church, which in turn was serving the human community. Intellectuals could find new meaning in their work by connecting with real communities, the church would become more intelligent, and the colleges and universities could talk to their students in new ways about knowledge, power, and responsibility, about vocation and citizenship. The vision, however idiosyncratic, has never left me.

This all came to a climax for me with the Call to Action Conference in Detroit in October 1976. Together with Sister Alice Gallin, I directed the work of eight committees, each chaired by a bishop and including scholars and people active in the ministries of the church. Our task was to assess the materials gathered during two years of national consultation, including eight dramatic regional hearings. The committees covered areas of church, humankind, nationhood, neighborhood, ethnicity and race, work, family life, and personhood. These reports, together with carefully constructed draft recommendations, were submitted to the 2,400 delegates selected to attend the first national convention of the American church. They debated and eventually voted on these recommendations, which were then submitted to the bishops.[18]

For a variety of reasons, the recommendations were for the most part shelved, but the experience did bear witness to the possibilities of combining faith, ecclesiastical unity, and social and cultural responsibility. The U.S. Bishops' later pastoral letters on nuclear weapons, racism, and the economy would not have been possible without the experience of the Call to Action Conference. The point here is that Sr. Alice and I experienced in the committees the process of intellectuals working with bishops and grassroots ministers to respond to the appeals of ordinary parishioners and to the problems of American society. Here was concrete proof that the tensions of postconciliar Catholicism could be overcome and intellectual life could be constructively connected to a church in service to the larger community. Others could find, as I had, new meaning in their intellectual vocations by locating themselves within a specific community of discourse.

Thus my interest in and approach to Catholic higher education. I come to the subject as a Catholic, committed to and working within this community of faith, understanding its meaning and mission within and not outside the human family at the end of the twentieth century. Pope John XXIII, in *Pacem in Terris* (1963), deliberately relocated the church at the heart of our historical situation, a shift confirmed at Vatican II. Thus the opening words of the Council's "Pastoral Constitution on the Church and the Modern World":

The joys and the hopes, the griefs and anxieties, of the men and women of this age, especially those who are poor or in any way afflicted, these too are the joys and the hopes, the griefs and anxieties, of the followers of Christ.[19]

Catholic higher education, to the degree it is Catholic, has something to do with the Catholic church, and the church exists not for itself, not in sectarian withdrawal from the common works of men and women, but, as the body of Christ, for the human family whose dignity and solidarity it affirms and in some sense makes present. And that understanding, for me, began and is nurtured not initially in texts or institutions, however precious, but in the encounters I have had, through the grace of God, with people and communities, many more than I have mentioned, who reveal and embody, who sacramentalize, that reality of faith.

FAITH AND CHURCH

Now, all this may beg the question. Granted that a believing Catholic might find the church enriching and church work vocationally enhancing, but what about belief itself? First, I am a Catholic by habit and conviction, and both derive from family history. So Catholic was the "web" of my existence (to use a wonderful Vatican II image)[20] until I was an adult, that I would not know myself apart from it. I say this in spite of the fact that my own family's later experience of parish life has been uneven, to say the least. But I am an historian, as I have said, and I feel far less uncomfortable with what some might call my "cultural Catholicism" than they think I should.

Knowing that the best defense is a good offense, I have developed some fairly sharp razors for dissecting the evangelicalism of some friends and the secularity of others. But there is another reason beyond the weakness of the alternatives to make me feel still at home with a Catholicism whose faith is shared in liturgy and sacrament. Although I know a great deal about the many inequities of pastoral, liturgical, and parochial life in the United States, I cannot imagine a richer and more interesting community of meaning and value to make one's own. I have known in my lifetime deeply committed, heroic Maryknoll missioners, enormously dedicated women religious, tough, cranky priests, brilliant teachers, and, most important, the men and women of the CCUM network. I have known about John XXIII and John Paul II, Lech Walesa and Oscar Romero. I need not extend the list. I have read Mary Gordon and learned from David Tracy and wondered at the ways that a Catholic sensibility still informs people who have consciously distanced themselves from the church. I honestly think that, when I urge people to read *Commonweal, America, Cross Currents,* and the *Catholic Worker,* I do so not because I am trying to get my own beliefs validated, but because they are intelligent, interesting, and worth reading.

Finally, I am not immune to industrialism's efficient use of resources. I may be a less faith-filled person than many of the Catholics I have met, but

I have been graced by the friendship of such persons and by their assurance that they appreciate that part of the work of the church I try to do. So maybe there is a rough division of labor in the mystical body of Christ. I recall an Oakland pastor at a liturgy speaking quietly at the prayers of the faithful of parishioners whose faith sustained his own. It is that kind of Catholicism, I suspect, that provides the best bridge to the liberal Catholicism of John Henry Newman. Perhaps it was the faith of his parishioners in working-class Birmingham that enabled him to remain honest and holy in spite of the times and in spite of what so many in the church did to him. Perhaps, then, the renewal of liberal Catholicism and the revival of its now shrunken and somewhat pessimistic adherents, lies in a similar recovery of connectedness with the Catholic people. David Tracy found the "classic" of liberation theology not in a written text, but in the people themselves;[21] perhaps we may someday learn to do the same. In any event, it is with and among people that I have sustained my faith and found meaning in my work as historian and professor. I hope that Catholic higher education can provide opportunities for others to do the same.

CHAPTER 2

Catholicism, American Style

CATHOLIC HIGHER EDUCATION AS AMERICAN

Several years ago, on the eve of Pope John Paul II's first trip to the United States, which was to begin in Boston, a friend asked me to speak to a faculty group at the Massachusetts Institute of Technology. When I arrived I found a rather full classroom, most of the group older adults rather than the students I had expected. Feeling a bit intimidated, I gave an overview of changes in the church since the Second Vatican Council, with particular attention to the growth of the church in the Third World and its developing role as a champion of human rights and world peace. When I was done, the first question came from the back of the room, from an older man I later learned was a distinguished scientist. "That's all very interesting," he said, "but let me tell you about the situation in my parish." He did, telling one of those all-too-common stories of an amazingly insensitive pastor. His question set the tone, and the rest of the discussion was taken up with problems of parish leadership, school closings, and birth control. No one showed much interest in the global issues about which I had spoken; there was not a word about science. I wondered if the situation would have been much different if the meeting had taken place at Boston College. American Catholics—maybe all American Christians—are very interested in the personal and community aspects of religion and a lot less interested in the religious dimension of things political and intellectual.

So the first thing to say about American Catholic higher education is that it is American as well as Catholic. It has developed and today exists within the community of Catholics in the United States. Debates about Catholic higher education in the United States invariably ignore that Americanness of American Catholicism. Instead, in dialectical fashion, academics and ecclesiastics talk about "the church" and "the university." One group stresses the proper Catholic understanding of human knowledge and, thus, of the university as the center where knowledge is preserved, extended, and

16

transmitted. At the other pole, academics emphasize the modern understanding of knowledge, and therefore of the university, held by scholars since the late nineteenth century. The one element is supposed to explain the Catholic adjective, the other the university noun; the first is concerned with faith and the church, the second with the intellectual life as structured around America's diverse array of colleges and universities.

At its best, the Catholic argument expands the understanding of Catholic Christianity's claim to universal truth in such a way as to embrace all of human life and culture; as religious faith and human intellect both strain for ultimacy, they are intrinsically related to one another. For those who adhere to the university pole — "a university is a university" — their reach also is universal. The university's intrinsic and necessary spirit is free; the university could not, without sacrifice of its essential meaning, be modified by any adjective — national, ethnic, or religious.[1]

Both ends of the dialectic may strain toward universality, thus pushing to embrace and subordinate the other. But there is almost always a missing piece — the piece needed to reconcile exclusive and universal claims with the fact of diversity. Ignoring the American context, the Catholic discussion is either abstract, dealing with theological explanations of Catholicism, or juridical, dealing with the location of the Catholic college and university in the structure of law and hierarchy. Little is said of the Catholic people; less is said of their understanding of the relationship between faith, knowledge, and education. Yet America's colleges and universities, including Catholic schools, are, more than in any other country in the world, the people's colleges and universities. And so they were, and are, American, very American.

"GOD, COUNTRY, AND NOTRE DAME"

In early June 1960, I graduated from the University of Notre Dame, and I thought I stood that day at the center of American Catholicism. The baccalaureate Mass was celebrated by Giovanni Cardinal Montini of Milan, who three years later would become Pope Paul VI. The next day, President Dwight D. Eisenhower delivered the commencement address, but our most enthusiastic cheers were given for medical missionary Dr. Tom Dooley, a Notre Dame graduate who had won fame by bringing basic medical care to poor people fleeing the communist menace in Indochina. Dooley was dying of cancer, and his youthful blend of Catholic heroism and American idealism touched something deep inside us. In a few months we would cast our first ballots in a presidential election, most of us for John F. Kennedy, who challenged us to get involved in public service during a visit to Notre Dame earlier that year. We went forth from Notre Dame that day filled with enthusiasm that was partly Catholic and partly American. Chiseled over the door of Sacred Heart Church on campus are the words "For God, Country, and Notre Dame." On that day, those words made complete sense.

We were not alone. Most Americans, Catholic or not, loved their church or synagogue, and they loved their country, as we did, with a heady blend of innocence and hope. Change was exploding all around us, but we believed with all our hearts that change was good, for history was on our side. Almost without trying, it seemed, we Americans had gained that world power that, in George Kennan's words, "history plainly intended we should bear." As Kennedy told us, we were "watchmen on the walls of world liberty," required to ask not what our country could do for us, but what we could do for our country. At the same time, we Catholics were on the move, poised to take our place at the center of American society and culture: it was our turn.

Belief that the historical process is headed in the right direction—in our direction—is no small thing. It means that when I give myself to satisfying and rewarding work, I not only do good for myself but good for others. In other countries class conflict might be a zero sum battle over fixed resources; here it was a struggle in which everyone could win because the economy kept growing through our efforts. Racial segregation was simply, in another Kennedy phrase, "the unfinished business" of American democracy. As for us, the children and grandchildren of immigrants from Europe, we had lost or were rapidly losing our old identity as Irish or French or German; we would not go home to the old neighborhoods, nor would we bring our families to ethnic churches. But we gained in melting pots like Notre Dame a new and richer identity, American and Catholic. So full and rich was American identity that it could embrace and not destroy the religions of the people; Notre Dame was living testimony to the fact that one need not cease being different in religion in order to be considered a first-class American.

So you could be and I could be, as enthusiastically as one can be, Catholic and American. Once those terms had raised problems, for some Americans wondered about Catholics, though very few Catholics wondered about America. Maybe we should have. When I was in school, a serious professor asked a question he heard from European Catholic visitors: were we Catholics who happened to be American or Americans who happened to be Catholic? We insisted that we were both, that each confirmed the other, that it all fit together. But when the professor pushed the question, I kept quiet, honestly unsure of how I should answer. For the moment, I could not imagine conflict. If proof was needed that American Catholicism and

Catholic Americanism were equally good, the proof was right there, in family stories about grandparents and parents who had very little, almost lost that in the Great Depression just a few years earlier, went to war, worked hard, kept the faith, valued education, and produced Notre Dame and Dr. Tom Dooley and, eventually, me and my classmates.

REINVENTION?

I was dimly aware in that setting that Notre Dame was changing, its modernizing drive for "excellence" another episode of our Catholic arrival. The Holy Cross priests who ran Notre Dame, especially the university's young president, Theodore M. Hesburgh, C.S.C., defined the meaning of the university and our experience; its quest for excellence, respectability, and power, like ours, was the logical and apostolic extension of our Catholicism. We were moving toward the center of American society and so was Notre Dame.

But in a very short time something happened, something that made the journey from margin to mainstream seem less exciting, even a bit sordid. I would sit at many more Catholic graduation ceremonies and hear messages as far removed from that day at Notre Dame in 1960 as that day was distant from the moment in 1843 when Edward Sorin decided to start a school at the mission of Notre Dame du Lac. America and Catholicism and American Catholicism changed, and in nothing did it all change more dramatically, or more significantly, than in our feeling about our Americanness. The taken-for-granted blend of Catholic and American righteousness, the unexamined intimacy of their relationship inside us, once shaped our church and its universities. But a new day arrived so suddenly that it shattered lives. On that day anything but a "Catholic-who-happens-to-be-American" answer to my professor's question would look like blasphemy. At Notre Dame, a decade after my departure, students demanded that the university recover its critical distance from the nation by opposing the Vietnam War; as at almost every university, these demands led to conflict with their administration, as well as with the government.

When the earthquakes of the 1960s were over, the mission and identity of Catholic colleges and universities, once so obvious and compelling, was hard to find. Having come from the heart of the American church, their fate had become bound up with a community undergoing historic transformation. When history is no longer moving in the right direction—in our direction—faith and work are disconnected, and everything looks different. In Mary Gordon's stunning novel *Final Payments*, the heroine exclaims after the death of her ever-so-Catholic father: "I would have to invent a life for myself."[2] It was a feeling shared by many Catholics, a feeling reflected in the energetic but vaguely uneasy and strangely confused culture of Catholic higher education.

TRINITARIAN CHANGE

The Catholic experience of this perilous new situation resulted from the convergence of three streams of historical change. First, there was the gradual collapse of the American Catholic subculture—the immigrant church—long made up of families, neighborhoods, parishes, and ethnic groups, all sustained by a shared sense of being a religious minority. As late as the 1930s, Catholics were predominantly blue collar workers, their incomes among the nation's lowest. After World War II, millions of Catholics went to college, many with the help of the G.I. Bill of Rights, then entered management and the professions, intermarried with one another, and moved from city neighborhoods to the automobile suburbs, building churches that were no longer Irish or French or German, but simply Catholic and American. This process of arrival—of economic and social outsiders moving inside, many helped along by rapidly expanding Catholic colleges and universities—changed the immigrant, working-class church into a community whose class composition corresponded more and more closely to that of society at large.

Over the years, sociologist Andrew Greeley regularly documents this astonishing record of improved income, education, and status, a success story without historical precedent.[3] Measured against the situation of immigrant families a few generations earlier, it was a story of authentic liberation. Economic security, educational advancement, and political participation are surely characteristics of a community freed from the harsher constraints of poverty, ignorance, and powerlessness. Put this process of social mobility together with the remarkable unity, orthodoxy, and prosperity of the post–World War II church and we have a success story—a liberation story—in need of theological reflection.

Perhaps that story never got told as liberation because it intersected with two other, equally complicated stories. One was the story of what was previously an oxymoron, Catholic renewal. In the United States, Catholic Americanization reached its climax with the Kennedy election, and at about that same moment the immensely popular Pope John XXIII decided to call an ecumenical council, Vatican II. Pope John apparently hoped to move the church from its defensive resistance of modern culture to a sharing of responsibility for the fate of the human family. Non-Catholic Christians were welcomed to the Council, which endorsed Pope John's affirmation of human rights and made its own declaration in favor of religious liberty, reversing the longtime Catholic condemnation of these liberal ideals. Theologically, doctrine was put to pastoral tests, and historical and scriptural scholarship modified liturgical and pastoral practices dominant since the Reformation. Even the Papacy challenged itself to become more collegial. The church, its boundaries with non-Catholic Christians and with all persons, now blurred, recentered itself as "the people of God" in the midst of human history. A Eurocentric Catholicism turned outward, sparking an awakening of local churches in Latin America, Africa, and Asia whose consequences none could foresee.

For U.S. Catholics, who were innocent of the tragedies of the church's European experience of fascism, anti-Semitism, and war, and were more organized, prosperous, and, in terms of doctrine and discipline, faithful than any other national church, the Council was a tremendous surprise. In a short period of time, English replaced Latin as the language of religious ceremonies, new forms of religious education emphasizing scripture and personal commitment replaced the doctrinal statements of the long popular catechism, hundreds of Catholic parochial schools closed, and a large number of sisters and priests left their ministries. While Catholics generally approved of changes in the liturgy, improved ecumenical relations, and the new scriptural piety, they were disturbed by the sharp decline in Catholic school attendance, the declining numbers of priests and religious, and the passionate public controversy over birth control. As Vatican II, with its call to renewal and reform, intersected with the social transformation of the American immigrant church, the pace of change was remarkable and increasingly troubling.

And, if all that were not enough, a third pattern of change converged with these others as the United States itself underwent the cultural upheaval of the 1960s. Whether it was the advent of a new religious pluralism with the collapse of denominational subcultures, the sexual revolution, the racial crisis, or the war in Vietnam, something happened. Catholics, their patriotism charged with an emotional quality aroused by years of nativist suspicions, loved America and found the new divisions within the civil religion enormously painful, especially when Catholics themselves were divided, as they were on race and war. The bishops belatedly endorsed the civil rights movement and attempted to combat racism in and out of the church. Spurred by Vatican II's support for the right of conscientious objection, the church attempted to guide its people to make up their own minds about the Vietnam War. In 1971, the hierarchy collectively determined that the war could no longer be justified. Some Catholics resisted this new critical distance between the church and the country until, in 1973, as the Vietnam War ended, the Supreme Court struck down laws prohibiting abortion. By then almost everyone had been forced to rethink that question my professor had asked about the priority of Catholic or American commitments.[4]

In order to understand Catholic higher education, it will be necessary to look closely at the impact of the first two strands of change we mentioned: the Catholic success story and the Second Vatican Council. But the third may be the most important, and least noticed. For how one feels about the country will in great measure determine the balance one strikes between the religious and academic dimensions of college and university life. It is the difference between the word "Americanization," used in the 1950s and early 1960s to describe the modernization of Catholic schools (that was usually thought a good thing), and the word "secularization," now almost universally used to describe these changes (that most definitely is not a good thing). Critics say the difference is the degree of commitment to the Catholic part of the identity of Catholic schools, and there is likely some truth in that. But a case can be made that the real difference is the change in attitude toward the larger culture — American culture — in which these schools, and we ourselves, live. If our America and our people prove unworthy of our faith, hope, and love, where will we turn, after all, but to church — to our church and to our true people — if we can find them? Finally, the answer to my professor's question was clear: Catholics who happen to be American.[5]

LIBERATION AND/OR DISINTEGRATION

The combination of these three streams of change left in their wake a new and more complicated American Catholicism. There are less priests, many fewer nuns, and fewer laypeople at Mass, although many more engaged in the work (now we say the ministries) of the church. There has been open dissent by theologians and massive resistance of people to Catholic teaching on sexuality. Church leaders speak with occasional wisdom about problems of public morality. A steadily increasing Hispanic population and large numbers of immigrants have brought renewed diversity to the church and changed its center of gravity a few degrees, from the industrial northeast and midwest to the west and south. Some of its older groups are now quite prosperous; many of the newcomers are at least as poor as immigrants of the last century. The bishops of the United States began to find a collective voice in the 1970s, before a conservative resurgence in Rome reined in what seemed venturesome independence. In recent years, debates about the role of women in the church have divided the hierarchy, angered if not alienated large numbers of women, and put at risk many church programs that depend upon the contributions of women.

Most of all there is a new voluntarism throughout the church. Less and less can be taken for granted, consensus and community are harder to find, self-conscious choice has become the norm, and people have been thrown on their own religious and spiritual resources. This new voluntarism, and the self-consciousness from which it springs, now pervades the church in:

- renewal programs focused on small groups sharing personal responses to scripture, now seen as essential to vital parish life;
- personal prayer, growing from the heart of one's own experience of God, a piety in sharp contrast with the novenas and insistently public ceremonies of the past;
- the widespread popularity of the new Rite of Christian Initiation of Adults, in which both catechumen and community become self-conscious about the conversion to which all are called;
- the widely noticed gaps between church teaching and popular practice on birth control, in the widely perceived inability to be prescriptive about matters of sexual and social morality; and
- the emergence of the word *ministry*, unknown among Catholics a few years ago. Standing in some tension with hierarchical, clerical church organization, ministry brings with it themes of community, mutuality, and equality, as well as a theology of gifts, even participatory democracy.[6]

Andrew Greeley sums up this vital, if confusing, Catholicism with his characteristic combination of irritation and affection:

A Rembrandt landscape after a storm: ineffective, confused and conflicted, if sincere, church leaders; poor religious education; disheartened priests; unenlightened preaching; angry women; a vigorously independent laity; a moribund sexual ethic; economic success; cultural resurgence; distinguished theologians; increased religious devotion; shortages of priests; democratization of local institutions; fads; conflict; shouting; anger; hope, and a new religious sensibility among the young—thus American Catholicism 20 years after Pope John XXIII's breeze became a whirlwind after crossing the Atlantic.[7]

Greeley calls it "do-it-yourself" Catholicism, others, less sympathetic, "cafeteria Catholicism."

Birth control led the older generation to question church teaching and rely on conscience; for younger people there is less conflict as they adopt the individualism of American culture. Personal choice is inevitable for a generation without a subculture of their own and directed by their parents toward the center of society. A teacher at one Catholic high school reports what could be repeated on many a campus: "One cannot encourage young people to develop habits of mind that go along with being good students at an elite institution without also promoting autonomy" and what one scholar calls "moral protestantism," the primacy of personal conscience. Paulist Michael Hunt reports that among incoming first-year college students in 1992, 30 percent were Catholic, and they were more religious than expected and differed widely in their views. Of that group, for example, 84 percent had been to church at least once in the previous year, 33 percent described themselves as "born again" Christians, and almost 66 percent favored legalized abortion under some circumstances. One observer reports that religion teachers in schools and parishes adapt very effectively to this diversity among the young. They have authority when students see them as being motivated by a desire to understand more than to control and to offer not clear answers but moral categories and guidelines. But their very adaptation may unintentionally reinforce the selective Catholicism they often want to avoid. For two-thirds of the students interviewed in one Catholic high school, "being Catholic" was simply a matter of choice, including the right to affirm some specific teachings while rejecting others.[8]

Such assessments, and they could be multiplied endlessly, make a cliche of the statement that the church has changed. The point is that in order to understand Catholic higher education and what the Catholic adjective requires of the college and university noun, one has to make sense of this new, very diverse, sometimes conflicted, now altogether free church—no simple matter. In fact, the pace of change has been so rapid, and at first glance at least seems so far reaching, that all assessments must be tentative. Nevertheless, to proceed to make judgements about American Catholic higher education without attending with appropriate modesty to this changing church would be a serious mistake.

MAKING SENSE OF RENEWAL

Historians have yet to offer a thorough analysis of the post-conciliar period. The most common explanation is that this new situation is the result of Americanization. Historians like the late John Tracy Ellis, Philip Gleason, Jay P. Dolan, and James Hennessy agree that the American church, once "the immigrant church," now stands at the climax of assimilation.[9] For awhile this "revolutionary moment" seemed promising; Catholics were finally at home in America. They still retained "a special sense of themselves," so Hennessy was typically confident that the American church would approach its new challenges "out of its own tradition, its own social memory, its own special understanding of reality."[10] But do Catholics really retain enough "social memory" and "special understanding of reality" to shape their own future? Monsignor Ellis grew uncertain in his later years. Philip Gleason became convinced that renewal brought not liberation but "disintegration." Indeed, as Gleason sees it, Americanization became a synonym for secularization: Catholics joined the mainstream, but at the cost of their rich heritage and distinctive self-understanding. It is fair to say that this pessimistic view, once confined to a small minority, has now become a near consensus. Renewal, in practice, meant adaptation to American secular culture, and it has gone too far. This is the charge stated more or less directly in almost every criticism of Catholic higher education.

There are, however, serious problems with the Americanization/secularization hypothesis, not least the insistence of older generations as far back as John Carroll, the nation's first Catholic bishop, that they were as American as anyone else (to say nothing of the preoccupation of church leaders with money, buildings, growth, and other more or less "secular" matters). Carroll's confident Anglo-American Catholicism was overwhelmed by the masses of European immigrants who arrived after 1820, but even the immigrant church's most militant Irish or German or Polish leaders invariably took pains to insist on the patriotic loyalty of their people and of the church, even as they worked hard to retain religious customs and commitments that had originated in Europe. The self-conscious effort to do so, expressed in churches, schools, and hospitals, all with American flags prominently displayed, along with dozens of other elements of a growing Catholic subculture, was a bootstrap, self-help experience that was quintessentially American. So it is not at all clear that the heart of recent experience was the Americanization of non-American, presumably European, Catholicism.

Instead the story involves an ongoing process of interaction between individual and group values and the changing social and cultural landscape of the United States. Support for such an argument is found in the work of historian Timothy L. Smith. Concentrating on the experience of later immigrants from southern and eastern Europe, Smith is convinced that parishes often owed their origin to lay initiative and that the laypeople and pastors who built the churches, like the priests and religious who founded the colleges, were only modestly alienated if at all; instead they were usually optimistic, hopeful, and ambitious, determined to take advantage of the new opportunities America afforded. At the same time, they saw no reason why they should not hold on to the values, traditions, and religious faith they had brought with them from Europe. They could be themselves and they could be American. Why not?

For Smith, therefore, the ethnic group—and ethnic parish—was a corridor through which people passed, not a room that walled them off. Within it, men enjoyed new opportunities for education, self-improvement, and leadership, while women enjoyed new status by sharing responsibility for family income and household management. For the children of such settled families, who dominated churches and ethnic organizations, the group provided identity, affirmation, and a ground for active, assertive engagement with the amoral but not necessarily impenetrable world beyond the group. Smith therefore challenges those who have held that "the religious and ethnic sentiments of immigrant minorities are anachronisms that must give way to the processes of assimilation and modernization." Instead he argues that ethnic identity "gave both to faith and to the sense of peoplehood a fluid and instrumental quality that was more future oriented than backward looking," as, in a stunning image, "folk memories were brought to bear upon new aspirations."

Smith consciously rejects metaphors of melting pots and mosaics in favor of "kaleidoscopic change." This fluid, undogmatic, and compassionate understanding of social history suggests that the contemporary Catholic search for group identity and a sense of mission is not new but a normal, persistent response to the experience of pluralism.[11] Ambivalence, as in the famous image of W.E.B. DuBois of "twoness," American and African, American and Catholic, may be built in. It can be resolved on one side (Catholic) or the other side (American) only at the peril of personal and ecclesial integrity. And realization that the meaning of each of the terms, *Catholic* and *American*, is always changing, and always in some large measure a human construction should moderate quick judgements about secularization and the loss of Catholic identity.

The suggestion of this interpretation of U.S. Catholic history would be that the superficial unity of the American Catholic community—and the apparently solid identity of Catholic institutions—in the postwar years, a unity that gave the changes of the sixties that peculiar sense of "disintegration," was a temporary and quite uncharacteristic moment. For all the diversity of the immigrant church, the dream of Christendom lived on in a sectarian Catholic ideology that claimed that the Catholic church was *the*

Church and the custodian of true culture. In the colleges and universities, this was the Catholicism that supplied a Catholic gloss on an education designed to prepare people for middle-class life. The church could, in the 1920s and 1950s, decry the selfishness, materialism, and secularism of American culture while taking immense pride in the numbers of communicants, the size and splendor of its buildings, the worldly success of its most rich and famous members, and the victories of its football teams.

That particular Catholic and very American subculture is gone, because its people, its self-definition, and its cultural setting changed, less because of external pressures to conform or unworthy desires to belong than because Catholics wanted to be at home at the center of their world. Of course, pressures for change came from the outside, as they always do, but the Catholic community in the United States exploded from the inside more than it collapsed under external pressure. Perhaps the United States wanted to integrate its Catholics, perhaps they were seduced by secularism or capitalism or materialism. But I suspect that Catholics also wanted America, and they wanted and needed the openness and honesty made possible by Vatican II. They broke out of the subculture more than they watched it disintegrate. If Smith is right, Catholics were almost never passive victims, almost always (even in the depths of poverty) active and responsible agents. They were certainly that in the 1960s, and they still are, and nowhere more than in higher education.

So the bewildering variety and complexity Greeley described, made dramatic by the unity that preceded it, may not be declension at all, but merely a return to normal. Constructing a unified church organization, forming communities appropriate to the needs of individuals, families, and social groups, and creating institutions through which to support those communities are projects for us as they were for our predecessors. Like them, we carry out that work in some combination of memory and hope; starting over is never an entirely new experience. What they found and what we have lost, perhaps, is neither faith nor ecclesial loyalty, but that key for Smith, peoplehood. Thus the Catholic and American questions intersect: who, after all, are our people? If they are Americans, and in another way Christians or Catholics, is there not truth in that and danger in choosing one over the other?

My teacher Hayden V. White once suggested that modern historiography crippled itself by clinging to notions of Darwinian science and Victorian literature despite the radical transformation of twentieth-century understanding of art and science.[12] Could the same thing be said of our understanding of American Catholicism and American religion? If Catholics are now Christians first, if they prefer religious experience to organized ritual practice and Scripture to catechisms, if they believe the dignity of the human person means freedom for believers as well as nonbelievers, and if they doubt that their nation or world will become Catholic in the near future, then the neat patterns that once grounded distinct identity will not be recaptured, save at the price of isolation and irresponsibility. We Catholics have arrived, to be sure; arrived not as Americans, because we always were, but arrived into the center of that America which, like the ancient holy of holies, turns out to be empty. Spiritually on our own, we are socially and organizationally not in the Kingdom of God, but in a pluralistic world and a diverse and conflicted church for whose current life and future prospects we share responsibility.

DECENTERING CATHOLICISM

In many ways, the challenges of pluralism were already evident in the universal church around the world when John XXIII decided to summon his Council. Thoughtful European Catholics had been asking since the end of the war whether the church's exclusive claims and harsh rejection of modern cultural and political values had contributed to the tragedies of twentieth-century history. Faced with the cold war, the nuclear arms race, the awakening of non-European peoples, and a host of global problems, Roman Catholicism groped for a new image of itself. With John XXIII it came: "Now more than ever, certainly more than in past centuries, our purpose is to serve man as such, and not only Catholics, to defend above all and everywhere the rights of the human person and not only those of the Catholic church."[13] John's words were echoed at the Council. After centuries of preoccupation with its own integrity, unity, and survival, the church would become, in the Council's words, "truly and intimately linked with mankind and its history."[14]

Later, in parts of the Third World, the proposition would be made that this option for the human family should be made more concrete as an "option for the poor." In clarifying that phrase, theologians and the Popes have reaffirmed the basic option for the people above all. It is a case of decentering, locating the center of God's care and the church's life, outside the formal boundaries of the church, in the middle of the human family.

But this new option has its price. Karl Rahner argued that the historic significance of Vatican II lay in the transition from a western dominated Catholicism, present in branch plant fashion throughout the world, to a "world church" with authentic new Christian churches emerging from every continent and culture.[15] Faced with this emerging global pluralism, the church's leaders now seek a balance between "indigenization" within diverse cultures, with its risk of fragmenting the universal church, and the unity of the church, achieved by the authority of Rome. Pope Paul VI's "Apostolic Exhortation on Evangelization" called for the insertion of Christianity into the very heart of world cultures, seemingly affirming the diversification of theology and pastoral practice, but a reaction toward Roman centralization has taken place under Pope John Paul II.

In the United States this worldwide effort to come to terms with pluralism is intensified by our nation's own distinctive emphasis on individualism and freedom, which makes Rome nervous and Catholic identity especially precarious. Before the Council Rahner argued that, in what he called "diaspora," where the church sees itself as a more or less permanent minority, there is a natural reaction to deny that such a situation can or should exist. "What, after all, does a person do if he sees the diaspora situation coming and thinks of it as something which simply and absolutely must not be?" Rahner asked. "He makes himself a closed circle, an artificial situation inside which it looks as if the inward and outward diaspora isn't one; he makes a ghetto."[16] At the time, this was an interpretation of the sources of the integral Catholicism of the pre–Vatican II church, but it now appears a more general phenomenon in situations of pluralism and freedom, where the church must always fear seduction by the culture. After all, it is said, the church must be the church.

So rapid and complete was the collapse of the American Catholic subculture that such attitudes were bound to reappear. Avery Dulles, one of the more moderate American theologians, has been among those who have responded to the current situation of the church with a critical reassessment of the whole process of renewal. In his view, Vatican II was "essentially a compromise between the vision of the church as a hierarchical and divine society oriented toward eternal life and the newer vision of the church as a free society called to serve the human community." Unfortunately, as Dulles sees it, advocates of the latter view controlled the post-conciliar era and went too far in their option for everybody, in the process endangering the very existence of a distinctive Catholic church and community. Dulles joined with a number of prominent Protestants and Catholics in signing the Hartford Affirmations, a set of orthodox Christian propositions they felt needed reaffirming.[17] Before long he and others turned their attention to Catholic colleges and universities, finding there the same insidious surrender to "the world," what Dulles called "the slippery path" to a complete secularization that "competent observers" regarded as "now inevitable in practically all Catholic colleges and universities."[18]

Such concern to affirm what is distinctively Catholic, whether in the church or in Catholic higher education, is at first glance a concern for integrity. It links moderates like Dulles with radicals like Daniel Berrigan, Pentecostals like Ralph Martin, and even many extreme conservatives. These factions may not like each other much, but they agree that the church and the Catholic university, and by implication most middle-class laypeople, have been compromised by immersion in the surrounding culture, in this case American culture, popularly called "the world." Even the American bishops use such terms, as in the following passage (paraphrasing Avery Dulles) from their 1983 pastoral letter on nuclear weapons:

> As believers we can identify rather easily with the early church as a company of witnesses engaged in a difficult mission . . . To obey the call of Jesus means separating ourselves from all attachment and affiliation that could prevent us from hearing and following our authentic vocation . . . This means, of course, that we must regard as normal even the path of persecution and the possibility of martyrdom. We readily recognize that we live in a world that is becoming increasingly estranged from Christian values. In order to remain a Christian, one must take a resolute stand against many commonly accepted axioms of the world. To become true disciples, we must undergo a demanding course of induction into the adult Christian community. We must continually equip ourselves to profess the full faith of the church in an increasingly secularized society.[19]

So strong is the need to recapture a distinctive Catholic ground that it leads to such sharply negative judgements on American culture; in early drafts of the pastoral, the bishops used Dulles's word "neo-pagan" to describe American society.

What distinguishes these positions is their common lament of worldliness and their call for Catholic separatism. The church and its members have become at home in their world—Americanized, if you will. The boundaries between the church and the world have become all but invisible. Laypeople at home in the world have surrendered to the siren call of modern materialism; bishops who take on a public role without reference to a specific Catholic agenda have surrendered to "secular trends." And the Catholic university, now so unsure of its Catholic identity, has been yet another victim of secularization. Understanding this attitude is absolutely essential to grasping the problem of the identity of Catholic colleges and universities. While the schools are prospering, they are beset by uncertainty about their mission because attitudes like these have undercut their historic mediating role between faith and life in pluralistic, secular society. They have helped make Catholics into Americans and now must help the church recall them to Catholicism. There is truth in this formulation, but it is also profoundly misleading. Untempered by more careful reflection on recent experience, it becomes practically, if unintentionally, restorationist.

REMEMBERING RECENTERING

Is the choice for Catholic integrity justified by a reading of the signs of the times in light of Christian faith? Was Vatican II's call for service within human cultures too risky? And were the last generations of Catholics, our parents and grandparents, bent as they were on education, economic advancement, and social respectability, pursuing false gods? After all, how can the follower of Jesus live comfortably, indeed perhaps even live at all, in a world marked by injustice, poverty, political oppression, and violence? Can any reason be given to try to influence American public life from the inside toward a "seamless garment" of pro-life values, an effort that implies an activist engagement in worldly activities? Can there be any religious, theological, or ecclesial value placed upon the laity's work in the world? And how can any serious Catholic, loyal to the tradition, be at home in a world of abortions, drug abuse, sexual kinkiness, and God knows what else?

One answer, perhaps too simple, is that it is, for better or for worse, our world. Not ours as bishops might have said in the middle ages or in Franco's Spain not too many years ago, but ours in the sense of the shared responsibility of citizenship in a pluralist democracy. If the United States is, in fact, "increasingly secularized," it must be partly our fault. We might argue that, as immigrants and outsiders, we never really had any constructive role in American society and therefore do not bear responsibility for its problems. Most of us need only reflect on our own family histories to know that is not entirely true. This is, in the end, our country; we have helped to make it what it is and by our choices we will help determine what it will become. Walt Kelly's Pogo had it right: we have met the enemy and it is us.

Making sense of the historic situation of American Catholics is the first step toward making sense of Catholic higher education. In the end, it is a question of responsibility. Thomas Merton, among the better guides, found at the heart of the central modern problem of war and violence a pervasive lack of responsibility. The lover of justice, the good person, was tempted, Merton said, "to remain quietly at his own work, like a traveller caught in a storm who retreats behind a wall to shelter from the driving gusts of dust and hail. Seeing the rest of the world full of iniquity, he will be content to keep his own life on earth untainted with wickedness and impious actions, so that he may leave this world with a fair hope of the next, at peace with himself and God." Even pacifists, Merton noted, often betray such a "world denying and individualistic asceticism. It is perhaps true that sometimes individuals may be forced into this position, but to view it as normal and to accept it as preferable to the risks and conflicts of public life is an admission of defeat, an abdication of responsibility," Merton argued. "This secession into individualistic concern with one's own salvation alone may in fact leave the way all the more open for unscrupulous men and groups to gain and wield unjust power."

Merton did not want to move the monastery to the prophetic edge of the church and the world, but rather to their center, there to engage in the midst of pluralism with the central issues of public life:

> We must judge and decide not only as individuals, preserving for ourselves the luxury of a clean conscience, but also as members of society taking a common burden and responsibility. It is all too easy to retire into an ivory tower of private spirituality and let the world blow itself to pieces. Such a decision would be immoral, an admission of defeat. It would imply a secret complicity in the overt destructive fury of the fanatics.[20]

It is this realization of responsibility that informed the effort of the Catholic bishops to participate in reshaping a public dialogue about war and economic justice and abortion. In different ways Cardinal Bernardin, Archbishop Rembert Weakland, and Cardinal John O'Connor have attempted to affirm the prophetic impulse present within the church and yet to remain within this political community, accepting responsibility for its current life and precarious prospects. As Bernardin put it in describing the overall thrust of the 1983 pastoral letter, "The Challenge of Peace":

> Historically, the moral issues of war and peace have spilled over into ecclesiology; today the cosmic dimensions of the nuclear question have moved many to say that the Christian posture can only be one of separation — personally, vocationally and ecclesially — from the societal enterprise of possessing nuclear weapons. Despite the radical moral skepticism of the pastoral letter about ever containing the use of nuclear weapons within justifiable limits, the bishops were not persuaded that this judgment should lead to an ecclesial posture of withdrawal from dialogue or participation in the public life of the nation. Rather, in accord with the traditional Catholic conception,

they affirmed a posture of dialogue with the pluralistic secular world. I am the first to say — after the past three years — that it is a precarious posture, but one I find more adequate than either total silence within society or absolute separation from society.[21]

These bishops explicitly recognize, but do not resolve, the problem posed by Dulles and so many others: how can the church be the church, with its own distinct identity, and at the same time undertake with full seriousness its mission to society, to humanization and justice and peace? There are some strong theological answers to that question that we cannot explore here, but we should at least question the concern with distinctiveness, so strong in discussions of Catholic higher education. Always we must remember that in discussions of church integrity and responsibility, church and world are not two entities, separate and apart from one another. Here and now there is no church without a world, no world without churches. In Joseph Komonchak's suggestive description:

> The world is not that which lies outside the Church; the world includes the Church, and without the Church, the world would not be what it is. Christian believing, hoping and loving are political acts, moments in the realization of the world. If this is the case, then there is not some first moment in which the Church becomes the Church and a second moment in which the Church considers its relation to the world. The Church's self-constitution is itself an act within and with reference to the world.[22]

So Americanization is not so easily reversed, and Americanism should not be so easily discarded. It is one thing to insist upon the independence of the church, its right to be the church; it is quite another to make that church the sole or dominant center of value in any particular culture. For in any particular culture, be it Poland, Chile, or the United States, the church is at one and the same time a community of faith and a constituent element of its particular world; it is responsible for its own fidelity and integrity, but also for the moral well-being of that society in which it is a participant. If it is neither the only church for a society, as it once was in so many places, nor a sect set off on the margins of society, as the dominant metaphors suggest it should be, then it is one church, with universal claims, set among others within, and sharing responsibility for, a pluralistic society and world. The church and each of its members, then, must necessarily be bilingual and bicultural, capable of forming Christian communities of conscience and conviction, but capable as well of sharing with fellow citizens responsibility for neighborhood and nation. That is as it should be, at least for now. Perhaps this dilemma of pluralism—that the church must be the church while also being "truly and intimately linked with humankind and its history"—is what American Catholics as Americans have to offer the universal church. In any event, it is why it is so very important to speak of the *American* Catholic church and the *American* Catholic university, and pause before judgements about secularization and disintegration. And it is why Catholic higher education—this meeting ground of faith and culture where, in very concrete ways, "folk memories" are still brought to bear on "new aspirations"—is of the greatest importance for the American Catholic people.

CHAPTER 3

Ex Corde Ecclesiae Americana

HANDING ON THE FAITH

Religion and education go together in the United States. It would be hard to find a religious congregation whose activities do not feature a heavy dose of religious education, with innumerable volunteers directed by one or two professionals, passing on belief to the young. No religion, it seems, is without education. Nor are we entirely convinced that there should be education without religion. Only after long, bitter debate did we Americans allow public schools without explicit religion, and many of us are still uncomfortable with that decision. Our discomfort arises from worry about our children, but also about our communities and our country. Religious people and some not-so-religious people believe that somehow national well-being seems tied to the vitality of our people's faith, and separating religion so sharply from our common life may work to the detriment of both.

Pluralism makes the relationship between religion and education particularly passionate. In more homogeneous areas, family and community may unite with formal education — with school — to make the young aware of what is important to their parents and to the society around them. But where things are changing rapidly, as they always are for migrants and for many of the poor, or where society is composed of diverse groups with different values and beliefs, as it is in so many parts of this country, education becomes a very self-conscious, deliberate, and contested process. The young must be instructed about almost everything, and on some of the most important matters, adults do not agree.

At the very least, we are aware of change, and some of us — most of us — know we are different, so we need to articulate the differences and pass on those we think important. From the start of America's immigrant history, or at least from the point when migration was considered permanent and not temporary, generational continuity, community coherence, social dis-

35

cipline, the whole transition of the child from family to community became problems to be solved by deliberate action, by education. Self-conscious community formation to support families and enable education provided the very fabric of American social life. This process was repeated in one form or another for every succeeding group of newcomers.

Of course pluralism is not all; there is the *unum* to be forged from the *pluribus*. American society and every local community needed to act to insure some degree of unity and stability, while accommodating as best it could the diverse needs of the dynamic ethnic, religious, and regional communities of which it was composed. Public schools became, at least in popular belief, important instruments for achieving that unifying purpose. Particular communities had their own needs, among them integrity. To meet those needs they could supplement the public schools with their own educational programs, centered on families and congregations, but sometimes they decided that family continuity, community solidarity, and cultural survival required them to conduct their own schools.[1]

Education became a political and cultural battleground because it was so important, to society and to its diverse peoples. It was a profoundly political matter, for it involved one of the few things that Americans decided, early in their history, to do together through their government. Diverse groups might live and let live, except when it came to the common life, like erecting and maintaining schools or, later, making war. When called to work together, differences mattered.

The history of American Catholic education reflects this complicated reality. As one minority among many, Catholics had to insure that their children remained Catholic. But they were also Americans, with the same rights and responsibilities as others, and they wanted their children to participate in the larger society. The bishops had their own interest in education. They had to unify the church and insure its integrity amid the country's — and the church's own — bewildering pluralism. Simple accommodation to American culture could result in division, doctrinal latitudinarianism, and general indifference, as the present generation is relearning. Knowing what makes Catholicism different and valuing that difference enough to sacrifice on its behalf were, for the bishops and clergy, essential educational goals.

To achieve those goals did not necessarily require Catholic schools, for the church here did not want to be entirely separated from society. But public education, requiring at least toleration, risked encouraging indifference, deadly to a struggling voluntary association. It was pluralism, not secularism, that pushed the church toward separate schools. But it meant a heavy burden, and priests and bishops and people squabbled for a century before making parochial schools more or less mandatory in 1884.

So the history of Catholic education turns on the combination of pastoral and organizational imperatives. Catholic schools were deemed necessary to the degree that a) they enabled Catholic communities to meet their twin objectives of preserving traditional culture and improving their economic and social conditions, and b) they helped the bishops and clergy build an identifiably Catholic church and secure for it a respected place in the larger society.

This combination of popular and organizational appeal was evident throughout the history of American Catholic education. Maryland Catholics sent their sons abroad to receive an education that would reinforce fidelity to family tradition while providing the skills and contacts necessary for economic survival, a combination that would long characterize Catholic education.[2] After the revolution, the American clergy, now free to establish their own institutions, agreed that one of the "most effectual ways to promote religion" would be to establish schools "for the general education of Catholic youths and the forming of ecclesiastics to the ministry." John Carroll and later bishops worked hard to establish schools, for decades bringing a wide range of ages under one roof. But they placed the highest priority on identifying and educating candidates for the priesthood. Thus Carroll established Georgetown University almost as soon as he began his episcopate. Gradually, the work of advanced education was turned over to religious orders. In the process, "the colleges took on a greater degree of detachment from the concerns of the church's official leaders."[3] Instead they reflected the aspirations of the Catholic middle class and the traditions — and ambitions — of their founding religious orders.

BUILDING A CATHOLIC SUBCULTURE

Catholic institutions then as now reflected the experience of the Catholic community. Historians have delineated a sharp change in nineteenth-century American Catholicism, a change that preceded but was confirmed by the flood of immigrants who began to arrive in the 1830s. The Anglo-American Catholics who founded the church in the United States shared many of the values of their better educated contemporaries. Their religious life was marked by an enlightenment piety, an optimistic anthropology, a rather open, tolerant view of the church, and even a hesitant acceptance of lay control of church property. But the realities of pluralism and, later, mass immigration displaced this republican style in favor of a more pessimistic view of human nature, a piety centered upon the sacraments and a more clerical, authoritarian, and institutional view of the church.[4]

This shift had a profound effect on the evolution of Catholic higher education. At first the colleges included all ages, from small children to young adults. In their programs of study, rather than building bridges between Catholics and the larger American community, they usually affirmed the clerically dominated subculture shaped by conservative theology abroad and the immigrant influx here. When convert Isaac Hecker visited the newly established Holy Cross College in 1843, he was disappointed to find that the Jesuit faculty were unfamiliar with modern literature and unable to converse on the problems stirring the religious world he was leaving behind.[5] A few years later, Hecker's friend, Orestes Brownson, was appalled when his son reported from Holy Cross that his philosophy teachers relied on anti-intellectual appeals to faith, despite their claim to base philosophy entirely upon reason.[6] In fact, Holy Cross and most other schools were little concerned with addressing the problems raised by contemporary culture, giving rise to complaints from Hecker, Brownson, and others about the primitive state of Catholic intellectual life.

Behind the controversies were real and persistent differences in understanding the church and the role of higher education within it. Liberal Catholics throughout the century retained some of the earlier generation's emphasis on reason and intelligibility, and they believed that the church should engage the problems of the age in order to forward its evangelical mission. Catholics should understand their age and nation, affirm popular hopes, and correct national failures. Most bishops and religious orders, however, were preoccupied with pastoral and organizational needs, less concerned with conversions and evangelization than with preserving the faith and loyalty of the immigrants and their children. That stance of Catholic social and cultural (though not economic) detachment from society was eventually reinforced by the triumph of ultramontane Catholicism in Europe.[7]

This broad division eventually climaxed in the Americanist episode of the 1890s. After the Civil War, educated Catholics once again complained about the intellectual shortcomings of the clergy and the weakness of seminary education. Bishop John Lancaster Spalding revived a campaign to establish a national university as a center of higher studies for clergy. Spalding and his supporters hoped that the new Catholic University of America, established by the Holy See in 1886, would be a "true university," confined to graduate instruction and research, "at once a scientific institute, a school of culture, and a training ground for the business of life."[8] When Leo XIII issued his long anticipated endorsement of the university in 1895, he seemed to affirm Spalding's dream:

An education cannot be deemed complete which takes no notice of modern science. It is obvious that in the keen competition of talents and the widespread and in itself noble and praiseworthy passion for knowledge, Catholics ought not to be followers but leaders. It is necessary, therefore, that they should cultivate every refinement of learning and zealously train their minds for the discovery of truth and the investigation, so far as possible, of the entire domain of nature.[9]

However, Leo set his endorsement of the university in the context of another project—the appointment of the first Apostolic Delegate, or papal representative, to the United States. The ecclesiology with which that office was surrounded stood in marked contrast to the open and liberal thrust of the university:

We had in mind to draw more closely the bonds of duty and friendship which connect you and so many thousands of Catholics to the Holy See. . . . For the Roman Pontiff, upon whom Christ has conferred ordinary and immediate jurisdiction as well over all and singular churches as over all and singular pastors and faithful, since he cannot personally visit the different regions and exercise the pastoral office over the flock entrusted to him, finds it necessary from time to time . . . to dispatch legates into the different parts of the world . . . who, supplying his place, may correct errors, make the rough ways plain, and administer to the people entrusted to their care increased means of salvation.[10]

The Pope hoped that the Delegate, representing his authority, would "possess no slight weight for preserving in the multitude a submissive spirit." Leo left little doubt that the American church was not to be encouraged to engage the larger world in dialogue, but to concentrate on strengthening its own subculture:

Wherefore, we ardently desire that this truth should sink day by day more deeply into the minds of Catholics—that they can in no better way safeguard their individual interests and the common good than be yielding a hearty and submissive obedience to the church.[11]

Americanists, like Spalding, saw Catholic higher education as part of a larger strategy of evangelizing American culture. In a pastoral letter of higher education in 1898, Archbishop John Ireland of St. Paul, perhaps the nation's most famous bishop, insisted that Catholicism had a public responsibility to bring her wisdom to bear on society:

> To be equal to her whole mission, the Church must possess social and political influence; she must be an intellectual and moral power, present in all fields of activity and disposing successfully of all forces that are serviceable in the cause of truth and virtue. . . . She is to be a public power, not merely in quietude with individual souls, but also controlling, by the strength and sweetness of her doctrines and her teachings, the public life of men and of peoples. . . . The Church has not fulfilled her mission, has not established the reign of Christ, where she does not direct and inspire the social and public life of the community as well as the private life of the individual. Indeed unless she does inspire and direct the social and public life of the community, it cannot be said that she really directs the private life of individuals, or that of a larger number of them, for a man's convictions are not deep and sincere unless they bear fruit in his public as well as his private life.

If the church had failed in this respect, it was because she did not have "sufficient alliance" with "intellectual culture." Now, by providing its men and women (Ireland was a strong supporter of higher education for women) with "a high order of instruction in secular branches of learning, but also a high order of instruction in matters of religion," it had the opportunity to secure "the social and public influence" that it required in order to win respect for religion and a hearing for Catholicism. To date, too many had seen education as "providing nothing but the means of making money," but now Ireland hoped Catholics would choose a "superior education" and thus become "champions of truth in the open arena of the world."[12]

But Ireland, of course, joined Spalding among the losers in the struggle to define the mission of the American church. Liberal Catholicism suffered continuous defeats. In 1899 the Vatican condemned the supposed heresy of Americanism. A few years later came the condemnation of modernism and a systematic campaign to police theological education. These steps doomed the dialogue between religion and culture, and with it the sense of an apostolic role for the laity. Left in its place was a peculiarly Catholic form of anti-intellectualism that subordinated inquiry to ecclesiastical power and imposed theological and philosophical orthodoxy on seminaries and universities.

SUBCULTURAL HIGHER EDUCATION

The American church of the twentieth century set clear boundaries to Catholic life and provided Catholics with a sense of assurance and confidence. By 1900 a combination of ethnic commitment, Vatican pressure, increased investment, and pastoral conviction solidified support for Catholic elementary schools, laid the basis for expansion of Catholic high schools, and provided a rationale for Catholic higher education. Preserving the faith of the growing middle class meant insuring opportunities for education under church auspices, encouraging Catholics to marry one another, and doing so in ways that did not inhibit economic and social advancement. A combination of religious and secular objectives, enabling social and economic advancement while insuring continued loyalty to the church, dominated American Catholic higher education. The Association of Catholic Colleges in the United States, formed in 1899, defined the purpose of higher education as forming "citizens for the city of God" while fitting "them for the business of life."[13]

It took awhile before Catholic colleges and universities became a major means of achieving these objectives, for the resources were not yet available for them to compete with secular schools. As a result, some bishops offered pastoral services to students at state or private colleges and universities, such as the Catholic center established at Cornell by Rochester Bishop Bernard McQuaid. But McQuaid's experiment was not well received. More characteristically, in 1906, the Archbishop of New York charged students attending public universities with "unpardonable disloyalty and grossest ingratitude." The pioneers in the Newman club movement, attempting to provide spiritual and intellectual support to students at non-Catholic colleges and universities, met determined opposition from Jesuits and others engaged in Catholic higher education.[14] They hoped the bishops would make attendance at secular schools as unacceptable in college as it was in grade school. By the 1920s, they almost succeeded. As a priest wrote in an early issue of the liberal lay publication *Commonweal*: "The Catholic man who would sacrifice lightly the Catholic atmosphere of the Catholic college for the ephemeral advantages of pagan culture has failed to realize practically the finest things in Catholicity. He is to be pitied."[15]

The emphasis on males accurately reflected the official church's own perception of higher education, but after 1900 there was a remarkable if often unnoticed expansion of Catholic higher education for women. The College of Notre Dame, in Maryland, founded in 1895, was the first four-year college for women. By 1910 there were thirteen, and women could be found in summer programs of graduate schools of several university campuses. For the most part, the women's colleges featured educational programs thought appropriate for women destined for careers as middle-class wives and mothers or, in a few instances, specific training in education, nursing, social work, and other fields open to women. But a few colleges, sometimes taking their models from the best private women's colleges, self-consciously sought to offer women opportunities for serious intellectual growth and service to church and society. In those instances, as at St. Catherine's in Minnesota or Notre Dame in Maryland, they more closely resembled the colleges and universities of the post–Vatican II period than they did their contemporary male counterparts. The religious orders of women themselves, of course, provided opportunities for study, service, and leadership rare for any women in American society.

Ideologically, at least, Catholic higher education was one expression of a Catholic subculture, "certain and set apart," as historian James Hennessy put it. Rather than appropriate the best of secular culture, as the Americanists hoped, the U.S. church and its colleges gloried in their distance from modern society. "To me it is of little importance" if a college "turns out a genius," historian Peter Guilday wrote Archbishop John T. McNicholas in 1928. "But it is of prime importance in the intellectual world of today, that we should be recognized as *orthodox*, that is, showing to the nation the *right* way and the *straight* way amid all the mental unrest around us."[16] Catholic educators regarded the depersonalized, commercial, and vocational orientation of secular higher education with contempt. Instead, Catholic education offered a unified vision of life that successfully insulated Catholics from the corrosive effects of modern historical consciousness.[17] As a resolution of the Committee on Educational Policy and Program of the College and University Department of the Catholic Educational Association stated in 1935:

> The Catholic college will not be content with presenting Catholicism as a creed, a code or a cult; Catholicism must be seen as a culture; hence the graduates of the Catholic college of liberal arts will go forth not merely trained in Catholic doctrine, but they will have seen the whole sweep of Catholicism, its part in the building up of our western civilization, past and present.[18]

The basis for this radical difference in the Catholic college curriculum, however, was not theology or history, but scholastic philosophy, which was defined as the only "Catholic philosophy." Undergraduate religion was rarely taught for academic credit. Students were offered catechetical instruction and pastoral care. Only in 1939 did reformers, led by Jesuit John Courtney Murray, begin urging the introduction of theology courses as the basis for unifying the undergraduate curriculum. Some women's colleges responded, but most men's colleges continued to rely on philosophy. All agreed with Murray, however, that neither Catholic philosophy nor theology admitted any error. As historian Philip Gleason put it, both would stand forever as "an intellectually integrated vision of the natural order and its relation to the order of transcendent truth." All this was very self-consciously meant to be an alternative to the scientific, specialized instruction that came to characterize secular colleges and universities. As Philip Gleason puts it:

To an age whose education was secular, scientific and technical in spirit, particularized in vision, flexible in approach, and democratic in social orientation, [Catholics] opposed a system that was religious, literary, and humanistic in spirit, synthetic in vision, rigid in approach, and elitist in social orientation. There was no place in it for interchangeable parts, electivism or vocationalism. These were simply the educational heresies that sprang from the radical defect, the loss of a unified view of reality. To tell a student that he could "elect" anything was to admit that one was no longer sure what was worth knowing . . . and to award a degree . . . for 128 credits was utter academic and intellectual irresponsibility.[19]

Organizationally, colleges and universities for the most part were under the control of religious orders, resulting in a great deal of institutional proliferation and little cooperation. The relationship between the college or university and the hierarchy was intimate but, in a peculiar way, undefined. Juridically, some colleges, sponsored by dioceses or religious congregations established under diocesan auspices, resembled parochial and diocesan elementary and secondary schools, but those under the control of religious orders enjoyed a certain autonomy. Yet there were few public conflicts during these years in part because religious superiors kept tight control. In the 1950s faculty contracts, when there were contracts, allowed for summary dismissal for offenses against Catholic doctrine or morality or American national security. The statutes of Marquette University, for example, declared that the faculty were to teach nothing contrary to Catholic doctrine nor to American principles as these are embodied in the Declaration of Independence and the Constitution of the United States.[20]

For the most part bishops seemed proud of the colleges and gave them consistent moral, though little financial, support. They urged the necessity of Catholic higher education in terms indistinguishable from those in which they demanded attendance at parochial schools. In many dioceses, bishops and people had come to regard large private universities like Chicago, Syracuse, or Harvard as enemies, though relations with the popular state universities in the mid-west were warmer. Still, there was little in higher education before World War II to disturb the ecclesiological stability that had settled on the American church after the Americanist crisis of the 1890s.

THE CATHOLIC PEOPLE'S COLLEGES

In practice, of course, Catholic higher education was less conservative and isolated than the rhetoric suggested. From the start, the colleges and universities, with few exceptions, changed their curriculum to meet the demands of their ever changing constituencies, especially to meet admissions requirements of secular professional schools. Departure from the classics, establishment of women's colleges and admission of women to men's colleges, a vast expansion of professional education, standardization with adoption of credit hours, accommodation to regional accreditation agencies, and introduction of social sciences and other specialized fields — all came, though all were denounced by some as secularization. Only the strong philosophy programs, dominated by neo-scholastic or Catholic philosophy, allowed continued emphasis on Catholic culture and curricular integration. As Gleason explains, the schools engaged in organizational adaptation while holding fast to a conservative ideology. As a result, when vast expansion and a drive for academic excellence came after World War II, they posed — and continue to pose — more problems in theory than in practice. The colleges prospered, and still do, but today they are less sure than they once were that they are doing something specifically Catholic.[21]

After World War II, ambitious veterans demanded — and the government paid for — college education that would lead to productive life in a thriving industrial society. Catholic graduate and undergraduate programs in education, law, nursing, medicine, business, and engineering grew rapidly. More and more lay, professionally trained faculty were recruited, the liberal arts curriculum changed and shrank, and integration through philosophy or theology became more a prescription for reform than a description of Catholic distinctiveness. A few purists clung to small programs in Christian culture, but most Catholic educators weren't worried. These were the boom years, as higher education shared the expansiveness of the American church, whose population doubled between 1945 and 1965 and whose resources of money and personnel grew almost as rapidly.

At the same time an intellectual revival inadvertently began to erode the once secure theoretical foundations of Catholic higher education. Its origins were also social. One reason Spalding, Ireland, and their friends were defeated at the end of the previous century was that there were simply not enough educated, relatively assimilated Catholic laypeople with a self-interest in a more intelligent, respectable Catholic culture to offset the enormous demands of the exploding immigrant, working-class church. Now there was a rapidly expanding middle class and a widespread feeling that educated, middle-class, suburban lay Catholics were the wave of the future. They could hardly be outdone in their loyalty to the church: Mass attendance was higher than ever, few questions were raised even about the most distinctive moral teaching, such as on birth control and divorce, and educational and charitable work flourished. But the separatism (frowning on mixed marriages, celebrating the Catholic novel — or college — just because it was Catholic, or newspapers with the perhaps apocryphal headline: PLANE CRASH IN KANSAS! NO CATHOLICS KILLED!) and exclusivism (summed up in a ditty by lay theologian Frank Sheed: "We are the sweet, selected few/ the rest of you are damned/ There isn't room enough for you/ We can't have heaven crammed") of subcultural Catholicism seemed increasingly anachronistic to men who had fought on malaria-infested islands with comrades from the American melting pot and watched with their wives and daughters wonderful movies about America's triumphant diversity afterwards. If the United States had once been a Protestant culture, it was now the America of Protestant, Catholic, and Jew, and Catholic parochialism, charming on the trivial, was simply embarrassing on matters of significance.[22]

Self-criticism, long buried, gradually forced its way into the open. Catholics were embarrassed by the repression of religious freedom in Franco's Spain and in democratic Ireland, their embarrassment sharpened by Paul Blanshard's best-seller *American Freedom and Catholic Power*, which blasted away at contradictions between Catholic teaching and American values. Jesuit John Courtney Murray began a careful campaign to reconcile American religious liberty and church-state separation with church teaching, long opposed in principle to these cherished American practices. Echoes of the new thinking and increasingly open dissent from the old appeared in the more sophisticated Catholic press. Silenced for a time, Murray renewed his work when Pope John XXIII arrived in 1958, and saw that work vindicated by the "Declaration of Religious Liberty" approved by the Second Vatican Council in 1964.

Even more significant for Catholic higher education was the controversy that erupted following the 1955 publication of an essay on "American Catholics and the Intellectual Life" by historian John Tracy Ellis. Ellis decried the absence of significant intellectual achievement by American Catholics. Well aware of the former poverty of Catholics and of the anti-Catholicism that remained an important feature of American culture, especially among intellectuals, Ellis also noticed that the post-war intellectual climate was surprisingly receptive to religion. The blame for the absence of a strong Catholic voice could be placed partly on Catholics themselves. There were too many colleges and universities, there was too little cooperation among them, and the priests and religious who ran them gave too little support to serious research. Ellis unlocked the door, and numerous others came through with their own explanations of why there were "no Catholic Salks or Oppenheimers." The open debate helped make criticism of Catholic institutions possible again, it centered attention on the intelligibility of the faith in the minds of fair-minded outsiders and newly critical Catholics, and it awakened consciousness of the need for change that would stand the church well a few years later when the Second Vatican Council began in Rome.[23]

THE DRIVE FOR EXCELLENCE

The debate about Catholicism and the intellectual life also helped sanction a drive for academic excellence on many Catholic campuses. Years later a Jesuit, one of those "strong presidents" who reshaped Catholic higher education, told me that his vocation was decisively influenced by the message of the older generation of Jesuits, Murray, ecumenist Gustave Weigel, cosmopolitan editor John LaFarge, and polymath Walter Ong, and that message centered on one word—"excellence." These men inspired him to study theology with reference to contemporary philosophy and culture and with an ecumenical orientation fed by Protestant scholarship. Later, when he was called to teach at and then lead a Jesuit institution, he noticed that the sign at the entrance said "college" not church, and he set out to make it the very best college it could be.

It was a common theme, the quest for excellence. "Making it" meant more than making money or achieving respectability, though for the children of immigrant parents whose lives were shaped by depression and war, these were by no means unworthy goals. But it also meant fulfilling the opportunities that history and God and those who went before had placed in front of you: For God, Country, and Notre Dame (and our parents).

But what did "excellence" mean for Catholic higher education? Most looked around at what were by consensus the nation's best colleges and universities and tried to be like them, at least in academics. That meant changes in curriculum, opening up the philosophy department to approaches other than neo-scholasticism, placing new theology departments and their offerings on a "sound" academic basis, being less confessional, more ecumenical, and always "scientific," and hiring Catholics (and if need be non-Catholics) coming out of the best secular graduate schools. Later, some Catholic intellectuals, a bit estranged after this quest for supposed excellence, recalled Notre Dame's Frank O'Malley as an exemplar of a really Catholic university, one who had stood against the supposed trend toward secularization. While O'Malley organized networks of Catholic intellectuals, taught inspiring courses on Catholic writers, and directed a small discussion group of promising Catholic undergraduates, he also had another agenda, felt by those of us who passed his way: he did everything he could to encourage us to attend the nation's top graduate schools, none of them Catholic, and he worked hard to find us the fellowships to make that possible.

But when we and many others who had never gone to Notre Dame or its equivalents arrived as professors, we brought more than the secular university's credentials of excellence. We also brought those structures of specialized learning that had worried Catholic academics from the start, sixty years earlier. In the most comprehensive study of American higher education written in those years, David Reisman and Christopher Jencks described an "academic revolution," at the heart of which was "the triumph of the graduate school."[24] For most of us, our intellectual homeland was our discipline; we thought well of ourselves when we published in its journals and gave papers at conferences within our field. We preferred teaching graduate students and, if we came to undergraduate education, our enthusiasm was about our department and our majors. If we taught courses for nonmajors, we insisted that those courses provide an introduction to our discipline and its "methodology" rather than examine its place in our culture or the relationship between the knowledge we developed and things in general. And many of us who had come from and returned to Catholic schools saw ourselves as crusaders, champions of modern, rigorous, and "serious" intellectual work against the long legacy of antiquarian, amateurish, moralistic, and mediocre teaching that we believed had characterized our schools before our arrival.

Thirty years later I asked several well-known leaders in the modernization of Catholic universities whether they had any reservations about the path they had pursued; all of them were familiar with the criticism that had eventually been directed at them for allegedly secularizing their schools. While they acknowledged mistakes on many things, they had no reservations whatsoever about their drive for academic excellence. Perhaps it was this confident self-assurance that made the revolution possible.

THEOLOGY TO THE CENTER

Revolution it surely was, and it began with theology. Almost before anyone noticed, theology became the heart and soul of Catholic higher education. It provided the bridge between the older Catholic identity and the newer, more excellent version of Catholic higher education. The pursuit of excellence meant imitation of the prevailing academic models. One result was departmental divisions and academic specialization. This threatened to leave "theology and philosophy attached to the academic body like a kind of veriform appendix, a vestigial remnant, neither useful nor decorative," Notre Dame's young president Theodore M. Hesburgh wrote in 1962. If this happened, Catholic universities might become great, Hesburgh said, but they would no longer be Catholic.[25]

As Hesburgh's words indicated, theology had joined philosophy as the central elements of Catholic identity. It was their job to maintain a sense of integration and orthodoxy, to engage the other disciplines, explain their meaning, and insure their subordination to sound doctrine and morality. Both departments, sustained by strong administrative support, enjoyed a central role in the curriculum. Before long, the newly diverse philosophy departments lost their way and theology was left alone to provide the distinguishing intellectual component of Catholic higher education.

So it was a heady time for teachers of theology. Back in 1952, teachers of undergraduate religion had organized the Association of Catholic Teachers of Christian Doctrine, later renamed the College Theology Society. They hoped to improve the teaching of undergraduate religion and, as laypeople and women religious, they felt excluded from the heavily clerical Catholic Theological Society of America. With the arrival of the Second Vatican Council, more and more schools decided to establish or expand undergraduate programs in theology, sometimes called religious studies to distinguish it from the theology taught in seminaries.[26] Accordingly, in 1964, Jesuit Bernard Cooke at Marquette began the nation's first Ph.D. program in theology, "oriented to contemporary needs and to thorough and up to date scholarship" and open to laypeople and religious.[27]

Cooke's program, academically rigorous, drawing on the dramatic expansion of Catholic theological and biblical studies in Europe, and grounded in the drive for excellence of the post-war generation, reflected the vast acceleration of self-examination and self-improvement occasioned by Vatican II. The Council's affirmation of freedom of conscience, the dignity of the person, the freedom of the act of faith, and the autonomy of secular culture all called into question confessional, paternalistic, and authoritarian practices on campus. The Council brought theological self-understanding under the scrutiny of scholarship in history and scripture studies; it opened dialogue with other Christians and even affirmed the dignity and value of non-Christian religions.

"The Pastoral Constitution on the Church and the Modern World," published in 1965, located the church within human history and placed great emphasis on dialogue between the church and human culture. The Council's tone of Christian humanism echoed the long-repressed voice of liberal Catholicism. Now the bishops acknowledged that the church could learn from as well as teach human cultures, that it was necessary to study the concrete situations in which people found themselves if the church was to announce the Good News effectively, and that God acted outside as well as inside the church. The "Pastoral Constitution" became a kind of *magna carta* for Catholic higher education in the United States. Its words affirmed all that the reformers were trying to achieve, including the study of the human sciences, respect for non-Catholic, secular culture, dialogue with those beyond the church, and service to society. Now the drive for excellence had become the church's own.

In 1967 a group of church leaders gathered at Land O'Lakes, Wisconsin, in order to define the Catholic university in the new postconciliar setting. The university would be Catholic because theology would make Catholicism "effectively operative" within it. A Catholic university should have scholars in all branches of theology able to explore the depths of the Christian tradition "and the total religious heritage of the world" in order "to come to the best possible intellectual understanding of religion and revelation, of man in his varied relationships to God." They should be engaged in "constant discussion" with other disciplines. "There must be no theological or philosophical imperialism. All sciences and disciplinary methods, or methodologies, must be given due honor and respect." Hopefully, there would also be in those other fields "Christian scholars who are not only competent in their own fields but also have a personal interest in the cross-disciplinary confrontation." All learning should be integrated around "relevant, living Catholic thought." The presence of non-Catholics was necessary "to bring authentic universality to the Catholic university." By their active participation, they would "help insure the seriousness and the integrity of the search for understanding and commitment." Then the

Catholic university would help shape "the critical, reflective intelligence of the church," a role it had hardly played in the recent past, but now its most important function.[28]

The shift to theology arose from and legitimized the drive for excellence and the structural changes that institutionalized the newfound academic respectability of Catholic higher education. No one noticed how linking the intellectual and curricular elements of institutional identity to theology raised confessional issues, like what is Catholic theology and who is authorized to answer that question. Some may have questioned the quality of Catholic higher education, and many ignored clerical advice and attended non-Catholic schools. But no one doubted that Catholic schools were Catholic or that theology, properly taught, began from and eventually affirmed the teaching of the church. The visible presence of priests and religious and their practical control over nearly all that happened on campus guaranteed fidelity to the Catholic tradition and obedience to the magisterium. But if the priests and sisters stepped aside, the Catholic adjective in Catholic higher education might be followed by a question mark.

CHAPTER 4

The Catholic Academic Revolution

SEPARATE INCORPORATION

Bishop John Carroll and his successors occasionally founded colleges as a way to build a native priesthood. But their interest waned when they were able to establish their own free-standing seminaries, ideally beginning with the high school years. With self-interest reduced, they adopted a pastoral stance, encouraging religious orders to found schools, supporting fund-raising drives, and generally affirming, though not quite requiring, Catholic higher education. As long as the religious orders controlled the schools, bishops and religious superiors generally got along and no serious problems arose.

Only after World War II did tensions emerge, most from the desire of the schools for greater autonomy from ecclesiastical control. As individual schools became larger and more complex, their presidents invariably resented interference, even by their own religious superiors. Efforts within religious orders to bring about modest cooperation among the order's schools were often seen as threats to the independence of individual institutions. Jesuit provincials, for example, exerted direct control over Jesuit schools in their provinces and attempted to shape them into a system through the Jesuit Educational Association, established in 1934. But there was persistent tension with the presidents, whose resistance stiffened as the universities expanded and diversified after World War II. By 1970 they had thrown off provincial control, and the new Association of Jesuit Colleges and Universities, which replaced the JEA, was composed of presidents, not provincials.

The revolutionary change that made this and much else possible was separate incorporation. By the late 1960s institutional autonomy, presidential authority, and academic excellence seemed intimately connected. Many schools now had professional faculty and staff, modern management and personnel policies, and increasingly complex bureaucracies. The authority

51

of religious communities and provincials, with their primarily pastoral responsibilities, seemed potentially disruptive and organizationally anachronistic. In addition, state assistance to higher education and prospects for increased federal funding encouraged efforts to detach colleges and universities from ecclesiastical structures. Vatican II seemed to give permission for separation by affirming the autonomy of the human sciences and encouraging recognition of the expertise of laypeople.[1]

Under the leadership of Paul Reinert, S.J. and Hesburgh, St. Louis University and Notre Dame led the way in 1967 by establishing independent boards of trustees with full authority over those universities. Within a few years, the vast majority of Catholic colleges and universities followed suit. Thus, in a move that seemed remarkable at the time and seems even more remarkable today, religious orders turned over the property and the charters of their thriving colleges and universities to these new boards. They gave them the schools!

Separate incorporation meant establishing two distinct legal entities: the university and the religious community. A few schools, sponsored by bishops, remained directly under ecclesiastical control, and lay boards were ultimately advisory, though they often exercised considerable delegated authority. Some schools created a two-tier board system, with the religious community retaining control — or considerable influence — over areas like the election of trustees, alienation of property, and preservation of the Catholic character of the school. In most places, there were formal agreements between the order and the college or university, spelling out mutual rights and responsibilities. For example, the religious order might agree to continue to assign men and women to work at the school and to make an annual contribution from the salaries that members received; the university might promise to appoint members of the order to the office of president, to provide housing and medical benefits, and to maintain religious services and a campus ministry program from university funds. Still, with the exception of the few diocesan schools and the Catholic University of America, established by a Vatican charter, lay-dominated boards of trustees now constituted the corporation of almost all Catholic colleges and universities.[2] It was a revolution whose full impact is still to be felt.

ACADEMIC FREEDOM

It is hard now to recapture the pace of change in American Catholic culture and on Catholic campuses in the 1960s. In the last academic year of the war there were 92,000 students in Catholic colleges and universities. In the fall of 1948, 220,000 enrolled. By 1970 that number had almost doubled, to 430,000. At the same time the church and the country changed dramatically. When Fordham launched an experimental undergraduate college in 1967, the announcement said that its participants would "rethink the whole of education, in this day and age, from top to bottom." Father Vincent Yanatelli, S.J., of St. Peter's College, a year later described the mood on Catholic college and university campuses as "a kind of ecstasy of hope."[3]

But there were bombshells waiting to explode. As late as 1960, few people had doubts about the exclusively Catholic character of Catholic higher education, and almost no one believed there was room for discussion of what Catholic meant. The president of St. John's University in Brooklyn simply stated a broad preconciliar consensus when he told his faculty senate:

> The University is committed to Catholicism and, since the great majority of the students are Catholic, the tone of the lectures certainly should be Catholic. The content of the texts should be Catholic, or at least they should not run, in any way, contrary to Catholicism. . . . St. John's University is committed to pure Thomism as a system of philosophy. . . . It is the handmaid of the Catholic theology which we teach. . . . Whatever is said in any course may not, in any way, contravene pure Thomism or Catholic theology.

Six years later, these were fighting words. In 1964 Catholic University denied four distinguished theologians the right to speak about Vatican II, and similar actions took place during a lecture tour by theologian Hans Küng the following year. In the next few years conflicts over academic freedom and tenure ripped St. John's, Catholic University, and the University of Dayton. Another president, reeling under the shock waves rolling over "pure Thomism and Catholic theology," told a reporter: "These people come along and say they're going to teach what they want to teach — complete license, that's what it is. We're not going to have it. We're not going to have it."[4] In a calmer moment a few months later, Apostolic Delegate Egidio Vagnozzi agreed that "we're not going to have it" as he told a Marquette graduating class that the "usefulness" of Catholic colleges and universities lay "in the necessity of constructing an orderly and solid body of doctrine and of creating a purely Catholic cultural environment." There was no question of infringing on a "healthy academic freedom," he argued, but only of "preventing an unhealthy license and chaos."[5] His was a last-ditch effort to salvage an attitude and way of life composed of preconciliar Catholic orthodoxy and the American Catholic subculture that was rapidly disappearing.

By then such questions almost never arose in departments other than theology and philosophy; even at the Catholic University of America, structurally the most Catholic of the schools, an observer reported that the faculty felt that the clerical administration of the school obscured the "basically secular character of the education offered at the university."[6] This was probably an exaggeration, but the content of the curriculum or its integration around Christian ideals had ceased to be a problem, at least for awhile. People studied many subjects, most professors and professional staff felt quite at home, administrators, as in all private institutions, struggled with rising costs, and in most fields academic freedom was simply presumed.

The problem came in theology and, to a far lesser extent, philosophy. A major study of church-related higher education completed in 1966 posed the question clearly: "how can a college do justice to its avowed purpose as a Christian institution, a purpose which carries with it commitment to a set of beliefs, and at the same time maintain the freedom of inquiry which most academic people feel is necessary for a good education?"[7]

One St. John's faculty member put the Catholic slant on this issue directly: the church could not subsidize error, yet no faculty member would be safe until the church agreed that it ought not to interfere with the research and teaching taking place in its universities "even though this entails permitting the teaching of heresy."[8] When Archbishop Karl Alter attempted to intervene in a dispute at Dayton, where faculty in the philosophy department were charged with just that crime—teaching heresy—university officials were forced to resist on the grounds that the bishop had no authority to override the statutes of the university.[9] At Catholic University, when young moral theologian Charles Curran was denied a contract in 1966, faculty and students closed down the university, and the bishops who controlled the university surrendered; Curran was granted promotion and tenure. In 1968, after publication of the papal encyclical *Humanae Vitae*, upholding the church's ban on artificial birth control, Curran helped organize a national dissent by hundreds of Catholic theologians. When Catholic University attempted to discipline some of its professors who participated, a faculty committee determined that they had acted within their rights, a decision affirmed when the American bishops spelled out guidelines for permissible dissent in their 1969 pastoral letter "Human Life in Our Day."

The move toward academic freedom was encouraged by court decisions.

In 1968 many New York schools, worried about state financial assistance, took steps to distance themselves from the institutional church. That same year, watching challenges to federal assistance in the courts, national officials urged Catholic institutions to adopt the 1940 statement on academic freedom of the American Association of University Professors (AAUP) and incorporate it into their faculty handbooks. The following year the courts rejected *in loco parentis*, requiring new attention to student rights. In *Lemon v. Kurtzman* (1971), the courts laid down a three-pronged test, including academic freedom, to insure that public money was not given for sectarian purposes. In *Tilton v. Richardson*, a few months later, the Supreme Court by a 5–4 decision upheld grants to four Catholic colleges in Connecticut under the 1963 Higher Education Facilities Act, which allowed such grants when they were not directly used for a religious purpose. The court said that such grants could be made provided there was evidence that religion courses, if required, were taught according to academic requirements intrinsic to the subject matter, that teachers had a sense of professional standards, that the schools had adopted the AAUP policies on academic freedom, and that there was at the school an atmosphere of academic freedom "rather than religious indoctrination." By this time almost no Catholic colleges had difficulty passing these tests.

But, however frequent the victories of academic freedom, many still believed that the conflict with Catholic identity remained complete: a Catholic university was impossible. John Cogley, probably the country's most respected layman, argued that advocates, like Father Hesburgh, who insisted that you could have real universities integrated around Catholic theology, were pursuing a contradiction. They were really trying to preserve "the old Catholic culture, at odds with the modern world." Of course Notre Dame was doing university work, Cogley agreed, but to do so it had to surrender many of its claims to distinctiveness: "the facts in South Bend are not the same as the theory in South Bend." Cogley did not argue that major Catholic universities should close their doors, but that religious orders and the new lay boards should be satisfied with sponsorship, perhaps offering programs of interest to Catholics, but ending the contradiction of maintaining that theirs were distinctively Catholic universities, that they were different. They could adopt academic freedom and hire professionally trained faculty and ultimately become true universities, or they could privilege Catholicism and Catholic theology and remain Catholic, but they could not do both.[10]

Cogley knew that it was a question of university work—teaching and research—more than of structures of control. Philip Gleason asked the question: in what sense was a school Catholic if it was "composed predominantly of lay professionals who employ the same methods and norms as their counterparts in secular universities, and who are engaged in the pursuit of knowledge in autonomous spheres that are in no way dependent upon an overall Catholic position?"[11] The movement was clearly away from dependence upon "an overall Catholic position." A decade after Gleason posed his question, a careful study of Marquette University indicated that the process of change had led many students, professors, and supporters to feel that an increasingly professionalized faculty had eroded the school's Catholic identity. "The successful efforts of the university to improve its academic quality were seen to move the institution towards academic professionalism to the detriment of its Catholicity," Gregory Lucey, S.J. wrote. "The dynamics of appointments, rewards and faculty development reinforced the values of academic professionalism while not supporting goals more appropriate to the Catholicity of the university. Thus rather than developing a synthesis of academic professionalism with concern for questions of ultimate social and moral importance, Marquette had allowed academic professionalism to displace Catholicism as the dominant value orientation within the faculty."

Another study indicated that Loyola University of Chicago, like many others, had modernized its curriculum to resemble that in nonsectarian universities, adopted disciplinary policies that reflected legal and social realities rather than Catholic viewpoints, and begun to emphasize the school's Jesuit rather than Catholic character. The "fragility of this new corporate identity" was evident in widely differing perceptions within the university of the meaning of "Jesuit liberal arts education."[12]

As Cogley saw it, there was a gap between what the universities were doing and their explanation of what they were doing, their ideology. Philip Gleason agreed from the start and summed up his views of the process years later. The changes occasioned by the Second Vatican Council brought to a climax a long process of academic modernization in Catholic higher education. But they also created an ideological crisis. "Whatever one may think of its intrinsic validity," Gleason wrote, "neo-scholastic philosophy and theology functioned for two generations before the Council as the agreed-upon Catholic system for reconciling the claims of faith and reason, establishing the rational grounds for religious claims, and articulating the implications of faith in the areas of personal morality . . . social ethics . . . and even international relations. Neoscholasticism, in other words, constituted the *intellectual foundation* on which the Catholic identity of Catholic institutions of higher education rested in the half-century before the Second Vatican Council." When neo-scholasticism no longer functioned that way, nothing took its place. As Gleason saw it, "the nature of the crisis can be put in a nutshell by saying that a working consensus no longer exists among Catholic academics and administrators about what it means in intellectual terms to be a Catholic and about how Catholic faith should influence the work one does as a scholar and teacher."[13] Catholic institutions would eventually have to decide whether they wished to remain Catholic and, if so, how they would make that decision operational.

WHAT ABOUT CATHOLIC?

What sharpened Gleason's challenge was not so much events on campus, where academic freedom was usually sustained and academic excellence remained the operative goal, as it was the determination of church officials to remain connected in a meaningful and effective way to Catholic higher education. Separate incorporation meant that decisions about the life of any particular institution would from now on be made within the institution, through its own procedures, and that officials and agencies external to the institution would have no direct role. Of course, the schools had always valued their independence. John Leary, S.J., president of Gonzaga University, argued in 1968 that religious orders that operated colleges and universities always wanted church approval, but they had also kept their distance from the bishops, fearing "that even a slight embrace might turn out to be a bear hug." But now, as Father Yanatelli of St. Peter's correctly responded, new questions required a new approach:

If the institutions of higher education must be autonomous, that is free of any authority external to the process pertaining to the pursuit of truth, what happens to the relationship of the bishop to the Catholic college? What indeed happens to the relationship between the teaching magisterium of the church and the Catholic college? Further questions arise on the legal level. . . . We have been laboring under an historical illusion just because we have never been forced to sit down and think much of this through.[14]

Thinking it through meant defining for the first time the relationship between the institutional church and its colleges and universities, a thinking through that for the most part came after, not before, separate incorporation. First came the 1967 manifesto, drawn up by a group of twenty-six bishops, university presidents, and Catholic intellectuals gathered at Land O' Lakes, Wisconsin, which gave its name to the statement. They put the matter directly: "The Catholic University today must be a university in the full modern sense of the word, with a strong commitment to and concern for academic excellence." To perform its functions, "[it] must have true autonomy and academic freedom in the face of authority of whatever kind, lay or clerical, external to the academic community itself." Thus "institutional autonomy and academic freedom are essential conditions of life and growth and indeed of survival for Catholic universities, as they are for all universities." Independence did not mean secularization; voluntary commitment and the study of theology would be vital links to the Catholic heritage and the Catholic community. The university would remain Catholic, the signers affirmed, for Catholicism would be "perceptively present and effectively operative" by means of scholars in theology who were to "engage directly in exploring the depths of Christian tradition."[15]

Five years later, international delegates meeting under the auspices of the Sacred Congregation for Catholic Education and the International Federation of Catholic Universities echoed these words, urging support from the hierarchy and promising "frank and confident collaboration" in return. They spoke of the "delicate balance" between the university and the bishops and the "complicated and delicate question of orthodoxy." Bishops had no right to intervene in university affairs contrary to the statutes, the university leaders insisted; they could deal with persons as members of the church, but this could not involve "juridical intervention." For its part, the university had the "responsibility to take the necessary and appropriate steps to maintain its Catholic character."[16]

This rather ambiguous middle ground, which left "Catholic character" a matter of voluntary policy within an independent and self-governing institution, quickly found its way into the self-definition of American schools. At Marquette in 1969, for example, a special committee stated the "delicate balance" clearly:

> Whatever a Catholic University does must be true to the idea of a university as open and a scene of free inquiry in which the pursuit of truth is unfettered except by accountability to the truth itself, but what specifically it does it may choose to do. And in this act of choosing and specifying its efforts and emphases, it may select alternatives which are especially appropriate to the commitment it assumes in calling itself Catholic.[17]

It cannot be emphasized too strongly that the institutions had become self-governing; therefore, the Catholic commitments of their officers and boards, unquestionably sincere, were also voluntary. Whether this was legitimate or not, it was certainly different from what Catholics were used to.[18]

Later, critics unhappy with the outcome wrote as if people arrived at this new situation without attention to their Catholic responsibilities. This was rarely the case. At some schools, pursuit of academic excellence may have temporarily pushed Catholic matters to the margins. A very few, like Webster College in Missouri and Manhattanville in New York even abandoned their Catholic affiliation. And anecdotal evidence suggests that the new lay trustees tended to take Catholic identity for granted or leave such matters to the president, usually still a member of the sponsoring religious community. And the presidents, with many other problems and opportunities before them, undoubtedly tired of endless, often repetitious arguments about Catholic identity.

But by no means did the Catholic issue pass unnoticed. The leaders who wrote the Land O' Lakes statement and the many officials and professors who discussed that document clearly were wrestling with the problem. The question of Catholic meaning and identity regularly appeared on the agenda of the national Catholic educational bodies. Still, after weathering a severe financial crisis in the period from 1969 to 1972, the schools enjoyed a long period of growth and improvement, they gradually modernized their internal systems of administration and governance, and their presidents and friendly bishops were able to deal with controversial questions without raising a fuss on most campuses. Priests and, in a few cases, sisters still occupied the presidency of many schools, theology was energetically taught, and campus ministries offered pastoral and liturgical services, so the Catholic issue did not seem pressing. There were a few complaints and a few more worriers, but nothing very much was done.

THE VATICAN STEPS IN

Only Rome, it seemed, was not satisfied. The Vatican pursued a long, behind-the-scenes campaign to insure that Catholic higher education remained Catholic on its terms. In 1986 the Vatican brought this process to a climax by publishing the draft of a proposed Apostolic Constitution intended to define the relationship between Catholic colleges and universities and the hierarchy. The document, which reasserted the need for Catholic institutions and theologians to be directly accountable to the church's bishops, arose from Rome's persistent anxiety about the changes in American Catholic higher education. Sister Alice Gallin, then executive director of the Association of Catholic Colleges and Universities, argues that the Vatican's determination to call forth a clear statement of mission and accountability from the colleges and universities in the United States arose in response to the gradual surrender of control over these institutions by religious orders. Established as apostolic works of religious communities, they were clearly linked to ecclesiastical authority. But, with separate incorporation, "church officials now had to deal with the universities as independent autonomous corporations rather than being able to work quietly behind the scenes with Religious Superiors to monitor theological studies, speaker policies, honorary degrees and various student issues." Rome was worried. As Pope Paul VI told the Jesuits:

> The Catholic University should be open to the world and to modern problems. They should foster and sustain dialogue with all forms of culture . . . but this should be done while fully maintaining the character of Catholic universities. . . . In teaching, in publications, in all forms of academic life, provision must be made for complete orthodoxy of teaching, for obedience to the magisterium of the church, for fidelity to the hierarchy and the Holy See.[19]

As early as 1974, the Congregation on Catholic Education called upon Apostolic Delegate Jean Jadot to express the Vatican's concern that property was being transferred to lay boards without securing the permission required by canon law, leading officials to wonder whether the schools were still Catholic. Oral history suggests that these transfers that accompanied separate incorporation were justified by the argument of a canon lawyer that the schools were civil institutions, so canonical permission was not required, an argument never approved by the Vatican.[20] The Congregation instructed Jadot to arrange for the establishment of a joint committee from the bishops' conference and the associations of major superiors of religious orders of men and women to study the matter. The new committee was to ascertain from those responsible which schools remained Catholic, and until that was done, no further changes were to be made.

On the basis of this request, it seems, a committee of bishops and presidents was formed that became the major channel of communication between the academic community and the hierarchy. The committee worked very well; after its first meeting in December 1974, one of its bishop members reported it had been a "splendid meeting held in a spirit of mutual trust, respect and concern" with emphasis "on service rather than definitions." This informal, trusting relationship—practical, impatient with canonical technicalities—seemed quite appropriate. For some years bishops almost never felt called to interfere with the universities, and university leaders felt they enjoyed the active support of key members of the hierarchy. They were especially pleased by the publication by the bishops of a very affirmative pastoral letter on Catholic higher education in 1986 and by the support the bishops gave them when dealing with Rome on questions of canon law. The dialogue and bonds of trust built by the committee, it seemed to some, provided a typically American solution far preferable to drawing hard and fast definitions that would limit academic self-government or establish clear-cut structures of ecclesiastical accountability that might jeopardize government financial support.

But Rome was never satisfied with the informality of this arrangement. The reforms in the United States left church authorities on the outside of the new structures of control, and Alice Gallin, who was as close to these questions as anyone, believes that the highest authorities in the church were determined not to be considered outsiders. In negotiation over texts, the Vatican regularly bristled at phrases indicating that it and the bishops were "external to the structure" of Catholic higher education. In 1976, Monsignor John Murphy, Gallin's predecessor, attended a meeting in Rome where final touches were put on a constitution to govern universities chartered by the Holy See, a category that included only a few faculties in the United States, Catholic University of America among them. He became alarmed when he heard rumors that the Vatican planned to develop a similar constitution for all Catholic universities. He visited Vatican offices to argue that such a move would be less than helpful in the United States. He told Rome: "the terms cooperation, mutual respect and support more faithfully reflect the historic and fruitful relationship American institutions have had with the Church than those implying a canonical or juridical relationship."[21]

Murphy's fears were realized in 1979 when Rome began work on a constitution for all Catholic universities. At the same time, the Vatican published the new Code of Canon Law, a redrafting initiated at Vatican II. Again American officials were alarmed by provisions that required anyone teaching Catholic theology to secure a "canonical mission," official permission to teach Catholic theology to be granted by the proper church authorities, presumably the local bishop. When high-ranking American officials, including Hesburgh, Bishop James Malone, a key figure in the Bishops and Presidents Committee, William Byron, S.J., president of Catholic University, and Sister Alice visited Rome to explain American church-state problems, they were stunned by the apparent unwillingness of Vatican officials to adapt to American conditions.

A short time later, Rome showed that it meant business by pushing to completion a long investigation of Catholic University theologian Charles

Curran. The Vatican's Congregation on the Doctrine of the Faith, under Cardinal Joseph Ratzinger, had previously penalized such outstanding theologians as Hans Küng and Leonardo Boff and investigated Edward Schillebeeckx and Gustavo Gutiérrez, so Curran was in good company. Ever since the faculty strike forced Curran's retention at Catholic University in 1966, some American bishops and conservative activists had lobbied for his removal. Yet Curran enjoyed tremendous respect among his fellow theologians; he served as President of the Catholic Theological Society of America and the American Society of Christian Ethics and received the former organization's John Courtney Murray award for distinguished service to Catholic theology. Moreover, his tireless service to priests, religious, and laypeople working in pastoral ministry made him very popular with the church's staffs and with many pastorally oriented bishops. Nevertheless, Curran's public opposition to the 1968 encyclical on birth control and his carefully stated dissent from prevailing Roman teaching on a number of issues in sexual morality made him vulnerable.

In 1989 the Congregation on the Doctrine of the Faith concluded that Curran could no longer be allowed to teach Catholic theology. Because the theology faculty at Catholic University was established by papal charter, this meant Curran's dismissal from his post. A long series of negotiations followed, aimed at finding Curran a different post at the University, but in another, nonpontifical faculty. Those negotiations failed, in part because Curran wanted to force the issue of academic freedom in theological schools, in part because his case had become tied up with a larger effort to discipline the supposedly too independent-minded church in the United States. A civil suit brought by Curran also failed, the judge finding that Curran's contract ceded authority to determine his fitness to teach to ecclesiastical authorities. Later, there was evidence that church officials helped keep Curran from positions at other universities.[22]

Thus, when the Vatican in 1985 published a draft constitution for Catholic universities and requested comments from officials around the world, the academic freedom question had been rekindled, dramatically so by the time the long negotiations began to make an impact on campuses in 1989. American university officials almost unanimously found the preliminary Vatican text both untimely and, for American schools, dangerous. The college presidents stated boldly that the shift of responsibility for orthodoxy from boards of trustees to the bishops "has nothing to recommend it." The schools are "de facto recognized by our bishops and the ecclesial and civil communities as Catholic—and have been for a century—but have no juridical links with the ordinaries," they explained. "The university is the home of the theologian, not the bishop," they noted, "and the bishop must respect that fact." Moreover, the text's definitions of Catholic universities made no provision for the American type, structured by church-state separation. The text also contained stringent provisions for controlling the teaching of Catholic theology, provisions bound to raise more academic freedom problems. Worst of all, the entire text rested on the assumption that the university was "part of the church" in a juridical sense and thus ultimately accountable to the hierarchy. Joseph O'Hare, S.J., President of Fordham University, located the problem right here. If the Catholic university was part of the church in that sense, then it simply was not a university as Americans understood that term. If the Catholic university was institutionally autonomous, as it had to be, then it simply could not be part of the hierarchical church.

In an unprecedented show of unity, the presidents of almost all American Catholic colleges and universities submitted a collective, strongly critical commentary on the draft. Later, a delegation of presidents and bishops visited Rome to explain the American situation and their objections. For a time, they thought the text might have been put aside, but that was not the case.

EX CORDE ECCLESIAE

In 1990 Pope John Paul II proclaimed *Ex Corde Ecclesiae* ("From the Heart of the Church"), an apostolic constitution on Catholic higher education. Since this is the most authoritative official statement of the meaning and mission of Catholic higher education, it deserves to be widely read. The text itself, as distinct from the general norms for legislation with which it concludes, is very affirmative, claiming for the Catholic university a central role in the mission of the church. John Paul II's vision, shaped in part by his own extensive university experience as student, graduate student, teacher, and chaplain, centers on integration:

The Catholic university, by institutional commitment, brings to its task the inspiration and light of the Christian message. In a Catholic university, therefore, Catholic ideals, attitudes and principles penetrate and inform university activities in accordance with the proper nature and autonomy of these activities. In a word, being both a University and Catholic, it must be both a community of scholars representing various branches of human knowledge, and an academic institution in which Catholicism is vitally present and operative.[23]

Well aware of the difficulties posed for the integration of knowledge by the intellectual specialization of modern research, the Pope insists that the Catholic university seeks to determine the relative place and meaning of the various disciplines within a Gospel-enlightened vision of the human person and of the world. It pursues this end through a continuing dialogue between faith and reason, a pervasive "ethical concern," and by offering a vigorous theological perspective.

A theme of the Pope's leadership has been the dialogue between faith and culture. He has little in common with the pre–Vatican II popes, who always counterpoised a superior Christian culture against contemporary culture. Instead, he insists the "there is only one culture: that of man, by man and for man." What he calls the dialogue *with* culture is really a dialogue (almost too soft a word for the vigorous intellectual combat in which the Pope seems to delight) *within* and about the future of that one human culture; John Paul II believes that it is there that the future of the church and the world is being played out. He wants Catholic intellectual resources enlisted in this cultural and spiritual struggle to shape the future of an increasingly interdependent human family. And the Catholic university, distinguished by its "search for the whole truth of nature, man and God" and following "a kind of universal humanism" is "a primary and privileged place for a fruitful dialogue between the Gospel and culture."

The Pope does not ignore the issues of institutional autonomy and academic freedom that preoccupy Americans:

> Every Catholic university, as a University, is an academic community which, in a rigorous and critical fashion, assists in the protection and advancement of human dignity and of a cultural heritage through research, teaching and various services offered the local, national and international communities. It possesses that institutional autonomy necessary to perform its functions effectively and guarantee its members academic freedom, so long as the rights of the individual person and of the community are preserved within the confines of truth and the common good.

Nowhere does the Apostolic Constitution come closer to accepting the position of the university communities than in its use of the language formulated by an international Congress of academic leaders almost twenty years earlier. Quoting from that text, the Pope writes:

> Since the objective of a Catholic university is to assure in an institutional manner a Christian presence in the university world

confronting the problems of society and culture, every Catholic university as Catholic must have the following essential characteristics: 1. A Christian inspiration not only of individuals but of the university community as such. 2. A continuing reflection in the light of the Catholic faith upon the growing treasury of human knowledge, to which it seeks to contribute by its own research. 3. Fidelity to the Christian message as it comes to us through the church and 4. An institutional commitment to the service of the People of God and of the human family in their pilgrimage to the transcendent goal that gives meaning to life.[24]

But, as these words make clear, autonomy and freedom are in fact limited, for the university is within the church by formal profession, which should be expressed in a formal document, and the Pope considers it to be intrinsic to the nature of theology that the theologian respects the authority of bishops and assents to Catholic doctrine "according to the degree of authority with which it is taught." At the end of the document, the Pope expresses some of this in general norms, leaving further specification in law to local episcopal conferences. Those norms suggest a close working relationship between the university and the local bishop, episcopal supervision of the university's Catholic identity and especially of the teaching of theology, and, in a new and controversial provision, efforts on the part of the university to insure that a majority of its faculty are professed Catholics.

At first American leaders responded to this text with relief. As Alice Gallin put it: "There are no surprises. We were not anxiously looking for any document, but if there had to be one, this is as good as we could get." Some of the more troublesome language had been modified, the definitions now left room for American institutions, and the norms were sufficiently general that they posed no immediate problem. Presidents Joseph O'Hare, S.J. of Fordham and Edward Malloy, C.S.C. of Notre Dame told the press that the key had been an April 1989 meeting of university personnel in Rome, when some of the improved language was hammered out. Malloy said that the experience demonstrated that things could be worked out within the church if there was "a good process of consultation." But they agreed with Boston College President Donald Monan, S.J. who noted that there were still some ambiguities, the most troubling being the provision that seemed to require that a majority of the faculty should be Catholics.[25]

But the sigh of relief was quickly followed by renewed alarm. The American hierarchy was changing as Pope John Paul appointed more conservative men to key sees. A number of issues, most dramatically a proposed pastoral letter on the place of women in the church, drove a wedge of division into the hierarchy. And some bishops, anxious to follow the Roman lead, arranged the appointment of a new committee to draw up legislation to implement *Ex Corde Ecclesiae*. For the moment at least, this new committee took precedence over the Bishops and Presidents Committee. With a number of university leaders joining the committee as consultants, a long debate took place about the need for norms and their content, the most contentious issue being the need for theologians to secure a canonical mandate from ecclesiastical authorities.

On May 4, 1993, Bishop John Leibrecht, Chairman of the Committee to Implement the Apostolic Constitution *Ex Corde Ecclesiae*, reported to his brother bishops a proposed set of ordinances applying the Constitution's general norms to the United States.[26] They had been drawn up by the bishop members of the committee. The university consultants had participated fully in the discussions, but there had been some issues on which they had been in unanimous disagreement with the bishops. It was not hard to see why. Using the constitution's language, the text defined Catholic colleges and universities as "those which, through their governing boards, freely commit themselves to the Christian message as it comes to us through the Catholic church and, together with the bishops, seek to preserve and foster their Catholic character and mission." Each institution was expected to undertake, every ten years, an "internal review of the congruence of its research program, course of instruction and service activity with the ideals and principles in *Ex Corde*." Academic officials would be required to advise those who were teaching theological disciplines of the church's expectation that they seek a mandate from the bishop or his delegate. That mandate involved "recognition by competent ecclesiastical authority of a Catholic professor's suitability to teach the discipline." Bishops and university leaders were invited to submit their comments or proposed amendments so that the proposals in final form could be considered by the entire hierarchy in 1994. If adopted by the U.S. bishops, any legislation would then have to be approved in Rome.

At a panel discussion held during a meeting of college and university presidents in February 1994, Bishop Leibrecht reported that the bishops had no desire to interfere in the internal governance of the schools. They hoped to preserve the "informal and dialogical" relationship of the recent past. But each bishop had a responsibility to safeguard authentic Catholic teaching and practice in his diocese. Bishop Oscar Lipscomb, a member of the committee, went a bit further, insisting that there were real problems of theological dissent that endangered the "integrity" of Catholic witness. The mandate, or something like it, was required by canon law and by Rome and, in the bishop's view, was needed. Bishop James Malone, a member of the committee and a veteran of these discussions, assured the presidents that the discussion would continue. He hoped that the deadline for submitting ecclesiastical ordinances would be extended and that participation in the process would be broadened beyond bishops and presidents to include a wider segment of the Catholic community. Responding, the presidents restated their opposition to the mandate. Boston College's President Donald Monan, S.J. described the dialogue as having reached an "impasse."

Thus, a quarter century after separate incorporation, tension persists between the American Catholic academic community, with its commitment to institutional autonomy and academic freedom, and the Vatican and its supporters, insisting on some juridical connection between the schools and the hierarchy. In order to avoid a clash that might be damaging to their colleges and universities and to the U.S. church, academic leaders and their episcopal supporters are forced to equivocate. By participating in seemingly endless meetings, expressing their own voluntary Catholic commitment and that of their institutions, clinging to power by filling top offices with religious, and seeking ways to be of service to the local church, presidents attempt to satisfy ecclesiastical officials that their schools are indeed Catholic. On the other hand, they are also forced to find ways to explain Vatican actions that will not arouse their faculty or the courts. They point out, for example, that the proposed ordinances contain no provision requiring submission of the ten-year review to the bishops and that the university as such need only notify Catholic theologians of the church's "expectation" that they seek the canonical mandate; it is then a matter between the bishop and the theologian, with the institution uninvolved. Or, in the case of Charles Curran, where academic freedom was clearly violated at Catholic University and rumors abounded of pressures to keep Curran from being hired by other Catholic schools, a great deal of rhetorical effort was expended to demonstrate that his case was not typical and that, on any one campus, it "could never happen here." Theologians did little better, passing a few resolutions of support but generally acquiescing to the Vatican's right to control teaching within the church, within pontifical faculties, and presumably in seminaries and other institutions forming people for ministry.

In discussing these matters, presidents and theologians alike express the same sense of powerlessness as most Catholics, rarely noticing that these pleas, by suggesting that only the Holy Father or the bishops are responsible, justify their own inaction. That these actions might be the result of internal church politics, at which some prove more adept than others, is rarely considered.

The other unfortunate consequence of all this is that the battle over accountability, understandable from an ecclesiastical point of view, constantly pushes other important matters into the background. Few forums are created for dealing with pluralism and polarization within the church, few programs are developed for carrying on the much heralded dialogue between religion and culture, and few resources are expended on research and development aimed at significant reform of undergraduate and graduate curriculum to incorporate theological reflection and ethical concern as called for in *Ex Corde* and many other texts. Instead, the valuable work of campus ministries and theology departments and the visibility of Catholic symbols too often substitute for serious engagement with broader issues of ecclesial and social responsibility. In short, if one asks, in teaching and research, what is being done that is Catholic, rather than what is being said that is Catholic, the record, although not meagre, is not close to what it might be. One reason is the atmosphere created by the need to wage a defensive battle against ecclesiastical interference. The church needs more from its universities, and it has much to offer in return; both church and society benefit when there is vigorous Christian and Catholic intellectual life. Building on those truths will require us to go beyond the chronic contentiousness that so often surrounds "the Catholic university."

CHAPTER 5

What's Catholic about Catholic Higher Education

JUST TELL THEM IT'S CATHOLIC!

Father Theodore M. Hesburgh, C.S.C., long-time president of the University of Notre Dame, once told a group of parents who sought his advice regarding the threatened closing of their local Catholic parochial school: "You take on the total responsibility for financing and operating it, but you assure [the bishop] that it will be a completely Catholic school." Ten years later, under lay control, the school was prospering. The lesson for Hesburgh was clear: "I firmly believe that this is the pattern for the future. We have long since gone this route in Catholic higher education." Universities like Notre Dame, under independent boards, responsible for their own funding, and recognizing academic freedom, "are not a direct arm of the church," Hesburgh argued, but they are "if anything, more professedly Catholic than ever."[1]

Catholic colleges and universities have indeed "gone this route." They are Catholic by profession; they say so. And most of the time their leaders share Hesburgh's confident enthusiasm. But, as the debate about *Ex Corde Ecclesiae* indicates, the Catholic question is not so easily resolved, and church authorities are not as easily assured as Hesburgh hoped. Just as the central problem in the church now is what it means to be a Catholic, so the central problem of Catholic higher education is the meaning of Catholic identity: what is Catholic about the Catholic college and university?

PROSPERITY

The first thing to say about Catholic higher education is that it is prospering. While Catholic elementary school enrollments dropped by 50

69

percent between 1965 and 1980, college and university enrollment climbed steadily. There are now 238 Catholic colleges and universities, with over 600,000 students. Among the Catholic schools are 91 predominantly undergraduate institutions, 12 two-year colleges, 1 historically black university, and 49 women's colleges, half of all the women's colleges in the country. Catholic schools are located in 40 of the 50 states, Puerto Rico, and the District of Columbia. A careful study in 1988 reported on 229 Catholic colleges and universities, with a total enrollment of 609,350 students. 378,000 students (336,000 of them undergraduates), were enrolled full time, 231,000 were part time. Ten schools had more than 10,000 students, 42 had fewer than 1,000. There were 41,000 full-time and 94,000 part-time students in graduate and professional schools. Nearly 36 percent of all students were of "nontraditional" age. There were 127,000 in universities which grant doctoral degrees, some 100,000 in liberal arts colleges, and the remaining 367,000 in schools which fell somewhere in between.

While some urban schools like Seton Hall and DePaul University are very diverse, only 6 percent of students are African-American and 7.7 percent Hispanic, a great many of them in three Catholic institutions in Puerto Rico. Most schools are making major efforts to attract minority students. Notre Dame, for example, doubled its minority enrollment, from 7 to 15 percent, between 1988 and 1993. The College of New Rochelle, long known as an undergraduate women's college, now has thousands of older persons enrolled in its College of New Resources at sites around the New York area. Three-fourths of its 18- to 22-year-olds are Catholics, but less than one-third of its older students are; many are Black and Hispanic.

Catholic institutions are only 14 percent of the total number of independent institutions of higher education, but they grant 20 percent of the degrees, including 16 percent of the first professional degrees, 20 percent of the masters degrees, and 22 percent of the bachelors degrees. The so-called Neylan colleges, founded by religious orders of women, enroll 27 percent of the students in 128 schools. In 1990, 39 percent of the students were the first generation of their family to attend college, evidence that many still provide an avenue to a better life. As compared with other private colleges and universities, the Catholic schools are more heavily dependent on tuition and fees and award less scholarship support. Catholic schools derive nearly 60 percent of their income from tuition and fees, as compared to 45.2 percent at all independents and 16.3 percent at state schools. In the 1992–93 school year, 34.4 percent of the schools charged between $6,000 and $9,000 for tuition and fees; the average of 154 schools surveyed was $8,799, well below the average for independent institutions. Financial aid doubled during the

1980s. Government assistance provides 12 percent of total income, compared to 17.3 percent at other independents.[2]

There are still 4,000 priests and sisters at work on Catholic college and university campuses. The gifts and contributed services of sponsoring religious orders amount to over $30 million. Their historic contributions reside, too, in land and buildings in local communities; together with the loyalty of alumni and immense good will, this is sometimes called "the living endowment." In a great many schools, members of the order still occupy important positions of administrative leadership and constitute either a strong minority on the board of trustees or retain considerable power through a two-tier board system. Some thoughtful observers believe that Catholic schools cannot survive as Catholic unless religious orders continue to play an important part.[3]

At one time, of course, these religious orders dominated the schools, but now they are struggling. To take the most dramatic example, in 1970 there were 7,775 Jesuits in the United States, over 4,000 of them involved in education.[4] By 1992 the number of Jesuits had dropped to 4,484 (25 percent of them over 70 years of age) and was expected to bottom out at 2,411 by 2010. The shaky status of vocations is indicated by the expectation of 2,338 deaths and only 1,140 entrances into the Society, with the latter almost canceled out by an expected 975 departures. In 1991, 878 Jesuits worked in higher education, only 709 in the 28 Jesuit colleges and universities. That latter number is expected to drop to 401 by the year 2001, when it is estimated there will be only 14 Jesuits at Fordham, 20 at Boston College, and 9 at Holy Cross. There is no reason to think that prospects are any brighter for smaller religious communities of men, and many believe that religious orders of women, with the exception of a few more conservative orders, will all but disappear in the next generation.[5]

Still, for twenty years, with more and more laypeople (many non-Catholics) filling faculty and administrative positions, Catholic higher education has prospered. More and better students arrive to meet an ever improving faculty on campuses filled with new buildings and talented staffs. The mood is positive; everyone seems convinced that they are engaged in valuable work and that they are doing it very well. Recently, at one of the country's best liberal arts colleges, not Catholic, an older professor whispered to a brand new colleague: "they complain a lot here, but it's very nice." That sentiment is widespread on Catholic campuses. A shrinking number of veterans can remember the dark days, when serious scholars had to defend their decision to teach at such schools. Now they are as academically respectable as private and state counterparts.

As recently as the early 1970s, most of the schools had their backs against the economic wall. Now most of them would acknowledge, if reluctantly, that things have changed for the better. Indeed, today there are few doubts about the value and improving quality of the higher education part of Catholic higher education.

THREE PUBLICS

The second point that needs to be made is obvious enough. Catholic colleges and universities are not just Catholic. Thirty years ago, when the big issue was religious order control, one study reported that the only agreement found at Catholic colleges and universities was the need to broaden self-definitions, for every Catholic college and university is an institution of higher education, a public servant, and a non-profit corporation, as well as a Catholic institution. While the public role may sometimes seem to threaten Catholic identity, federal courts have allowed Catholic colleges and universities considerable freedom, seeking only to deny public funds to pervasively sectarian institutions.[6]

Even more today, the church-university relationship is only one area of identity and mission. Most discussion in recent years has centered on the Catholic dimension of Catholic higher education. But Catholic colleges and universities resemble Catholic hospitals far more than they do parochial schools. The latter are entirely, or almost entirely, a church responsibility. They receive no direct public support, and their relationship with other educational institutions is limited. Catholic hospitals, in contrast, work closely with governments and with other health care institutions, their clientele and their staffs are usually very diverse, and they are accountable to a variety of public and private agencies. They stand solidly within three networks: the professional associations of doctors and other medical personnel, the health care system, connected by innumerable threads to governments and businesses, and the church. Like the hospitals, the Catholic college and university stands at the intersection of three distinct, overlapping publics — professional, political, and religious — within each of which it has responsibilities. Each brings something special to the enterprise, each has some serious problems that Catholic higher education might help address.

For higher education, the three publics are the church, the academic community, and the American people as a whole. The colleges and universities have responsibilities within the church, whose people have created them and continue to offer them remarkable support. They have responsibilities within the academic community, because they want their degrees to be recognized by graduate schools, professional and accrediting associations, and employers, because their faculty and professional staffs have credentials from and responsibilities within professional associations, and because they universally acknowledge a shared role with other institutions for preserving, extending, and communicating the accumulated wisdom of the human family. They have responsibilities within the political community as well, for each holds a public charter and receives considerable direct and indirect material support from local, state, and federal governments.

In varied and valuable ways, Catholic colleges and universities already render significant services to each of these publics. They continue to provide quality education to Catholics, they provide intellectual and cultural resources for the American church, and they often provide special services to the local churches in which they live. They have not yet made major intellectual contributions to American academic life, but they have provided American higher education with one component of its rich diversity and they stand poised to do a great deal more. And their services to society are innumerable and unquestioned; they are almost always highly valued institutions in their local communities.

Each of these publics today has some serious problems that the Catholic academic community might appropriately address. It is not by giving priority to one or another of these sets of responsibilities — religious, academic, and political — but precisely by attempting to address all three and seek creative links among them that the Catholic college and university can make its most important and distinctive contribution.

The church, as it settles into the evangelical piety that seems to mark democratic Christianity in a setting of pluralism, risks becoming not anti-intellectual but a-intellectual, understanding religion in personal and emotional terms with little serious intellectual content. Christianity makes claims on personal lives and sustains warm communities of mutual support, but it makes a shrinking contribution to our collective lives as Americans. The lack of intellectual content in popular piety has always been a problem for American Protestants, a problem that sharpened when so many churches allowed their links to higher education to wither. Today, there are many signs among Catholics that the intellectual preparation of priests, religious, and lay ministers is inadequate; networks of Catholic intellectuals are weak, and there have been sharp drops in circulation of intelligent Catholic journals. Even at Catholic educational institutions deeply committed to their Catholic mission, pastoral ministry enjoys far more success than even the best theology programs. If there is good news in all this, it is that the problem concerns both conservatives and liberals; on both sides heads nod when Father Hesburgh says that the Catholic university should be the place "where the church does its thinking."

The second public, *the university community*, also has some problems that might evoke a helpful response from Catholics. Everyone agrees that over the last generation Catholic schools have become more like their secular counterparts. Faculty and professional staff can now move back and forth between Catholic and private or public higher education with little serious readjustment. However, along with greater professional acceptance have come problems. Arguments about multiculturalism and political correctness are as common on Catholic campuses as on others; so are problems of drug and alcohol abuse and sexual harassment. Catholic schools struggle, as others struggle, to do the right thing in areas of race and gender. From wrestling with intercollegiate athletics to lobbying government agencies to sharing ideas about minority recruitment, Catholic schools are part of the academic mainstream.

Perhaps the two most important problems in undergraduate education today, at least judging by newspaper accounts of such matters, are the coherence and purpose of the curriculum and the problem of public morality. Critics like Allan Bloom and William Bennett emphasize the former, and, whatever one thinks of their analysis and prescriptions, they obviously have touched a nerve. It would be hard to find anyone who would not agree that more needs to be done to articulate general educational goals and find strategies to reach them. This means reforming the core curriculum and building bridges between the arts and sciences and more vocationally oriented programs, both undergraduate and graduate.

Catholic educators have long made claims about integration; by attempting to fulfill those promises, they may be able to contribute to resolving a common problem. And perhaps the way to begin is by taking up more confidently the once-cherished idea among religious people that somehow religious and intellectual formation should go together. Finding creative ways to reintroduce fundamental philosophical and religious questions into undergraduate education is a common task, not a specifically Catholic one. Catholic educators, faced with a Catholic population whose religious search increasingly resembles everyone else's, are compelled to find better ways to make religion intellectually challenging and personally compelling. What they have to do as Catholic schools, all schools need to do.

The potential for a Catholic contribution is even greater in the area of personal and social morality. Already, Catholic thought has made tremendous contributions in the areas of medical ethics and the ethics of war and peace. A century of Catholic social teaching—and almost a century of

American Catholic commentary on it—provides unique resources for developing social and business and professional ethics that go beyond the usual "how far can you go without saying no" approach characteristic of these subjects. So far Catholic schools have not been particularly creative, or even energetic, about incorporating these resources into curriculum. But by doing so they could serve their Catholic heritage and responsibility and simultaneously address some crucial issues in American university life.

The third public is *society* at large. The people through their institutions have chartered these schools; their degrees are recognized because the government has delegated accreditation (at least for now) to private agencies directed by the colleges and universities themselves. Fewer and fewer students could attend Catholic schools without government-backed loans and grants; very few people of low income could attend without this help, and these are students the schools very much want to attract. And when the students leave these schools they go to work, many in the surrounding community. So every school is connected to specific communities—local, regional, and in a few cases national. What is the responsibility of the Catholic college or university to these publics? In some cases, large, complex universities, with medical and law schools, are deeply embedded in their surrounding communities; they have become in some sense semi-public. Others have made a self-conscious decision to become more public: one thinks of the new downtown Minneapolis campus of the University of St. Thomas, a growing institution that awards the second largest number of M.B.A. degrees in the country.

Some would argue, incorrectly I think, that focus on public responsibility is what got the schools in trouble with their Catholic identity. But a case can be made that one way the schools can serve the public is precisely by being Catholic, by attending to the issues of meaning and value that are the particular domain of a church-related college. Another way is to help reinvigorate public moral discourse, as our bishops have tried to do in the area of abortion, nuclear weapons, ethnic diversity, racism, and economic justice. There is wide agreement that our country needs a more vital sense of civic responsibility, and there are resources in the Catholic tradition and its existing communities to help meet that need.

The Catholic college and university can help the Christian community *shape* its self-understanding within American culture, and it can *share* its wisdom with others in defining the meanings and responsibilities embedded in our common American and global experience, forming in pluralism what John Courtney Murray called the public moral consensus. The dual task requires suspicion of the sectarian temptation—by which the Catholic component controls the university—and the secular temptation, allowing the university dynamic to control and marginalize Catholicism in particular and religion in general. Trying to do *both* — to shape an intelligent Catholicism and to share in forming a common culture and language — in the same place, with others, is the challenge and the great opportunity before Catholic higher education.

MASKED ISSUES

Catholic higher education, then, has academic and political as well as religious responsibilities. It also has a variety of internal problems that arose with rapid change and are often obscured by the emotionally charged issues of academic freedom and institutional autonomy. Yet they must be understood before we can adequately address problems of mission and identity. Let us examine three among many:

Trustees

It is so remarkable that it should be repeated. In an act of unprecedented trust, religious orders of men and women gave their schools to lay-dominated boards of trustees. But so far there has not been a lot of attention given to the criteria for selection of trustees, their orientation to Catholic higher education, and their continuing education on issues of importance to Catholic mission and identity. Presidents who guided the early moves to lay boards admit that, even though they understood the change as a sharing of responsibility with lay Catholics in the spirit of Vatican II, they selected laypeople on the basis of the skills or experience they could bring to the school: lawyers, benefactors, key alumni, businessmen who could offer specialized advice, such as on investments or insurance. Only later did some religious orders begin to provide programs to orient trustees to their own specific concerns or, at crisis moments such as a law suit against Georgetown University that charged discrimination against homosexuals, to church issues as they touched the campus. Moreover, during the first generation of lay trustees, especially in the schools founded by male religious orders, strong presidents continued to dominate. Now, as trustees select their second and third presidents and as the pool of qualified religious shrinks, boards are clearly maturing. In the future trustees will play the most important role in the life of these institutions, which makes their understanding of Catholic mission and identity absolutely crucial.[7]

The Economics of Catholic Higher Education

One of the untold stories of recent years is the enormous increase in endowment of a few Catholic schools, including Notre Dame, Georgetown, and Loyola University of Chicago. Catholic schools also enjoy remarkable support from their alumni and alumnae. Some schools have become very expensive, a few having adopted the "meet need" admissions policies of the nation's best schools, but most remain relatively inexpensive and frequently are noted as good bargains in guides to prospective students. But all is far from secure. Catholic schools are very dependent on tuition and fees, but they also depend heavily on public support. Friends of Catholic higher education have all but obliterated memories of what things were like in the late 1960s and very early 1970s. At that time, Catholic elementary schools were in free-fall decline; their enrollment dropped by almost 50 percent in fifteen years. A major factor (though assuredly not the only one) was increased costs associated with more and more lay teachers and with parental demands for academic quality comparable to public schools.

Something very similar was happening in Catholic higher education: lay faculty multiplied; Catholics no longer felt required to avoid the quality non-Catholic private schools, which now welcomed Catholic students, making better quality a competitive necessity for Catholic schools. Costs rose accordingly. In every part of the country serious questions were raised about the survival of the weaker Catholic institutions, and even some of the best known Catholic universities were in very serious financial trouble.[8]

What saved the situation in higher education (in sharp contrast with elementary and secondary education) was a dramatic increase in federal tuition assistance for students, whether in private or public schools, brought about by a lobbying effort in which Catholic presidents played an important role. Federal and state grants and loans are what make possible Catholic higher education as we know it. As William Byron, S.J., former president of the University of Scranton and of the Catholic University of America regularly insists, federal financial aid policy is probably the most important factor that will determine the future of Catholic higher education. Intellectuals rightly ask about the impact of this assistance on the Catholic integrity of the schools; unfortunately, they ask fewer questions about the meaning of these policies of pluralism in higher education for American public policy, both in education and in other areas. If those questions were asked, a public service test might seem as important as the proposed tests for Catholic theological orthodoxy.

The financial aid issue ties in directly with several important aspects of Catholic identity. For example, in a stagnant economy, facing few increases (even likely declines) in government assistance to students, the self-financed student financial aid budget comes to dominate institutional priorities. Important questions then arise. For example, program changes designed to strengthen Catholic identity, such as hiring more faculty interested in Catholic studies, expanding Catholic theology, or developing innovative graduate and professional programs that take religion seriously, are all easily discussed when budgets are expanding, far harder when they can come about only by sacrificing other desirable projects.

And what about social class? Catholic colleges and universities played a very important role (though we should always remember that they played a less important role than state colleges and universities) in the upward mobility and social progress of American Catholic immigrants from Europe. Now some schools are trying to play a similar role in the lives of Latino and new immigrant Catholics. While schools can summon some private and foundation support, government tuition assistance programs are what make these efforts feasible. Similarly, many worry that the best and most expensive schools are now available only to the wealthiest families. This is a particular problem for religious orders like the Jesuits and many women's communities that have made a collective "option for the poor." How can they reconcile that commitment with their heavy investment in the education of middle-class and wealthy Americans? But, to the degree that they try to maintain multiclass and multiracial student bodies, Catholic institutions are again heavily dependent on government student aid support. Calls to reassert Catholic identity and question the supposedly secularizing decisions of the last generation need to be tempered by such realism.

Academic Governance

Almost everyone agrees that professionalization is a key to understanding contemporary American Catholic higher education. Academic freedom, institutional autonomy, emphasis on research and publication within the disciplines, and problems with general education have all come with this process. So has the demand for structural reform to recognize the faculty's primary responsibility for academic policy. Modern faculty not only expect to be left alone in the classroom and laboratory, but they also expect to shape policy on curriculum standards, hiring, promotion, and tenure. On such matters, trustees should interfere only in extraordinary circumstances. On other matters, from admissions and athletics to investments and building and grounds, the faculty and professional staff expect to share responsibility and the power that goes with it. I know of no studies of changes in internal academic governance, but I have the impression that administrators and trustees were slower to share responsibility than to affirm academic freedom. But gradually changes have been introduced so that at most schools it is simply no longer possible to mandate academic policy or define institutional identity without consulting the faculty and staff and winning their support.

Catholics, clergy and laity alike, have long been accustomed to change initiated from the top down, and Catholic colleges and universities have not been immune to this hierarchical style. Intellectuals with a project need only gain the ear of the Pope, the bishop, or the university president, like courtiers intriguing around the throne. Many arguments about the Catholic university betray such a distinctly Catholic tone, insisting that Catholicism requires a specific set of actions and then looking to those responsible for Catholic identity: the trustees or the religious order or the president or, in the case of extreme conservatives, the Pope, to mandate those actions. But universities are not like that, at least not any longer. Whether it is a matter of hiring more faculty interested in Catholic subjects, expanding programs in Catholic theology, or initiating cooperative research projects with the local church, any changes designed to better express the Catholic identity and commitment of a college or university will have to win support among a significant portion of the faculty and professional staff. Dialogue and persuasion are not the best way; they are the only way.

HIGHER EDUCATION, YES; CATHOLIC, NOT SO SURE

Even when we acknowledge the complexity of the situation and the multiple responsibilities facing each college and university, the Catholic question remains. Some once-Catholic schools, such as Webster College, Manhattanville, and a few others, are by choice no longer Catholic. A few, such as Christendom College and the Franciscan University of Steubenville, are trying to be very Catholic by insisting on adherence to Catholic teaching in all areas of college life. At a few there seems to be a gradual process of erosion as schools de-emphasize their Catholic affiliation, sometimes while reemphasizing their relationship with a particular religious community. But most, with varying degrees of enthusiasm, cling to their Catholic identity and, from time to time, in formal and informal ways, ask themselves what it means.

There is little doubt that these schools are different. When pushed to specify the difference, pragmatic deans and presidents point to the still prominent role of religious orders at many schools, the strength of departments of theology and religious studies, well-funded campus ministry programs, and overall campus "atmosphere," marked by personal concern for students, a warm and welcoming community, cooperative programs with the local church, and tremendous generosity in providing services to people in need, much of it attributed to Christian spirit.[9] While these practical responses rarely satisfy theologians or ecclesiastical bureaucrats, they obviously touch real experiences, for many if not most of the schools enjoy healthy enrollments, warm alumni relations, and wide support in their local communities, and, in my visits to many campuses, I have found faculty, staff, and student morale to be remarkably high.

Given the obvious successes of the schools and the widespread satisfaction with their performance, reflected in enrollment and alumni support, people naturally grow impatient with the constant recurrence of the identity question. Father Hesburgh, for example, seemed extremely frustrated by the effort to formulate the Apostolic Constitution for higher education in the late 1980s; he rightly felt that the issues had been fully aired a decade earlier. Veterans of Catholic higher education become accustomed to the amused resignation and touch of cynicism with which the faculty greets an announcement of yet another airing of Catholic mission and identity. The President of Fordham University says that essays on "what is a Catholic university" evoke "ponderous abstractions, some airy aspirations and very little reference to particular times and places."[10] Or else definitions of Catholic identity are phrased in the language of in-house Catholic dialectics, inaccessible to any but the best-informed Catholics: for example, the idea that, while Catholic theologians (a title far less clear than it sounds) must receive a "mandate" from "proper ecclesiastical authority," this poses no problem of academic freedom or institutional autonomy because the school need only remind said theologian of that obligation, nothing more.

The outcome is rarely constructive. William C. McInnes, S.J. has documented the depressing record of two decades of attempts to define Jesuit mission and identity in terms satisfactory to all twenty-eight of the academically and financially strong Jesuit colleges and universities. In the mid-1970s, I was able to examine records of one of those intiatives, Project One, when provincials asked local Jesuit communities to articulate a collective statement of their mission at each Jesuit school.[11] Very few were able to do so, most finally turning the task of writing a report over to an individual or small group. Later, the Association of Jesuit Colleges and Universities tried its hand, with no greater success. Failure to find consensus terms to define Catholic, or in this case Jesuit, identity and mission does not mean that effective work is not being done, work that in many cases arises from and expresses Catholic commitments and concerns. But it does suggest why some might want to shelve the discussion.

Aside from Vatican insistence, however, there are many other reasons why the question of mission and identity should be pushed. There is considerable evidence that successful private colleges and universities are marked by a campus culture that reflects agreement on a common purpose. So the quality of work has some relationship with the collective sense of shared mission. One can also argue that, while these schools do wonderful work right now, their impact on the church and on American society could be even more significant if they could arrive at some shared understanding of what they are doing and why they are doing it. The thousands of men and women who work at these schools might find greater satisfaction in their work if they could connect their personal aspirations with the institution's deepest commitments. Finally, there is what I believe to be the most important argument: if one believes that the Catholic community is important and that its future depends to some degree on its collective intelligence and its capacity to think and work together, then Catholic colleges and universities that act on their Catholicity can be extremely valuable resources.

THE REALLY CATHOLIC OPTION

One of the few schools to make things crystal clear is the Franciscan University of Steubenville, with about 1,800 students, located about 40 miles west from Pittsburgh.[12] When Franciscan Michael Scanlan, a graduate of Williams College with a doctorate from Harvard Law School, became president in 1974, he determined to reverse what he regarded as the school's rapid secularization and by deliberate policy make it "stand for Christian and Catholic values, spiritual growth and the Franciscan ideals of its founders." Scanlan is convinced that all policies should be tested by a Christian and Catholic standard. To do this, the president must have the authority "to pastor the Catholic life there and to oversee the teaching. He must . . . also submit to appropriate episcopal authority and the authority of the Holy Father."

In short, Scanlan aimed to "establish mainstream Catholicism as normal." This included the following actions:

1. To "change the school's environment to one that is overtly Catholic-Christian" by witnessing to the word of God, preaching the Gospel, and establishing the presence of committed Catholics in key positions.

2. To have campus structures support a Christian environment by making "small faith sharing groups mandatory for all resident students" and offering them the choice of small residential households as an alternative to dormitories. According to Scanlan, "households on our campus ease the isolation and loneliness common to many college students and provide a positive peer pressure toward growth in Christian virtues and values."

3. To publish a clear statement of the school's values and commitments. This "statement of convictions," endorsed by trustees, faculty, and students in 1983, reads: "Our University is dedicated to the Lordship of Jesus Christ. I believe that Jesus Christ is the Way, the Truth and the Life. I commit this university to pursue a way of education based on God's revealed truth and the teaching of the Magisterium of the Roman Catholic Church, and a life empowered by God's Holy Spirit and nurtured by sound pastoral guidance."

4. To base decisions about faculty and staff recruitment, development, and termination on support for the school's mission as well as technical competence. In May 1989, after lengthy deliberation, all the priests, the entire theological faculty, the dean of the faculty and the president took an oath of fidelity and made a profession of faith as requested by the Congregation on the Doctrine of the Faith.

5. To "develop a curriculum whose courses are based on Catholic truths." Here conflicts arose between a faculty who translated Catholic orthodoxy into courses in Catholic culture, expecting a critical appropriation of the tradition, and the more evangelical students and staff, who saw the Catholic life of the school in more spiritual terms, demanded a literal adherence to papal teaching, and showed some indifference, if not hostility, to the academic demands of even highly orthodox Catholic faculty.

Scanlan's approach is similar to that of the nation's flourishing "faith-related" Christian colleges. This group's explanation of their work evokes a warm response from many increasingly evangelical Catholics. Robert D. Pitts, Vice President for Academic Affairs at Taylor University in Upland, Indiana, contrasted his school's effort to achieve "the integration of faith, learning and living" with a Catholic university colleague's insistence that "'religion' is merely another branch of inquiry and has no business pervading [invading?] the domain of [what amounts to] secular studies." Because evangelicals "understand our conversion to Christ to be so all pervading," they combine core courses on religion with a philosophy of education that requires that "every course in our curriculum should be taught from a Christian perspective (i.e. integrating Christian truth with the subject matter) to the degree that this is possible." Seldom is this close to indoctrination, he insists; "it is never assumed as it often is in secular universities that any issue is foreclosed or unworthy of discussion." They "reject the fundamentalist mentality that all of the answers can be found in a simplistic reading of Scripture and the pagan view that religion has nothing to say about life, the world and meaning." Above all this approach "does not compartmentalize the discussion of faith and practice. We contend that faith is in the fabric of our beings and that it is inevitable [more so probably] that it should infiltrate our consideration of knowledge."[13]

THE MESSY ALTERNATIVE

It is surprising that to date so few Catholic schools have followed this path. But most do not have the homogeneous faculty and student body needed to make such a move, and most do not want to separate themselves so sharply from the American academic mainstream, so recently entered. So the question that so disturbs Rome is a legitimate one: how are these schools Catholic? Do they remain "part of the church" and, if so, in what way? Among theologians and educated Catholics, it is now commonplace to assert that there are several images or models of the church, each grounded in scripture, tradition, and experience, none exhausting the full mystery of God's presence. Perhaps it would be helpful to think about the identity question under three of those models.

First, the church as institution. Here the universities still fight a two-front war. In dealing with the state and the faculty, they insist that they are not part of the church, but are independent institutions chartered by the government that operate under boards of trustees and meet criteria of autonomy, academic freedom, and professional quality established by accrediting agencies. In dealing with Rome, the university presidents repeat this argument, but at the same time insist that they intend to serve the church and maintain their Catholic character, and they express this intention in formal documents. This is enough for the bishops, when Rome is not involved. As early as 1976, when the Vatican was pushing for some accrediting process to clarify Catholic identity, the Purpose and Identity Committee of the College and University organization favored instead "some kind of Conversation." A few years later, in their pastoral letter on higher education, the American bishops recognized the "delicate balance" between the autonomy of the university and the responsibility of the hierarchy. They professed to seek "a fruitful cooperation" and encouraged the universities "to develop ways which will bring bishops and theologians together with other members of the church to examine theological issues with wisdom, with faith, and with mutual charity and esteem."[14] In their response to the proposed schema, the college presidents agreed. Situations vary so greatly that clear specifications of Catholicity "simply confuse the issue," while "the important thing is the internal commitment to the values of the tradition and the external witness in terms of achievement and service."[15]

Yet, as we have seen, the problem will not go away. Rome and its American agents consistently argue for a structured form of accountability. They either cannot understand or simply reject the preference of many American bishops and all university presidents, who want to resolve problems in a typically American fashion, avoiding sharp definitions and depending on dialogue and *ad hoc* negotiation to overcome the uncertainty that arises from blurred lines of authority. It is not hard to see why American ecclesial and academic leaders prefer ambiguity. In the wake of the Curran case, William Byron, the respected Jesuit President of Catholic University of America, argued publicly that Catholic institutions had to acknowledge some limits on academic freedom. "To proclaim a Catholic identity without accepting an ecclesiastical limit on theological exploration and communication is to misunderstand not only the nature of church-relatedness but also the idea of a university and the meaning of academic freedom," Byron argued.[16] Naturally, this drew strong responses from scholars. The most moderate acknowledged the possibility of limits when doctrines held to be infallible were involved. Others acknowledged the need for such limits on theology within the church, but strongly resisted limits within the university, where the spirit and ethic of freedom and the absence of fear of reprisal were essential to research and teaching. Most still agreed with Father Hesburgh who, as early as 1967, insisted that the Catholic university, to do its job for the church and for society, needed to "disaffiliate from every influence which is not ecumenical, that cuts us off from each other and from the world."[17] So the debate about academic freedom is not over.

From Rome's point of view, the crux of the problem is theology. The Vatican is not questioning the role of nontheologians, though church authorities clearly hope that a majority of faculty will be Catholic. Nor are they challenging the place of non-Catholics or persons who teach other than Catholic theology in departments of theology or religious studies. Even the large demands in the proposed ordinances for periodic reviews of policy contain no provisions for enforcement. It is only on the matter of Catholic theology that a line has been drawn.

As Avery Dulles has pointed out, Rome apparently understands the theologian's task as a "subordinate and instrumental one," namely, "to set forth and defend the teaching of the papal and episcopal magisterium." Dulles suggests that theologians also have a responsibility to speak the truth, so they exercise a "complementary and mutually corrective" relationship with the pastoral authority of the hierarchy.[18] In other words, there should be a more collaborative relationship between theologians and bishops; in Richard McBrien's words, "it is indeed a matter of balance."[19] But, at the moment at least, the Holy Father and the Congregation on the Doctrine of the Faith reject the idea that the theologians should share in the magisterium and prefer a more direct subordination of theology to ecclesiastical authority, the kind of subordination that was common between the First and Second Vatican Councils.

Here, too, the majority of bishops and theologians, unable to resolve the dispute at the level of principle, clearly prefer a messier arrangement that reflects American values. Bishops, canon lawyers, biblical scholars, and theologians negotiated for years to develop a set of procedures for resolving disputes. The report links the call for dialogue and negotiation to the American context of the universities: "Our church can still learn much from our nation's civic values of freely expressed public opinion and constructive public debate. Issues that arise in our community should be addressed with prudence and discretion, but also with realism about living in a pluralistic society and learning from it."[20]

Unfortunately, there is a tendency to mystify events within the institutional church and avoid the human reality that its actions reflect the give-and-take of institutional politics. How the issue of church-relatedness is resolved — indeed the very continuation of Catholic higher education — depends upon the commitment of persons and on strategic decisions and deliberate action. This means concerted action in the church as well as in the university. Most religious people hesitate to act politically within the church. Avery Dulles, who has described the problem of theological freedom best, ends his essay with warnings against becoming a "party" or faction within the church, an attitude of distaste for church politics that sharply limits attentiveness to church reform and contrasts sharply with the vigilance and activism of conservatives. Theologian William Shea disagrees with Dulles and insists that academics need to organize and act deliberately within church structures if their balancing act is to prove successful. "It takes strategy and relentless pressure to move the ecclesiastical mountain," Shea writes. "Theologians must learn to act politically if the mountain is to be moved." So far they have left the battle for the most part to friendly bishops and Catholic college presidents.[21]

Clarity comes no more easily when one takes another model of the church — community. These schools remain deeply embedded in the Catholic community. Most Catholic colleges and universities still depend on the Catholic community for support, attract Catholic students, and seek to make the life of the school reflective of the faith and values of the Catholic people. Theologian Joseph Komonchak has argued most eloquently that both bishops and universities should continually recall their common responsibility in and for the people of God. More concretely, McBrien, in arguing the case for the ecclesial role of the university, attempts to move the discussion away from clerical control and hierarchical responsibility to a wider context of shared responsibility for the life and work of the church.

This would mean working toward a structure of shared responsibility in which the Catholic academic community would relate to diocesan pastoral councils and other bodies of clergy, laity, and religious collaborating in the work of the church. Yet, as Komonchak and McBrien well know, church reform has generally failed. There are in fact few structures of shared responsibility through which the local church and colleges and universities might build more constructive and mutually enriching relationships. There are instances of consultation, collaboration, and dialogue, to be sure, and there is enough experience of shared responsibility to demonstrate that it can work effectively. But church reform in general has stalled and in some areas is being reversed. Also, at the moment, a sense of shared ecclesial responsibility is understandably not very prominent among laypeople generally, nor among professors and academic personnel specifically. While many would like to share with the bishops responsibility for dealing with problems ranging from cultural diversity to women in the church, there are almost no ways in which they can do so. When such structures do develop, the issue of church-relatedness will take on a new form and new possibilities will emerge.

Then there is the model of the church as servant to humanity. McBrien contends that the church can test the orthodoxy and fidelity of an institution by its commitment to justice and peace, orthopraxis, as well as by its adherence to doctrinal teachings, orthodoxy. President after president has repeated the words of the American bishops insisting that pursuit of justice and human dignity is an essential work of a Catholic institution. The Jesuits have reaffirmed their commitment to integrated education in the context of their Society's affirmation of faith and justice and the option for the poor as the context of Jesuit ministries. "Any college or university with which Jesuits are associated must work for justice and educate for justice," according to the late Timothy Healy of Georgetown. "If this is not the burden of what it tries to accomplish in the heart of its students as well as

in its corporate presence . . . then it is not a Jesuit university."[22] Monsignor
George Higgins told a Catholic University of America graduating class: "the
real test of a university's success in promoting justice for the poor and
disadvantaged and for the minorities in our society is not what its professors
say in the classroom and publish in learned tomes, but what its alumni and
alumnae do as free and committed citizens directly involved in shaping the
policies of the republic."[23]

Like the argument about shared responsibility with the local church, this
position has to be confirmed by the faculty, which often proves reluctant.
Catholic colleges and universities are building numerous programs of
community service to give expression to their intentional Catholicity. These
programs are widely admired, but they are hardly distinctive to Catholic
schools and hardly touch the educational and research practice of most
institutions. So this is an area of still largely unexplored possibility.

Service could well be the key to future resolution of the identity issue. If
the church were clear about its mission and Catholics themselves were
committed to that mission everyone would want to enlist all possible
resources for the life and work of the church. That would place the higher
education question, and many other questions, in a new context. To
oversimplify, if the mission is largely for the church itself — to build up the
church as the ordinary means of salvation and convert others in the sense of
persuading them to become members — then one set of options is called for,
a set focused on the religious as distinct from the academic and political
publics the schools serve. If, on the other hand, the church's mission is
within and on behalf of the whole diverse, conflicted, creative, endangered
human family, then another set of options, giving more weight to the
political and academic among the school's tripartite connections, would
seem appropriate. But, for Catholics who engage the mission issue, the key
question is not simply defining what the church is, so that we can locate, or
relocate, the university within its organizational chart, but understanding
why the church exists, so that we can decide how academic resources can
best serve the church's work. The big question is why, not what.

For the moment, however, none of these models get us any closer to
clarity about the meaning of Catholic identity. It is understandable that
many would prefer clearer definitions. Conservative restorationists and
evangelical radicals alike would emphasize the church's difference and
distance from the prevailing culture, clarify the demands of church
membership, and sharpen the boundaries between the church and "the
world." That option would force Catholic colleges and universities into
more explicit confessional practices like those at Steubenville. Most would
simply not do that. Convinced that autonomy is essential to the university,

faced with a professional and religiously diverse faculty who expect to share responsibility for all decisions about academic policy, and dependent upon public financial support, most schools would regard it as irresponsible to accept external control and impractical to try to force specific definitions by administrative fiat. On campus as in the parish, voluntarism is here to stay, and serious Catholics have no alternative to persuasion.

MISSION AND IDENTITY

The consensus is that Catholic schools sustain their Catholic commitment by institutional profession (official texts that say they are Catholic), strong departments of religious studies or theology, vigorous campus ministry programs, and, in some cases, continued presence of religious in positions of administrative leadership. Almost all, nudged by Rome and their founding religious community, are dissatisfied "with a Catholicism so unobtrusive that Catholics and non-Catholics alike can pass through without being touched by it." But that very anxiety can "raise nervous goosepimples on the flesh of colleagues," including Catholics. Given the tension, it would seem best that lay faculty and administrators, both Catholic and non-Catholic, wrestle with the problem and not allow trustees and the religious community to do it for them. That conversation must begin with trust, respecting and taking seriously both Catholic and academic values. What has to be avoided, as one woman administrator puts it, is the suggestion "that people of different faiths and even of no particular denomination are on our faculties on sufferance or as tokens to so-called opposite views."[24]

But often it turns out that, first of all, people don't even know each other very well. Then, when conversations begin, it is not so easy to talk to one another about the meaning of academic work, much less about religion. Accordingly, many schools have initiated modest (often charmingly modest) efforts to bring faculty and administrators, both religious and laypeople, together for small receptions and brown-bag lunches, for prayer, and for talks about the concerns and traditions of the founding religious community, all as possible occasions for serious conversation about the mission and identity of their school. Some examples:

- Jesuit provincials and presidents have initiated a well-funded national seminar on higher education, with Jesuits, lay faculty, administrators, and trustees, that produces a biannual magazine, *Conversations*, intended to stimulate local discussion of Jesuit and Catholic identity.

- Jesuit schools also have launched a new organization of mission and identity officers, persons officially appointed, at a large majority of Jesuit schools, to provide leadership to local efforts to nurture Jesuit-lay collaboration.
- At the University of San Francisco, James E. Flynn, S.J. turned his doctoral thesis on Jesuit-lay collaboration rooted in Ignatian spirituality into a job description for his position as Assistant to the President for University Mission. He believes that building toward a future for Jesuit education with fewer Jesuits requires a full-time person who enjoys the respect of the faculty and is supportive of the academic work of the institution, who truly regards the faculty and professional staff as partners in the work, equal to the Jesuits, and who is deeply engaged with the spirituality of the Jesuit tradition.
- Gonzaga University has a Council for Partnership in Ministry whose activities include a faculty-staff orientation program and educational events dealing with Jesuit history, educational philosophy, and spirituality. Faculty and staff have opportunities to experience the Spiritual Exercises of St. Ignatius with a spiritual director in weekly group sessions or on retreats. Small groups meet for breakfast or lunch to discuss the school's mission, particular campus problems, or the latest issue of *Conversations*.[25]
- Loyola of New Orleans holds an annual five-day summer seminar on Ignatian spirituality and to discuss campus strategies for preserving Jesuit educational ideals. Creighton University has a well-staffed Collaborative Ministry Office working on similar programs. Their workshops include "Building Community," "Meet the Jesuits," and "My Job as a Ministry of Service." Marquette's Center for Ignatian Spirituality, sponsored by the Jesuit community, has a five-person staff offering a great variety of services to faculty and staff, both Catholics and non-Catholics. Its leaders report considerable interest not only on the part of Christians but also "seekers," persons of faith without a church identification. Loyola of Chicago, one of the largest Catholic universities, has established a Center for Faith and Culture under Sr. Gertrude Patch, R.S.C.J. to enlist faculty and staff in conversation and encourage research projects, not just on matters of Jesuit identity but also on wider issues of religion and culture.

In some schools this work has taken a step toward institutional policy, particularly around matters of personnel. St. Louis University, for example, has a booklet on university identity and mission, a "map of its heart and soul," that provides a basis for discussion with prospective faculty. It is a more Catholic statement than most:

Saint Louis University is a Catholic university sponsored by the Society of Jesus and dedicated to the Society's ideal of striving for academic excellence under the inspiration of the Christian faith. It recognizes the central importance of the principle of academic freedom to its life as a community committed to the discovery and sharing of truth. In keeping with its Christian vision of the dignity of persons as created in the image of God and as united under the Creator's loving Providence, the University seeks to establish a collegial environment in which those of diverse backgrounds and religious beliefs can participate in this community in a spirit of cooperation and mutual respect.

Persuading the faculty to affirm such words is obviously difficult, and the religious community sometimes finds it hard to accept texts developed by the university community. At Georgetown, for example, a 1992 strategic planning document[26] states that Georgetown is "a Catholic University in the Jesuit Tradition." As such, Georgetown holds that "faith expressed as wisdom" is central to its identity, and its leaders constantly seek to expand and deepen the conversation between faith and learning. This "self-description" serves as the point of departure for a statement of goals: Georgetown seeks to be "an international and multicultural academic community in which men and women of diverse backgrounds and religious beliefs can fully participate." The university seeks to "integrate the pursuit of excellence in research with effective and imaginative teaching. The University is also a place where learning and personal growth prepare and motivate individuals to serve their communities." Immediate needs include research support, improvement in the quality of teaching, need-blind admissions policies, and improved governance and communication. The university's Jesuit community praised the text, particularly the call for need-blind admissions as a step to insure class and cultural diversity. The Jesuits also wanted more emphasis on "integrative learning" and concrete commitments to recruiting Jesuits and others familiar with Catholic and Jesuit commitments. But, a year later, a Jesuit dean told the faculty that, while wisdom rooted in faith remained central at Georgetown, "a person's religion plays no part in hiring, tenure, promotion, the awarding of grants or the securing of funds. In fact, most of us don't know each other's religious beliefs."[27]

As thirty years of Notre Dame history testifies, the issue of identity never dies. As early as April 1966, Father Hesburgh was attacked in the pages of *Ave Maria*, published on the campus, by recent alumnus Ralph Martin, a Princeton graduate student and soon to emerge as a leader of a new movement of Catholic Pentecostals. Martin charged that Notre Dame was "no longer a Christian university in any way other than Yale and Harvard." He admitted that Notre Dame made it possible for someone to study Christianity as a subject, but he insisted that "there is a big difference between thinking about Christianity and doing it and students need to be shown how to do it. They need to be initiated into a Christian community where the life is being lived." In the years that followed, Notre Dame invested heavily in campus ministry and, with the help of the Congregation of the Holy Cross, maintained a substantial pastoral presence of priests and religious in the university dormitories, so that complaints about campus religious life were relatively rare.[28]

The big issue was faculty hiring, more or less ignored at some schools, but regularly debated at Notre Dame. Notre Dame committed itself without apology to becoming a national research university, and over the last thirty years it has raised its endowment to the point where that goal is now within reach. Recurrent self-studies regularly reaffirmed this commitment. The PACE (Priorities and Commitments for Excellence) report of 1982, for example, insisted that "we must excel as a university in the full sense of the word" and outlined an ambitious agenda for improving the quality of research and graduate education. The same report reaffirmed the university's determination to "maintain" its Catholic identity, but, from time to time, controversies broke out over the degree to which the university was realizing that objective. In 1992 a graduate student charged that many faculty and administrators at Notre Dame were "embarrassed by the fact that it is a Catholic university and are working to hasten the day when it is no longer." The writer also claimed that an even larger number provided support for the process by hiring professors based on academic qualifications alone.[29] This was untrue. In fact, Notre Dame did more than most to make religious affiliation and interest a factor in the hiring process and had a *de facto* affirmative action program for hiring Holy Cross (CSC) priests. In establishing an independent Board of Trustees in 1967, the university committed itself to building a faculty of "committed and articulate believers" and others who shared the desire to maintain the "Catholic character" of the university. At the conclusion of yet another campus-wide planning process in 1993, Notre Dame's President stated that the university had a special obligation to pursue the religious dimension of all human learning and to "insure that Catholic thought intersects with the work of the university's schools and departments." Accordingly, he directed that steps be taken to insure "the continuing presence of a predominant number of Catholic intellectuals" on the faculty.[30]

Hiring Catholics, even vaguely defined "Catholic intellectuals," is not enough. During the discussions that preceded the Notre Dame report, one engineering professor reported that a study of faculty demonstrated that most professors, Catholic or not, regarded their religious faith as a private matter, only indirectly connected with their work as scholars, teachers, and researchers. What was needed as much as believers on the faculty were Catholic intellectuals "inclined to think not only in [their] discipline but about their discipline, seeing it in relation to a larger world of ideas and faith." The university would never realize its hopes if there was not "a living Catholic intellectual community at its core."[31]

With the help of a handful of first-class Protestant scholars, vigorous conversation about this problem seemed to go on during the university's self-examination. A task force headed by John Van Engen, a distinguished medievalist and Lutheran, insisted that religious identity should not be a matter of checking a box on a questionnaire and that religious matters should not be brandished as a threat, as the policy of hiring Catholics might suggest. It was equally important that Notre Dame develop specific programs to *creatively and critically* develop the "various Catholic traditions of intellectual reflection." The university would have to be "a pluralistic environment safeguarded by academic freedom" where Catholic intellectuals could learn from those outside their tradition. If it did so, Notre Dame could help revitalize Catholic intellectual life, a task for which the university bore a special responsibility.[32] How to combine that specifically Catholic responsibility with its equally compelling responsibility as a research university remained an open and hotly debated subject.

PARADOX

The renewal of a sense of mission and clarification of Catholic identity is the goal that many schools are pursuing; conversation is increasingly the means. Notre Dame President Edward Malloy said in his report that what the university asked of all its scholars was not their "credal affiliation" but "a willingness to enter into conversation that gives [Notre Dame] its life and character." But not everyone has taken the full measure of what authentic conversation requires. In September 1992, St. John's University, a Benedictine school attached to a major monastery in central Minnesota, installed as its eleventh president Dietrich Reinhart, O.S.B. Not surprisingly, he used the occasion to begin what he hoped would be an extended conversation about St. John's identity as a Catholic university. But he startled his listeners by addressing bluntly some of the more treacherous elements that had entered the life of the church and threatened Catholic intellectual life.

Some at St. John's were super-orthodox. "There are Inquisitors in our midst," he said, "waiting for the tiniest slip of the tongue, longing to silence ideas which do not have a full and impeccable pedigree." In addition there were ideologues with a ready answer to all questions, scoffers convinced that nothing comes from conversations, and special interest groups around liturgy or social action who were fragmenting the community.

Reinhart insisted that, as president of the college, he would urge everyone to come to a sharper, more explicit awareness of the college's Catholic identity. To do so, he said, "we will have to engage in dialogue suspicious of all boundaries, a dialogue in which no one has hegemony as a specialist and none can be excused on the grounds that their special interest lies elsewhere. This is dangerous stuff. We will have to come to a sharper awareness of disagreement, let go of control, resolve no matter what to affirm persons, and bear with ideas which seem half-baked long enough to tease something worthwhile out of them. This will be a messy enterprise."

Capturing the ambivalence that is so much a part of the consciousness of serious American Catholics, Reinhart spoke of the Christian experience of paradoxes as "contradictions which tug against each other and, as they do, open up a reality more spacious than the sum of the parts." "A Catholic college must draw its life from this rich paradoxical soil," he said. With the church, Catholic scholars had to enter into human alienation, yet remain open to utter transformation. "At times we would all like a simple description of a Catholic college — one which would allow us to name names and establish some standards of measurement. There is something insidious in human nature, something which whittles paradox down to scale. Within a Catholic college there must be something which resists that drive."

It makes a great difference whether Christian communities hold to their self-definitions by stifling debate, for they are then likely to miss the signs of change and be overwhelmed. But if the community is confident enough to cherish debate and value the persons who disagree, then its members have the resources to bring their lives into dialogue with the new age and under the spirit's guidance break good ground within it. At times we would all like the Catholic college to put its feet down "and establish what ideas belong and what ones do not, to pickle and preserve what is most precious," Reinhart admitted. "But the dynamics of Christian history suggest that a Catholic college dare not enter into the business of pickling and preserving. A Catholic college ought to be confident enough about its way of embodying Christian tradition to cherish the vitality of debate about that tradition. . . . If a Catholic college is a place where the tug of contradictions can thus be sharply etched in public life, then its members become resilient, attentive to challenges and — most importantly — "able to respond to those challenges with creativity and vision." He prayed that his university would:

> have the wisdom to be faithful to the nature of Christian experience, to ground itself in the paradoxes of law versus prophecy, death versus life, order versus utter transformation, contradictions which tug at each other and, as they do, open up a reality more spacious than the sum of its parts. A Catholic college must be a place whose values and commitments are clear, but which resonates with a spaciousness greater than any formulations can provide. A Catholic college must also be courageous enough to embody Christian paradoxes in a particular time and place — to build a community which embodies the best understanding of the present, yet prizes personal integrity more than the herd and listens to all voices, especially the unexpected and dissonant. Out of these commitments, the Catholic college creates an atmosphere for studying the curriculum, assembling for worship and extending itself in service to others.[33]

Reinhart's is a messier option than Steubenville's, but, without the spirit it expresses, the Pope's soaring vision of integration and Notre Dame's concrete commitment to hiring Catholics will both end up in a sectarian box. Yet all are facing the need to debate the question, make some judgements, and take action. In the absence of deliberate and effective action by men and women committed to the mission of the American church and to a creative role for higher education within it, the lines will be drawn more sharply and the result will be that good institutions will no longer be Catholic, good people will be even more estranged from the church, and the church itself will be less intelligent and less effective than it must be. To make the church work in a free society has always been a challenge — once it was the challenge facing clergy, hierarchy, and religious; now it is a challenge facing the whole community. Ultimately, the future of the church and, with it, at least some part of the prospects for the human family depend on the ability of American Catholics, on campus and off, to accept that challenge.

CHAPTER 6

From Secularization
to Americanism

SECULARIZATION

My college roommate used to tell me of a favorite saying of his father: "Never want anything too much; you might get it!" Contemporary American Catholicism proves that wise man right. Catholics wanted to be American; now they are, but many think they paid too high a price. A Jewish historian says, semiseriously, that when Americans were hostile to Jews, they helped sustain Jewish identity; when they were friendly, they endangered Jewish communal existence. Catholics have become Americans and seem to have no obvious enemies, but now they wonder what makes them different. Catholic universities that offer quality education and pose no problems for non-Catholic students or staff prosper, but are told they have sold out their heritage.

Pope Paul VI put the problem directly to Jesuit university presidents in 1976. Some Catholic universities, in attempting to offer better answers to human questions, had obscured their distinctive Catholic characteristics, the Pope said. The result was "a gradual weakening and dilution of Christian values, putting in their place a humanism which might properly be called 'secularization.'" Catholic universities, like the postconciliar church, should be open to human problems and should engage in dialogue with all comers, but they should also maintain their character as Catholic universities. In teaching, in publications, in all forms of academic life, provisions should "be made for complete orthodoxy of teaching, for obedience to the magisterium of the church, for fidelity to the hierarchy and the Holy See." It was fine to invite laypeople and, in this case, non-Jesuits to participate in the work, but care should be taken to insure that "the Society retains the authority necessary for the discharge of its Catholic responsibilities."[1]

Well, the Society no longer has the capacity to insure orthodoxy, academic freedom endangers "obedience to the magisterium," and "fidelity to the hierarchy and the Holy See" has become for Catholics a matter of voluntary and measured choice. So, perhaps the dreaded secularization is complete. This is not a new argument, of course. Accreditation, introduction of professional schools or social science departments, loosening of requirements in scholastic philosophy, and hiring laypeople all seemed like secularization to some religious, whose vocations were so closely tied to the counterculturalism of the pre–Vatican II church. But academic reformers thought it important to adjust to the aspirations of the small but growing Catholic middle class, and more and more theologians and Catholic intellectuals agreed that it was a good thing to pursue academic excellence, as that term was generally understood in American academic circles. This practical, pastoral side won out after World War II, when many schools moved quickly to accommodate Catholic students funded by the GI Bill of Rights. And when, having achieved success, the schools were asked about "complete orthodoxy" and ecclesiastical control, they had to explain that success had its price, in the parish and on the campus. In some sense, perhaps, people, colleges and even the church itself became "secular" by becoming American, but everyone insisted that they remained Catholic as well.

But a steady voice of dissent, like Pope Paul's, persisted; and the Pope was not the only one who had doubts. A group of lay faculty at New York's St. John's University in 1967 denounced separate incorporation as "a blueprint for the complete secularization of Catholic higher education."[2] Self-confessed conservative Catholics vigorously criticized every move. They had long opposed accommodation to academic professionalism, and some never accepted the reforms initiated at Vatican II. Though small in numbers, this group gained disproportionate influence with the Vatican and demonstrated a surprising resilience. A larger number of self-described conservatives were sympathetic to renewal, but worried about the preservation of the tradition of Catholic thought, the church's historical memory. This group denounced modernist tendencies among liberals, but was no more comfortable with the enthusiasm of new forms of Catholic piety or with the mindless authoritarianism of the peculiar Catholic fundamentalism that rested faith on papal pronouncements.

Even more troubling for higher education leaders was criticism for alleged accommodation, even secularization, coming from scholars and moderates that one might have thought their natural allies. Jesuit theologians Avery Dulles, S.J. and Michael Buckley, S.J., former Notre Dame provost James Burtchaell, C.S.C., and *New York Times* religion editor Peter Steinfels and his *Newsweek* counterpart Kenneth J. Woodward joined a rising chorus of protest against the erosion of Catholic identity in Catholic colleges and universities.[3] It may be a matter of note that almost no women joined them, perhaps because Catholic women, for obvious reasons, are less apt to romanticize the Catholic past and more likely to affirm the changes of recent years.

THE "SLIPPERY PATH"

The central argument is that Catholic colleges and universities are in danger of repeating the history of once-Protestant schools that gradually threw off their church affiliation, moved religion out of a serious role in academic life, and ended up as secular institutions with no particular religious identity. Many became world-class research universities, but they no longer made any direct contribution to the intellectual life of the church, and, partly as a result, religion was no longer able to play a formative role in the intellectual life of the nation. Now Catholic schools are on the same "slippery path" that leads inexorably from "denominational to generic Christianity, then to vaguely defined religious values and finally to total secularization," to use the formulation of Avery Dulles.[4]

Historian Philip Gleason has been the most consistent exponent of this critical position. He knows that the process of academic modernization arose from trying to balance competing claims, to offer a distinctive Catholic viewpoint as defined by the countercultural church and at the same time meet the more worldly aspirations of the schools' lay constituencies. The former required resistance, manifested on the ideological level in commitment to neo-scholastic philosophy. The latter required accommodation to accrediting agencies and the admissions requirements of professional and graduate schools, the hiring of faculty based on their scholarly record and potential as judged by widely held academic standards, and the gradual marginalizing of scholastic philosophy, which long provided the central element of ideological self-understanding.

Eventually, as this process accelerated dramatically during and after Vatican II, Gleason thought it left many schools and many Catholics uncertain of the meaning of their Catholicism. "The main cultural tendency since Vatican II—in Catholic higher education and elsewhere in the Catholic world—has been toward embracing the world in a positive way, deprecating the peril of secularization, and treating dismissively the 'prophets of gloom and doom' who warned against it," Gleason argues. But he thinks the danger of "total absorption" by secular culture is real. After thirty years of discussion of the "identity crisis" in Catholic higher education, the expression is no longer in vogue, Gleason wrote in 1993, "but the assimilation of Catholic institutions to secular norms has, if anything, gathered momentum. In other words, the danger has not lessened, but increased."[5]

Gleason's historical analysis of secularization has been strongly reinforced by James Burtchaell, the brilliant Notre Dame theologian and former provost. Like Gleason, Burtchaell has worried about the loss of Catholic identity for many years. As a young scholar, Burtchaell was the spokesman for a national group of Catholic academics who insisted that the Land O' Lakes statement in no way diminished their commitment to integrated learning through theology. It did, however, express a determination that the Catholic university would no longer be an "enclave of orthodoxy," but would make the Catholic tradition available in the process of renewal and reform. It would avoid "sectarianism," which he called "that obsession which leads a group to define themselves by their stubbornly cultivated differences rather than by their convergence in Christ."[6]

In the early 1970s Burtchaell led a Notre Dame committee that defined maintenance of its Catholic identity as the university's top priority. Notre Dame, his report said, would not follow in the path of other Christian schools that had abandoned their religious roots as they sought academic excellence. A short time later, apparently worried about the direction that other schools were taking in response to the need for government financial assistance, Burtchaell persuaded a committee of the College and University Department of the National Catholic Educational Association to assign him to write a position paper on the subject of Catholic identity to provide guidance for the new lay boards of trustees. Here he once again insisted that Catholic schools were determined to remain Catholic, particularly by insuring the presence of a "faculty among whom seriously committed and intellectually accomplished Catholics predominate," a goal he believed could be combined with the effort to become excellent American universities, complete with academic freedom.[7]

Burtchaell was disappointed when the Board of the College and University Department decided not to adopt the statement, but simply allowed it to be circulated. It was printed in their publication only after a long delay.[8] Some years later, when the Curran case and the Vatican draft of the Apostolic Constitution stirred the waters again, Burtchaell wrote what proved to be his most influential statement in a pair of articles in the neoconservative journal *First Things*.[9] In the first article, he examined the secularization of Protestant higher education at the end of the last century, using Vanderbilt University as a case study. Here he found that the school's lay Methodist leaders gradually severed Vanderbilt's ties to the Methodist church, all the while insisting that Vanderbilt would remain a Christian school. But, as Vanderbilt ended its church affiliation, it also watered down the meaning of its Christian profession, making it a matter of private preference. Then, in the interwar years, militant secularists drove an already weakened Christianity from the campus.

With an eye obviously set on recent Catholic experience, Burtchaell hammered at the church-relatedness question. He found that Vanderbilt's "structural disengagement" from the church preceded, by at least a generation, the marginalization of religion; the university moved from Methodist to Christian to generically religious to flatly secular. Its president never understood that the breach with the church "began a process of alienation that inevitably would run its course in total secularization." So at Vanderbilt and elsewhere, "active Christians, not hostile secularists . . . were most effective in alienating the colleges and universities from their communities of faith." Or again: "Ambitious but improvident leaders had suppressed their school's Christian immune systems," leaving it powerless to resist "the virus of secularization."[10] Thus, secularization was the unintended consequence of actions taken to vindicate institutional autonomy, academic freedom, and supposed excellence in teaching and research, all familiar themes of recent Catholic experience in higher education.

In the second article, referring to mission statements and presidential pronouncements from Catholic schools, Burtchaell argued that Catholics had, in a very short time, repeated that process of separating their schools from any effective ecclesiastical influence; they had secularized themselves. "The Catholic colleges and universities were somehow the last great cohort to be drawn into the process," Burtchaell wrote, but "having once put their feet to the path, they are finding their way along it at unprecedented speed." As at Vanderbilt, the Catholic story featured a "nonchalant" if not ignorant church, universities bent on excellence, which they located in the best financed secular institutions, and leaders "whose ego . . . inclined [them] to neutralize all potential rivals." These strong presidents created boards that would follow their lead; indeed, by severing the school's ties to the religious order, the new arrangement left the presidents "effectively sovereign." They then tamed the faculty with money and the donors with a "rhetoric of reassurance." They cut their ties to the church, promising to maintain their Catholic identity, but then took no steps to do so. "The reformed institutions never had the principled nerve to make good on their claim that in asserting their independence they would nonetheless retain their character as Christian communities," Burtchaell charged.

Burtchaell's strong, at times bitter, language made his articles widely influential and useful to all those who believed that Catholic colleges and universities had sold out. Undoubtedly many believed they presented an accurate summary of the Protestant, and then the Catholic, experience in higher education. What was less noticed was how well they reflected the now widespread desire to recover a distinctive Catholicism. This became most clear in the pointed "lessons" Burtchaell drew from his analysis. The most challenging was his contention that "the only plausible way for a college or university to be significantly Christian is for it to function as a congregation in active communion within its church." As far as Burtchaell was concerned, if it was not a community that could worship together, it would inexorably become secular. Thus, in "every one of its component elements — governors, administrators, faculty and students — the academy must have a predominance of committed and articulate communicants of its mother church." For Burtchaell, the issue was one of church affiliation. And the crux of church-relatedness was not limiting academic freedom or even accepting the demand for canonical mandates for theologians, about which he said little, but the presence on the faculty of a predominant group of self-professed Roman Catholics, presumably interested not only in going to church but in carrying on the dialogue between theology and the other branches of knowledge.

CATHOLICISM AND THE INTELLECTUAL LIFE

Of course, there was much more to the secularization process than eliminating church-relatedness. Another important issue involved the transformation of Protestant and later Catholic intellectual life. Protestant intellectuals of the late nineteenth century allegedly had become liberals and modernists, subordinating the claims of faith to the demands of the new scientific method. Among Catholics, Monsignor Ellis's lament at the absence of Catholic intellectual achievement was an important moment in the revolution in Catholic higher education. By the late 1960s, evidence accumulated that, in terms of numbers graduating from college, attending graduate schools, and entering the learned professions, Catholics had attained at least parity with other Americans. Catholic names grew more prominent throughout American culture. When I was growing up in western Massachusetts, for example, it was an article of faith in my family, school, and parish that nearby Williams College was a hotbed of anti-Catholicism and left-wing radicalism. By the late 1980s, Catholics constituted the largest religious group at Williams, and the school had a Catholic president, as did the University of Rochester, another supposedly anti-Catholic school where I received my Ph.D.

But quantity was not quite what Ellis had in mind; he hoped that Catholic intellectual achievement would be really Catholic. If Catholics accomplished great things in intellectual life but did not read Catholic literature or were unfamiliar with Catholic thought or if they became as indistinguishable from secular scholars as Catholic universities supposedly were from their secular counterparts, then the problem was far from solved.

Burtchaell emphasized church-relatedness as being essential to preserving the Catholic character of the university, and some would make a similar argument about Catholic intellectual life: that it can be Catholic only to the extent it once again takes place within the framework of ecclesiastical authority. That argument is indeed made by the Fellowship of Catholic Scholars, a conservative organization of theologians and others disenchanted with mainstream Catholic learned societies. But there is another, more sophisticated argument against the secularization of Catholic higher education, more closely connected with Catholic intellectual life than Burtchaell's. And it is influential and challenging because it comes from theologians long considered moderates and supporters of post–Vatican II theological renewal.

No one argued this more forcefully than Jesuit theologian Michael Buckley.[11] He takes as self-evident Burtchaell's argument that Catholic colleges and universities are risking the loss of their Catholic identity, but he is more interested in Catholic intellectual life than arguments about church affiliation. And here he joins Burtchaell in finding the most dangerous enemies among the most prominent leaders of Catholic higher education. He gives the strong presidents more credit that does Burtchaell; Buckley knows that the isolated schools needed shaking up. What most disturbs him are, first, mission statements that minimize or ignore Catholic identity and, second, claims made by many leaders and implicit in many mission statements that the church is somehow "present" within the university, whose work is essentially secular, or that the church and the university relate to one another as two altogether distinct entities. "The understanding of the Church and the university has been framed as if they were two distinct, interacting institutions," Buckley writes. So, when asked how the church relates to the university, people respond that it does so by leading its own life of prayer and worship within the university and by "sharing in the life and work of the university itself." Buckley finds these answers "profoundly inadequate," for they treat religion and the intellectual life as if they were "fundamentally extrinsic to one another."

Instead, Buckley argues that the proper understanding of the Catholic university goes beyond the usual forms of theology, campus ministry, and presence of a religious order. Its "inherent promise" arises from the fact that both Catholicism and the inquiring intellect strain for ultimacy, each involving the other in an integral way. Catholicism's drive for ultimacy compels it to become intelligible and understandable, making sense in every culture. So it must engage human learning at the level of meaning and value. "The Catholic university is one form of the Church, one of the communities which are integral to the universal Church," Buckley writes. It is "that Catholic community in which the Church strives to relate all human culture to the gospel of salvation."

Similarly, the university has a universal, catholic impulse to find the deepest truth about the realities it studies, which forces it to confront religious questions, to intersect with the church's own quest. So, in a startling reversal of the usual arguments, the Catholic university becomes not John Cogley's contradiction, but a redundancy.

Buckley well understands that the segmentation of knowledge, with the dominance of departments and disciplines, all aping the sciences, is at the heart of the secularization of academic life. Theology, when it presents itself as one discipline among the others, indeed making its own modern ideas about science and scientific method, presumably has already given the game away. Just as Catholicity lies at the heart of the university, so theology's questions lie at the heart of each discipline, embedded in its search, at the edge of its explanations. So, too, the reverse—that Catholic faith in Jesus as God incarnate and the Spirit's presence in every expression of the human—means that the search for truth to be expressed in word and culture is of the very essence of the Catholic. So the Catholic university requires theologians who are alert to the movements of the disciplines as well as theologically informed scholars in all departments and faculties. Buckley presents this as a call for an integrated ideal for Catholic higher education; it is even more clearly a soaring vision and prescription for Catholic intellectual life.

THE HISTORICAL ARGUMENT

However, even those who share Michael Buckley's hope for Catholic intellectual and academic life, should take pause, especially when locating it next to the arguments of Gleason and Burtchaell. For one thing, Buckley's ideal—compelling and persuasive when thinking about Catholic intellectual life—cannot easily be translated into policy for a college or university as a whole. It is one thing to say that such persons should play a crucial role in all departments and schools, another to say that that deep integration should inspire institutional self-definition. In practice, it would be hard to disengage from simple control of the university by qualified Catholics and subordination of academic to confessional considerations in academic policy.

Yet the temptation to make that move is reinforced by the fact that Buckley and the other commentators noted above share Burtchaell's view that American Catholic higher education is caught in an almost suicidal repetition of the "secularizing history" of other American universities that were once affiliated with churches. Their reading of recent experience is decidedly negative, conveying, in Buckley's words, a "sense that the *decline* in some Catholic institutions may be already advanced, that the conjunction of a vibrant Catholicism and these universities seems increasingly faint, that vision is *fading*" (emphasis added).

No one familiar with Catholic higher education can deny a measure of truth to these now stock arguments. But secularization was a more complicated matter than appears at first glance. Sister Alice Gallin, the historian who led the U.S. Catholic colleges through their tortuous negotiations with Rome, has also examined the secularization argument. She begins with suspicion, for she thinks it self-serving. "The secularity of American culture is sometimes a scapegoat for the lack of coherence in disciplines like philosophy and theology," she writes. "The real culprit may be a loss of nerve on the part of administrators and faculty who lack confidence in their ability to present clear and compelling arguments for their own faith and values."

As an historian, Gallin offers cautious criticism of Burtchaell's comparisons. There are similarities, to be sure, between the two experiences, that of Protestant church-related schools at the end of the nineteenth century and Catholic schools since Vatican II. The founding purposes of both groups included the moral development of youth, preparation of leaders for the church, and commitment to classical liberal arts education. Both groups were closely linked to their churches and therefore changed as the churches changed. The leaders who made the changes in church-relatedness were men and women strongly committed to their churches: they did not intend to undercut its mission or to minimize the importance of religious traditions. Each group was influenced by prevailing church-state arrangements, but in different ways. Protestantism was long identified with the larger civil society and culture; Catholicism and Catholic schools were clearly alternatives to it. And both groups, throughout their history, faced "a continuing struggle between an affirmation of pluralism as a social value and a commitment on the part of the college or university to a single faith community." How to be open to the values of others without losing institutional identity was not an entirely new question for the Protestant schools of the 1890s or the Catholic schools of the 1960s.

But there were many substantial differences. They moved away from their churches at different moments. The secularization of Protestant schools was part of the larger disestablishment of religion. It coincided with, and was in part spurred by, an epistemological revolution that produced a new faith in scientific method as the only path to truth, rendering the denominational college an anachronism. In the late nineteenth century it was the scientific method that defined the university; in the 1960s it was academic freedom and institutional autonomy, and these shaped the changing contours of the Catholic church-university relationship. In addition, with science dominant on campus, the Protestant schools of the turn of the century sent theology off the campus and into the seminary, leaving the church with Sunday schools and sermons as its sole educational media for the laity. Catholics, at the very moment they were creating independent boards and diversifying their faculties, were expanding and strengthening their theology and religious studies programs, insisting that they meet standard academic criteria, and struggling to keep theology a vital element of the undergraduate curriculum.

The two clusters of institutions also related to their churches in very different ways. For the Protestant schools, the relationship was direct: synods, dioceses, even parishes contributed to their support; ministers and lay leaders controlled their boards. Catholic schools, in most cases, were the apostolic work, and thus the responsibility, of religious orders, who were in charge of religion on campus. When their role changed, the hierarchy and papacy felt called to insure that the schools remained accountable. If this posed problems of governance and finances, it also kept the question of mission and identity alive. In other words, for awhile at least, the break was far less clean.[12]

Gallin suggests the church-university question is more complex than Burtchaell allows, while historian Henry C. Johnson, Jr., raises questions about the secularization of Christian intellectual life. After studying the turn of the century experience of the University of Illinois, Johnson offers an historical assessment that at first glance confirms Burtchaell's case.[13] In 1905 the new president of Illinois summoned a conference of religious and educational leaders to confront the continuing erosion of what had been the "real and pervasive" presence of Christianity in American higher education. After extended discussion, the conferees agreed that it would be best for the church to end its struggle for power within the university and to withdraw to the edge of campus life, perhaps to a cordon of denominational houses erected around the campus. There Christianity could attempt to influence the personal commitments of university personnel and offer its own religious interpretation of the truths uncovered through scientific investigation.

This move resulted in part from changes in the university, changes that everyone, religious and nonreligious, endorsed. With the dominance of science, the basis of the new university, reality came to be understood as constructed rather than given, so creation is self-intepreting, society self-determining, and human beings self-defining. Secularism eventually turned that process into an interpretive principle and a sociopolitical agenda, but almost everyone involved in the process itself claimed to be religious. Indeed, the new university would never have succeeded in a still very pious society if there had not also been significant changes in how religious people understood the sacred. One change was the increasing tendency to separate the intellect from religious commitment, so that the latter lost theological coherence and was described almost entirely in spiritual and increasingly psychological terms. Another was that the Christian academic vocation came to be defined (and is still largely defined) in terms of persons and their individual situations. The church's mission was to assist individuals in coping with the demands of the changing intellectual world without losing their faith, "rather than bringing theological knowledge claims to the process of interpretation, judgement and critical application." There was now a great deal of emphasis on the moral life, but even that was "circumscribed within the boundaries of personal experience." Christians no longer claimed either a vocation or the competence to subject the totality of human experience, social as well as individual, to radical criticism.

The elaborate justification of this changed posture erected by the churches was symptomatic of the alienation of religion from learning; it was also an open admission of failure to achieve religious consensus in the body politic. The dream of a unifying Christianity embracing the many sects faded amid America's ever increasing diversity. Pluralism was here to stay, and if everyone was to have access to the culture and to the state university, a compelling but religiously neutral language was required. Christianity continued to make powerful claims, but now their "consummation would be personal and emotional rather than corporate and intellectual." Thus, "the religion that was moved to the periphery in 1905 had already been largely redefined as a personal concern. And so, severing the cord was in reality neither shocking nor painful."

There was another change that has echoes among contemporary Catholics. The older, classical position was that learning itself was a form of piety: "seeing revelation as the foundation of meaning in the process of inquiry—a belief that such notably generous and diverse scholars as Erasmus, More and Colet would have shared." But in the United States, as the industrializing, urbanizing post-Civil War society seemed increasingly antagonistic to orthodox piety, many "classical Protestants" who had retained a conviction about the connection of religion and learning became "modern evangelical Protestants." To think as a Christian now meant to think about religion as opposed to other topics; to act as a Christian was to perform religious acts, in particular to make and renew the act of faith—conversion. This definition of religion almost exclusively in terms of personal piety created an enormous problem for the institutionalization of Christian learning in seminaries or colleges. If learning was to be genuinely religious in an evangelical sense, schools could not merely be places where Christians thought about the world in a distinctive way. Instead, to be religious, any institution had to be "consciously focused on, and practically organized around, the central Christian activity of making, examining and renewing the act of faith." This left only two choices. One was sectarian—to form self-consciously Christian schools, an option that, in different ways, both Burtchaell and Steubenville's Father Scanlan adopt. The other is the option chosen by the Illinois savants—to redefine religion as a personal and private, not an institutional and public, matter. Theology gave way to campus ministry.

What Johnson emphasizes is that this was not simply a matter of moral or intellectual weakness on the part of Christian pastors and professors. Large issues were at stake. With the simultaneous appearance of a modern scientific worldview and the post-Civil War fracturing of social, cultural, and religious unity, religion, to retain a degree of legitimacy, gradually allowed itself to be privatized and psychologized and hence became only indirectly relevant to the intellectual life of the culture. Evangelicals and religious liberals agreed on the absolute centrality of the act of believing and (whatever its content) its essential divorce from the analytical work of the intellect. Evangelical fervor and liberal coolness came "to the same thing: the primacy of faith as an act distinct from inquiry, evidence and argument." Because the latter lay at the heart of the university, religion had nothing in common with it. The only real alternative was "amiable divorce so that what was now an essentially private (that is to say secularized) religion could be created and cherished without either interfering with the university or eroding the purity of [religious] commitment." Thus, too, the "virtually universal assumption . . . that if religion is given any place in education and schooling, its inevitable agenda is conversion of the students, not their intellectual development." The subsequent dilemma was the cultural assumption that to be religious hampers learning and to be learned entails at least religious neutrality, if not abandonment.

Johnson describes the loss of a Protestant, nonevangelical role in the higher learning with less of an ax to grind, as well as with more compassion, than Burtchaell. His analysis would leave one skeptical about Burtchaell's prescription of the Catholic university as a worshiping congregation. It suggests sympathy with Buckley's classical Catholic approach of theology integrated into all studies, but leaves the feeling that such a vision is hopelessly utopian if intended to define the Catholic university as a whole. This will persist, unless scholars emerge, in theology and in other disciplines, who integrate the religious and scholarly impulses that our culture and, in its own way, our church has so sharply separated. Confessional mission statements and increased budgets for academic theology won't do it.

THE COMMON PROBLEM

Yet perhaps Buckley's vision of Catholic intellectual life arising from within academic culture provides the basis for a vision of Catholic higher education richer than any presently available and, with modifications, one appropriate to the Catholic university's responsibilities, not only within the church but also within the academic community and the general public. The problems of mission and identity, of intellectual and curricular coherence, after all, are not just Catholic problems. Nor are they problems caused by the Catholic pursuit of false gods, secularization, to be solved simply by an act of will: recommitment to the authentically Catholic. As University of Michigan historian James Turner insists, Newman's ideal of a university where philosophy related the disciplines to one another and to a common core of knowledge was once everyone's ideal and its loss is everyone's problem — indeed, it is *the* problem of contemporary academic life.

Surely, if it is not to be simply a tactic of Catholic subcultural restorationism, reformulation of Catholic mission and identity needs a larger context, one that makes the university debate a subsection of larger questions of Catholic intellectual life. Turner has attempted to do that.[14] He argues that there are really two problems, which share the same genealogy. One is the fragmentation of knowledge, that makes it difficult for molecular biologists to speak to political scientists and for either to speak intelligibly to an educated public. The second problem is epistemological: the uncertainty about whether there can be any secure ground for knowledge, which has led to the subjectivism that characterizes much recent theory in humanities and social sciences. Turner is delighted that Catholic scholars and schools are trying to take on these crucial questions.

As Turner sees it, Cardinal Newman made the case for a Catholic university in circumstances quite different from ours, but he made two claims Turner thinks fundamental: that the university is not the church and that philosophy (not theology) is the keystone of university education. The first assertion, as we have seen, limits and disciplines the institutional church's authority over university life. It also calls into question proposals for insuring a majority of Catholic faculty or insisting that only a community that can worship together deserves consideration as Catholic. The second proposition, which recalls the earlier emphasis on scholastic philosophy, grounds the intellectual underpinning of the question of mission securely within the setting of contemporary culture rather than within the church alone. For if Catholic theology requires reference to the believing community, philosophy searches for common ground. If theology is the key to Catholic distinctiveness, philosophy is the link to the common culture we share with others.

According to Turner, Newman "thought [philosophy] would unify the curriculum, integrate all the subjects of study, provide (as it were) a map of knowledge." At the time, this was an unremarkable claim because the unity of knowledge was still an axiom among English-speaking intellectuals. Because all knowledge referred either to the creator or to creation, philosophy could, at least in principle, demonstrate how "the various specific bodies of knowledge related to each other and to the larger whole." The unity of all knowledge was a pillar of culture, but disbelief in God washed away the axiom that formed this unity and unleashed a flood of doubt that wiped out secure connections between disciplines and between faith and reason. It took almost a century for "Victorian epistemological certitude" to collapse, although Newman saw it coming.

Unlike the other critics of this shift, Turner thinks the change was not all bad, because an excess of certainty can be and was a barrier to the spread of knowledge. But believers and nonbelievers alike should recognize that "the Victorian crisis of faith turned out to be equally a crisis of knowledge." We are now living in its splintered postmodernist aftermath. Knowledge lies "scattered around us, in great, unconnected pieces, like lonely mesas jutting up in a trackless waste. That this fragmentation has impoverished public discourse is a more or less common lament; that it has emaciated education, both undergraduate and graduate, is too painfully obvious a truth to dwell on. So as we try . . . to navigate through waves of uncertainty from one disciplinary island to another, all universities, not just Catholic ones, face the challenges and dilemmas of remapping the world of learning."

Thus the problems of Catholic higher education are part of the larger problems of contemporary culture. And Turner is sympathetic with those who seek to make Catholicism itself an actor in this cultural work. Like many outsiders, he thinks Vatican II swept away the Catholic sense of a cultural heritage that reformers are now trying to recover. Like Alasdaire MacIntyre, he believes that tradition matters if we are to resolve "our common problem of the fragmentation of knowledge. For only within an ongoing framework of shared questions and axioms can we find common ground for coherent disagreement, much less mutual agreement." So renewal of Catholic intellectual life is important but it is only one step in a larger and more important enterprise. "If we are ever to reestablish communication among the scattered realms of scholarship, ever to find common ground of discourse, ever, in short, to build anew the lost unity of knowledge, we will do so only by constructing a new intellectual tradition that we can all share." Right now, that idea is "literally utopian."

The Catholic university is a natural home for this utopian quest because its sponsors retain convictions in which the unity of knowledge can comfortably rest, particularly the dual faith in God and in reason as the God-given tool for understanding nature. Why have these schools been so inept in their task so far? Not because of mindless adaptation to culture, but because they stumble blindly like everyone else into the problems posed to all by the unraveling of the seamless web of knowledge.

So Turner takes the secularization argument seriously, but removes it from its Catholic mooring to show that it signals a larger, common problem of the type that Vatican II called upon Catholics to address. Some, like the Protestants earlier, may have put their beliefs in a drawer that will be empty when they return looking for them. To the extent that Catholic scholars have done this, they have cut themselves off from any real hope of influencing the larger world of knowledge. Turner finds something quaint in the embrace of secular knowledge at the very moment "when secular knowledge has collapsed in an undignified heap of squirming confusion. One smells a question badly asked. In fact it is yesterday's question." Today's question is: "How can the Catholic university reconstruct itself to bring the resources of Catholic tradition to bear on our common task of rebuilding the house of learning."

He urges Catholics to remember, as did Newman, that the university is not the church; instead Catholic resources are enlisted in "a human enterprise which is by no means exclusively Catholic or Christian or even religious." But it is also true that Catholic higher education cannot fulfill its part in this enterprise without nurturing its own distinctively Christian and particularly Catholic intellectual traditions. Turner does not hesitate to suggest how such a mission might be put into operation. He thinks that at least half the faculty should be Catholic, although not necessarily in terms of their personal piety. What is needed is "reflexive familiarity with the intellectual habits and resources of Catholicism, so as to provide a distinctively Catholic matrix for debate and teaching within the university. To put it bluntly, it matters more that Catholic faculty members be culturally Catholic than sincere Christians."

In addition, a critical mass of the faculty should be Christians, while "secular-minded" professors are also required. "To be blunt, without ongoing synergy between Christians and nonbelievers, the experiment of a Catholic university will fail." So "Catholic and other Christian scholars will have to grope their way into a largely untried conversation. They must learn to talk as Christian intellectuals with colleagues skeptical of Christianity. They must persuade secular scholars that knowledge forged within the Catholic tradition illumines problems of universal import. . . . To pull it off, they must not only rediscover and reapply the intellectual resources of Christianity in unimagined ways, but they must do so with constant thought of speaking to the universal university, not just the Catholic university. Sallying forth to conferences four times a year will not suffice. Dailyness is the key. So a Catholic university will make itself internally pluralistic not by accident but by design; for only thus can it become effectively Catholic."

Turner's vision is not simply of theology in dialogue with the other disciplines, but of Christian faculty developing "broad and complicated ways of seeing reality in many fields." The curriculum might well include required courses in theology and biblical studies, but there must also be continuing efforts to relate the full range of studies to the Catholic tradition. Not that there is a "Catholic literature" or a "Catholic chemistry," but the faculty "need to explore how to locate modern knowledge within the broad and humane perspective of the Christian intellectual tradition and, still more broadly, within the perspective of theistic transcendence." In other words, the university and its professors are to live fully in the modern academic world and make themselves distinctive "not by their methods but by their questions." Perhaps, he adds, "the resurrection of Catholic ways of knowing" might "help even those of us who have no truck personally with Christianity bring the isolated islands of human knowledge back into fruitful communication." Everyone in higher education should worry about "the incoherence of undergraduate education" and "the incoherence of graduate education from which the former flows." Accordingly, he encourages outsiders to welcome and pay close attention to efforts to tie individual subjects into broader patterns of meaning and to encourage students to think coherently about the interlinkages and mutual resonances in their diverse studies. He offers this as a description of Catholic higher education; he means it, as he should, as a prescription.

AMERICANISM REBORN

Turner offers another angle on the "slippery path" to "total secularization" argument that is now almost consensual among commentators on Catholic higher education. That position represents a repudiation of the Americanist heritage of liberal Catholicism. One of the main themes of American Catholic history has been the steady march of Americanization, once regarded positively, now denounced as secularization. The ideology of Americanization, of course, was Americanism, the judgement that God was at work outside the church, at work most visibly through the American nation, so that reaching common citizenship with other Americans was a worthy goal. But before long Americanization threatened to destroy Catholic unity and orthodoxy, so Americanism became an intellectual enemy. And the Catholic university, now in its very success the exemplar of Americanization, giving it a vested interest in Americanist ideas, seems both an agent of eroding Catholic identity morale and a potential center for the recovery of the essentially Catholic.

Yet a minority voice, uneasy with such arguments and alert to the shared responsibility tone of Turner, is still heard. Moralists like Charles Curran, Thomas Shannon, and Richard McCormick, S.J., theologian David Tracy, sociologist John Coleman, S.J., the bishops' advisor J. Bryan Hehir, and a number of women scholars, most notably Rosemary Ruether and Mary Jo Weaver, all continue to defend a liberal, mediating view of Catholic responsibility. But no one expresses opposition to the retreat from Americanism more clearly and spells outs its implications for Catholic intellectual life and for Catholic higher education more constructively than William Shea, chair of the Department of Theological Studies at St. Louis University.

Shea believes there is a deep division among Catholic theologians. On one side are those who believe that only Catholic sources provide proper texts for theological consideration; materials from outside the church, including those from non-Christian religions, are useful in helping Catholics to better understand and express their tradition, but they are not "of God." At Vatican II this school hoped to recover the great Catholic tradition as it existed before the divisions with the Orthodox east and later with the churches of the Reformation. Theologians of this school are oriented, in David Tracy's terms, to "manifestation," articulating the distinct vision of God, the world, and the human person opened up by revelation, convinced that it corresponds to the deepest human needs.[15]

There are many places to find this kind of concern, so crucial to the identity of Catholic higher education. Robert Imbelli, a New York priest who heads the Pastoral Institute at Boston College, cites favorably English sociologist William McSweeney's argument that postconciliar change led Catholics to chaos and religious promiscuity, leaving many unsure of what it meant to be Catholic. In Imbelli's words, the Council "deprived Catholics of the language with which they had habitually ordered their religious universe and through which they had articulated their own self-understanding. It is no wonder that its loss created a widespread sense of anomie, a loss of personal and corporate religious identity." So the postconciliar quest was for a new language, a language Imbelli thinks will emerge from a deepening sense of sacramentality. In outlining the characteristics of a new language, Imbelli concluded that the answer to the question of Catholic identity was universality: the Roman Catholic tradition is the bearer of "a comprehensive language which combats our subtle tendencies to partiality, to the erection of our immediate and often distorted experiences into the measure of the whole."[16]

For Shea such pleas recall the fight about modernism a century ago, which drew a firm borderline between "those who know truth and try to live by it and those who do neither."[17] It explains the passion of Catholic philosopher J.M. Cameron, for example, when he calls Catholics to mount a prophetic attack on the "dominant culture of western society, filled with hatred of life and of human virtue, lost in a maze of ephemeral intellectual fashions."

The other school believes that there is much to be learned from sources outside the tradition. The church can learn from as well as teach the modern world; its dialogue with culture is a two-way conversation. By attending to such outside sources, Hans Küng, to take one example, has been a burr in the skin of Vatican officials, because he persists in reading what Catholic officials regard as alien texts and speaking in what they hear as an alien tongue. Shea believes that the battle in many ways is still about the Enlightenment and the willingness to subject all traditions, including one's own, to tests of experience and reason. David Tracy refers to this approach as "correlational," confronting the contemporary cultural situation as a critical and self-conscious necessity.

The latter approach receives additional support because so many non-

Catholics and laypeople have joined theology departments in recent years. They may be theologians (as opposed to scholars in religious studies) and they may care deeply about their faith and the church, but they are likely to draw on wider sources and to have less invested in the specifically Catholic intellectual tradition than their more ecclesiastically focused colleagues. "One of the many reasons why there are so many variations in theology today," John Haughey, S.J. reports, is because "lay theologians are using many texts, both figuratively and literally, to understand the faith that are not faith texts or part of the scriptural or doctrinal canon."[18]

Of course, the conflict between these two positions is not complete; the highly Catholic group needs to understand the culture if they are to present the Catholic message effectively, and the correlationists have to have a grasp of the tradition if they are to engage the culture in dialogue. But the tendency in recent years has been polarization. Drawing lines on such matters, as in the Curran case, has become common, divisions have become increasingly institutionalized in separate organizations, and the ecclesial community has been badly damaged by the conflict.

Shea gives this division an Americanist twist. His own work centers on the American naturalist philosophers, and he admits to learning from them. He learned to speak of democracy as not just a set of political arrangements, but as a quality of human relationships that should pervade all aspects of life, including religion. Democracy is based on freedom of inquiry and communication; these are not only means to an end, but constitute the very essence of democracy: "the consequent conversation and argument are democratic experience." Theology proceeds from faith and reflects on its meaning, but we learn from the Enlightenment that, in the modern context, belief is always accompanied by doubt, by questions about its truth that are there from the start. Indeed, dogmatism makes genuine faith and belief impossible. So theology mediates a two-way conversation between Christians and others. Moreover, Shea learned from democratic sources that "loyalty to the human community is an ideal that transcends loyalty to tribe, nation, class and to church. The human community is the fact, not the abstraction; individual self interest and tribalism, including Catholic tribalism, are the abstractions."

Much of this became for Shea matters of conviction, held with religious intensity. For holding such conviction, Shea believes he has been regularly "indicted for selling out." And, he admits, he still has big questions about his own position. Are liberals simply romantic Catholics whose intellectual vision and beliefs are essentially secular? Do they import alien standards of American political culture into the church? Are they a new class, whose interests lead them to espouse liberal causes and seek power in the church?

After three decades of such arguments and the need to defend himself, Shea came to believe that the problem was that he simply could not accept the view of theology, the single source view, that underpinned such questions. But he still could not fully answer the question haunting the Catholic university: how can he think of himself as a Catholic theologian and at the same time consider himself responsible to a secular tradition, whether the tradition of the Enlightenment or that of American democracy?[19]

Father Imbelli worried that Shea did not, or could not, answer his own questions.[20] It was one thing to suggest that theology becomes more catholic by embracing non-Catholic texts, Imbelli argued, another to suggest that in expanding the theological universe the Gospel is somehow transcended. Shea could speak of dual loyalties, but Imbelli denied that they were of equal value. "For among the loyalties of the Christian," he asked, "is there not a paramount, indeed identity-defining loyalty: to Christ and his gospel as proclaimed by and in the church?" So, he concluded, one can't be a Catholic theologian without being profoundly ecclesial. One could not put more clearly the problem of the Catholic university united around theology, with its ecclesial responsibilities, as opposed to a Catholic university also self-consciously and deliberately American.

Searching for an alternative to confessionalism or mere sponsorship is not easy. As Turner indicated, secular scholars are not enamored of religious types, while fellow Catholics call into question the loyalty of dualists like Shea. Imbelli went so far as to find, at the root of positions like Shea's, "Christological doubt." In the face of the Christ question, some stand mute and some confess other ultimate loyalties, thus eroding the one foundation for all baptized Christians on which all professional theologians stand securely. Shea, he suggested, like many feminist and ecumenical theologians and much of the "academic guild," was "decentering Christ."

Shea of course denied that he was on a slippery slope to doctrinal bankruptcy and repeated his argument: he held some convictions with religious intensity that did not arise from Catholic sources, some of which do not yet have ecclesial sanction. His points about democracy "have been steadily repudiated by our infallible magisterium for two centuries; they are now suffered by our leaders to exist in nonecclesiastical reality and are denied again whenever they appear inside the gate." Imbelli did not tell him whether he could believe these things "as a revelation of God's meaning for human beings" and at the same time regard himself as a Catholic theologian. If he can, then there are two sources of theology; those sources, and not Christological heresy, will create a new age for the church if there is to be one.

He then posed other questions, which could be addressed to Buckley and

Burtchaell as well as Imbelli. They go to the heart of the issue of the Catholic intellectual and the Catholic university. What, after all, are we to think of the others, the outsiders, including the others on our campus? Could one have an eastern guru as a spiritual director? Should Catholics seek the conversion of the Jews? More generally, "what does it mean theologically and religiously when theologians start to take the stranger seriously as a stranger" and stop trying to convert that person or appropriate his or her meaning and start to learn from him or her? Or, more poetically, what does it mean when, "rather than looting the Egyptians for the sake of the house of Israel, we begin to see God's grace for us in Egypt?"[21]

Shea's reflections on theology clarify the struggle surrounding the question of Catholic university identity. If we follow Burtchaell and Buckley and Imbelli, Catholic theology makes the university Catholic, the Catholic public takes precedence over all others, and non-Catholics, welcomed and valued as colleagues, are nevertheless outsiders in a community that can never be their own. If we follow Shea, then it is the ambivalence — the very effort to be both Catholic and American, to take the secularity and pluralism of our world into ourselves — that constitutes the Catholic university and serves the church, the academy, and the human family. In the one case the presence of so many non-Catholics and the intrusive demands of outside agencies are threats to Catholic integrity. In the other they provide new opportunities to understand faith and its demands, within the world and the human family, who are equally "of God."

Shea's discussion of pluralism is even more helpful. For many years Shea taught religion at a state university, the University of South Florida. There he daily encountered America's wide religious diversity in his classroom. He rightly centers in on the heart of the problem that pluralism poses for all churches and lately for the Catholic church most of all. When students who are mostly Christians realize that a fellow student is not Christian, they ordinarily revise their inherited conviction that the other religion is inferior. Equally important, by taking the other person's religious beliefs seriously, they come to see their own for what it is — belief — whereas previously they had thought it was religious knowledge. "I do not think this shatters their faith or causes them to stop believing," Shea writes. "But one is easily able to grasp one of the reasons why denominations have their own educational institutions and prefer to isolate their people, young and old, from direct conversation with people of different convictions; contact does permit conversation, and conversation is the great leveller."[22]

He found that years of teaching in church-related institutions had blocked his ability to understand the religious language and concerns of others. In those Catholic schools he had been considered a liberal, but he had never been liberal enough to allow, even for conversational purposes, the possible truth or value of the religious life and language of a shaman, such as the one who appeared in his class at South Florida. At first Shea used academic language to challenge this student; when he asked a Catholic theologian about it, he answered that the student provided Shea with an opportunity to evangelize. But he listened to the student and learned some things. His reaction and that of others whom he discussed the matter with led him to a conviction, an American conviction, shaped by pluralism and democracy, a conclusion very different from those of the Catholic restorationists: "I am now convinced that Catholics should not teach theology out of earshot of Protestants and that Christians should not chatter on theologically out of earshot of people of differing convictions." Pluralism, as William James had taught him, was a blessing, not a curse.

BOUNDARIES

The problem of the Catholic university, and of Catholic identity generally, is a matter of boundaries, then, their penetration and restoration. Perhaps the most important boundary is that between religion and culture. *Ex Corde Ecclesiae* claims that the Catholic university is a privileged place for dialogue between religion and culture. Many commentators believe that this means there must be the retrieval and interpretation of the Catholic tradition and then creative efforts to speak about that tradition in and to contemporary culture. But, as Shea points out, that culture is shaped by the Enlightenment, and so are we. In fact, both Catholicism and the Enlightenment are part of our heritage. Historical and literary methods in biblical studies, democratic politics and liberal political values, religious freedom and freedom of inquiry and communication, and the self-determination of nations — all were part of the Enlightenment movement, all were once opposed by the Catholic church, and all are now acknowledged as being among our own values. It is important to deplore the crimes arising from the Enlightenment heritage, as it is to deplore the crimes of the church. But it is a mistake to speak of the Enlightenment as if it were another country from our own or as if there is a culture, out there, beyond the borderline with the church. "If we are to draw on our Catholic heritage to evaluate the culture, are we not also to draw on the authentic values of the Enlightenment to evaluate the church? In addition to the Catholic rush to evaluate modernity by Catholic norms, there are pertinent and legitimate norms derived from modern experience to evaluate the church, without disguising them as 'gospel norms.'" Also, as Shea might have added, both the

Enlightenment and Catholic Christianity are in here as well as out there. We experience America (the secular world) differently because we are Catholics, and we know ourselves as Catholics differently because we are Americans. Each shapes and reshapes the other, in our own consciousness as well as in the many worlds around us.

So, Shea sees Catholic higher education somewhat differently from Burtchaell and Buckley. It is not only a place to recover and cherish the Catholic tradition, but also a place to recover the Enlightenment as part of the Catholic heritage as well. I would put it only a bit differently: to recover and cherish the Catholic cultural tradition, through which we have encountered and appropriated Catholicism, and to recover and cherish American culture, through which we have encountered and appropriated what Shea calls the Enlightenment.

In the usual formulation, Catholic higher education assesses culture outside the church for the sake of the church, or it mediates the Catholic tradition to the culture. But, as Shea sees it, the dialogue is not between outside and inside, but within and about ourselves and our dual rootage. His intellectual tradition includes modern Western culture, forged without and sometimes in opposition to the church. "In this sense, neither I nor Catholic higher education belongs solely to the church; it is as well an educational institution of the human community with responsibility for the traditions of that community." Once again, three publics, not one.[23]

Rather than lament its new diversity and openness to society, Catholicism should acknowledge these as outcomes of an altogether Christian and Catholic impulse. "Catholic higher education is dealing with American culture as it in fact is in all its plurality, and it has chosen to take that plurality into itself in terms of students and faculty," Shea writes. That is the real meaning of secularization or the more benign Americanization. "Although that poses a difficulty to the definition of its Catholic nature, it also affords us a unique experiment in understanding the public responsibility of academic institutions and the flexibility of Catholic identity." Instead of stressing the need to hire Catholics or to submit reports to bishops, Shea, using a distinction drawn by his colleague Jacob Neusner, urges Catholic colleges and universities to play the role of a holy community and "seek out, care for, and engage the intellectual and religious stranger as a religious value, with an additional end in view, that hospitality and its conversation bring a revolution in our own self-conception, founded on our taking the alien as a God-carrier in his or her alienness." Otherwise, the Catholic college or university risks becoming again a sacred society, defining the stranger as being outside its borders, a fit object for conversion or rejection.

Neusner says that the issue is no longer the survival of religion, that battle with the Enlightenment has been won. Now the big battle is over religious acceptance of the other. Before, religions have always formed their own cultures, with borders; Christian failures include invincible ignorance and anonymous Christianity. Shea concludes by turning the secularization and Catholic restoration arguments upside down: "I believe that the most important issue confronting Catholic higher education as Catholic is not its own abstract identity, but understanding the identity of everyone else and the relation of that identity to being Catholic. In fact, being Catholic in any significant and memorable sense may well depend on the Catholicity of our understanding of others. We Catholic intellectuals must answer the question 'who are these strangers?' and do so not merely receiving them in charity but in receiving them as God-carriers, and we must think through their place in our own theological world."[24]

CONCLUSION

Let me put the issue sharply. Separate incorporation, professionalization, and internal diversity all make it difficult to articulate a compelling Catholic position for the Catholic university as a whole. Raymond Schroth, S.J. was once driven from a school for his attempt to hire faculty committed to the dialogue of faith and culture. Later he remarked that declarations of Catholic mission "are not hard to make but very hard to live by."[25] To the extent that one disdains the loss of control (and the bland mission statements) that come with the increased numbers of non-Catholic faculty and staff and the demands that explicit Catholic ideals be placed by fiat at the center and in possession of the institution, then the problem of Catholic identity leads to a solution that can only sound sectarian and restorationist, whatever the intention. This in turn suggests that the integrating educational ideal so well spelled out by Buckley and by John Paul II needs to be detached from its ecclesiastical interests and subcultural preoccupations.

Most schools, as we have seen, articulate their Catholicity in terms of the leadership role of religious orders, the presence of strong theology departments (usually containing an emphasis on self-consciously Catholic theology) the presence of campus ministry and a strong pastoral and liturgical life, opportunities for spiritual growth and Christian service, and many specific programs and projects serving the local and national church. These features of the schools manifest a continuing commitment to remain Catholic in some sense. It is clear that these elements do not meet the responsibilities of Catholic colleges and universities. Pope John Paul II looks to the Catholic universities to promote the dialogue between Christian faith and human culture. Bishop James Malone, a leader in dialogue between bishops and academics, expects Catholic colleges and universities to serve the church by assisting Catholics to understand their new roles of leadership in American society and by participating in the public life of the Catholic community.

These appeals stumble over many of the same problems that beset the church generally. One exasperated lay academic, faced with yet another charge by a bishop that Catholic educators were not "turning out loyal and committed Catholics," snapped "neither are you!" Appeals to form Catholic lay leaders and to offer Catholic perspectives on contemporary culture ignore the yawning chasm between campus ministry and the research and teaching at the center of university life, as well as between theology and the other academic departments and professional programs. The separation of faith from the problems of daily life, and especially from the problems of public life, is institutionalized on Catholic as on other campuses. Effective strategies to overcome these divisions and develop programs to enrich the intellectual life of the church will thus require serious attention to some of the most perplexing problems of modern culture. More will be needed than simply recruiting new vocations to the sponsoring religious order, hiring more Catholic faculty, or enforcing orthodoxy on the theology department and sexual orthopraxis on the student services office.

As Bishop Malone says, "Catholic educators themselves must engage in a high level examination of their collective purpose and develop an overall strategy."[26] But that strategy has to be constructive, particularly in the wake of recent efforts to reestablish control. "When you bring up the word 'Catholic' it conjures up a whole set of images of the university ready to pounce on people," one well-known Catholic woman professor remarked.[27] Turner, Shea, and Buckley all suggest ways to turn that image around and make the Catholic connection a valuable resource for addressing basic problems of modern life. To turn that possibility into action people should focus less on mission statements and institutional controls and more on people and programs. For example, elements of an effective strategy might include:

1. Expansion of cooperative programming with the local and national church, bringing academic resources into more direct contact with church ministries, as has been done in programs to train lay ministers and religious educators. Areas in need of immediate attention include the education and formation of clergy, deacons, and religious; the

work of Catholic Charities, the Campaign for Human Development, and Catholic Relief Services; the need to foster and support independent lay movements; and the continuing effort to initiate national dialogue on the moral dimensions of public policy.

2. Faculty development programs aimed at strengthening and motivating those already on campus to relate their teaching and research to their faith and to the needs of the church, and projects to identify and support Catholic graduate students and junior faculty. Such efforts require time, for theological education, for intra- and interdisciplinary dialogue, and for simple conversation, all of which means money and other resources. Catholic identity has a cost.

3. Deliberate action to influence faculty hiring to insure a critical mass of faculty in all disciplines who are committed to the mission of the school, alert to the agenda of the American church, and ready to work on undergraduate and graduate programs that will bring fundamental issues of meaning to bear on the work of schools and departments, a step that will require courage and honesty from sponsoring religious communities and Catholic faculty and adminstrators.

Most important is the formation of leadership among trustees, administrators, faculty, and students. The number of religious and lay personnel, both on campus and on a national level, who are committed to a constructive ecclesial role for Catholic higher education and are willing to do something about it is limited. They must be willing to work together to influence the direction of particular institutions and Catholic higher education in general. Their effort should be open, honest, and constructive. Without such organized action, the balancing act between church and university may continue, but real and important possibilities to enrich the church and contribute to the pursuit of its public mission will be lost.

The implication of separate incorporation was that the Catholic laity could be empowered to live fully Catholic lives outside the Catholic subculture, at the heart of the modern world. Of course, one can argue that this idea was a mistake, that it is either not possible or not desirable to live fully in American — or modern — culture and that they should move back to church. But if one still believes that the U.S. church is called to bring the Gospel to life within American society, rather than in a Catholic counterculture, then theology and worship and learning and teaching have to be done in the midst of life, where laypeople live. And, whether we are talking of the reasonable articulation of the faith or of the spiritual formation of Catholic laypeople, that goal would seem to exclude using power and privilege to restore Catholic identity. Rather, it would seem to require awakening a sense of purpose based on the providential meaning and moral power of the movement of so many Catholics and of their colleges and universities to the many centers of contemporary human life, there to share responsibility for common human problems, none greater among them than the meaning of the intellectual life itself.

The usual answer to this classic Americanist position is the rather unscriptural but altogether commonsense sociological argument that the church must be the church before the church can be the church for others. The writers I have examined, along with Peter Steinfels in a widely reported 1993 commencement address at Fordham University, are understandably concerned that Catholics are losing their capacity to speak as Catholics. All of us need to do what we can to build a strong Catholic intellectual community. But I think we should worry even more if Catholics decide to solve the problem of pluralism, not by helping to define a common ground for the common good, but by locating and reaffirming a supposedly distinctive Catholicism. The option for distinctiveness is what got us in trouble in the first place, but at least before Vatican II it reflected the outsider status of Catholics and their church. Now we occupy a very different social and cultural location, as the last generation's reformers knew we would. We are now too far inside this culture and share too much responsibility for what it has become to think we can solve its problems, or ours, by symbolic options for Catholicism.

A few years ago liberal Catholics thought that distinctiveness was not a good idea unless it served wider human interests. They thought that Catholic schools were called by their history to try to "do theology"—that is, to think through the meanings of experience with God, in the midst of those wider communities within which we must live. For such schools, the most important thing to say about the world outside the church is not that it is secular or that it is not the church, but that it is ours. Such schools might value Catholic theology tremendously and cherish a close association with the Catholic tradition. But even its Catholic faculty might argue that one must find ways to speak of God and connect with the Catholic tradition, while standing outside church, in the various "killing fields" of our century, perhaps with the poor, as some friends elsewhere suggest, at least among this people, our people, with whom our fate is bound up.

CHAPTER 7

A Case Study: Holy Cross and Its Mission Statement

MISSION STATEMENTS?

In the fall of 1988, John E. Brooks, S.J., president of Holy Cross, asked me to chair a committee to draw up a mission statement for the college. I was surprised and a bit embarrassed. Only a few months before, I had addressed a meeting of college and university presidents and provincials of religious communities. While I encouraged the group to examine more seriously their identity and mission as Catholic institutions, I argued that writing mission statements was probably not a good idea, at least for now. Changes in trustees, faculty, and staff, declining numbers of religious, and increased dependence on public financial support, together with dramatic changes in the church, had created a very new set of circumstances for the schools. All these factors needed to be examined carefully before a good mission statement could be constructed. Furthermore, the Curran case had reawakened worries about academic freedom, especially among faculty unfamiliar with the fine distinctions of Catholic church law and politics. At the same time, new Vatican initiatives designed to tighten relations between universities and the church had brought a nearly unanimous negative response from leaders of American Catholic higher education. The Vatican draft of the constitution for Catholic higher education and U.S. response received featured treatment in the *Chronicle of Higher Education,* further arousing faculty anxieties.

Perhaps in part because of these controversies, there was a tendency, evident at Holy Cross, to increasingly emphasize the word "Jesuit," translated quickly into liberal arts education with an ethical orientation, and to downplay or even omit the word "Catholic." Indeed, at Holy Cross, as elsewhere, the issue of Catholic identity often translated into the number of Jesuits on campus. (The college had an affirmative action hiring policy for Jesuits, as well as for women and minorities.) It was my impression that the Jesuits were no more comfortable than lay faculty with the Catholic dimension of institutional identity and mission, except as it translated into a strong campus ministry program and some presence of Catholic theology in the religious studies department, though even that was a matter of some continuing discussion. Such discomfort was understandable in light of Vatican actions regarding Jesuits, theologians, and universities and in light of the presence on some campuses, though not significantly at Holy Cross, of a small but vocal cadre of faculty, students, and alumni who still defined the Catholic character of the institution in terms of the orthodoxy of its theology and philosophy departments, the presence of practicing Catholics and the absence of public dissent. All this made lay and especially non-Catholic faculty nervous. It became harder to discuss collaboration with the local church, integration of religion into the curriculum, examination of problems of social and political responsibility, and institutional support for Catholic intellectual life.

The Catholic connection was a problem, then, one usually discussed in terms of juridical connections with the hierarchy, the status of academic theologians, or the religious composition of the faculty. In that climate, it would be hard to be constructive in defining Catholic identity in a text. Finally, I argued that mission statements were almost always constructed without the full participation of faculty and staff. They were almost always extremely abstract and, with their characteristic references to papal and other official Catholic texts, all but unknown to the faculty, misleading as well.

Instead of writing mission statements, I argued, it would be better to spend the next few years developing concrete projects in curriculum, faculty development, research, and other areas that would express the positive links between Catholic faith and the teaching and research that constituted the work of the community. Far better than mission statements, I thought, might be initiatives aimed at linking Catholic identity and mission with the intellectual interests and educational vocation of the faculty and professional staff. For example: projects to combine vigorous student service programs with Catholic social teaching, Catholic Charities and the Campaign for Human Development, and faculty research interests in urban affairs. Or summer institutes, modeled on the popular programs of the National Endowment for the Humanities, to enable faculty to study Catholic theology as it relates to their disciplines. If successful, such projects might stimulate discussion, make the Catholic aspects of the institution more attractive and interesting, build awareness of the resources that the Catholic Church and the Society of Jesus brought to the college, and build a climate of dialogue more favorable for mission statements that would be more than just material for public relations.

DO IT ANYWAY!

I thought that all of this was particularly true at Holy Cross. But the president and dean made their own persuasive argument. Holy Cross in recent years had made enormous progress in its quest to become a truly excellent national liberal arts college. Recently, it had even cracked one list of the nation's top 25. Now Father Brooks and Dean Frank Vellaccio wanted to use an upcoming reaccreditation process to build support for taking Holy Cross to the next level. They hoped the community would make a systematic study of curriculum and student life, which, combined with the work of a committee studying faculty resources, would provide a profile of the college and suggestions for further reform aimed at reaching the very highest levels of American liberal arts colleges. But to guide the process, they believed the college needed a new mission statement, one that would reflect the profound changes that had taken place in the last twenty-five years as well as the aspirations of the men and women who had come to Holy Cross during that period.

So I agreed to take part and our small committee of five set out to construct a mission statement. We spent a semester investigating mission statements from other schools, consulting with experts, and meeting with small groups of faculty and staff, the Jesuit community, student leaders, and the executive committee of the board of trustees. We then produced a first-draft statement, held hearings and more small group sessions, refined the text, and, at the end of the year, presented the president with a report and another draft mission statement.

We recommended that the draft be discussed by the community as it deliberated through the reaccreditation process. For two years this was done, as the college considered changes in curriculum, student life, and governance. Finally, in the fall of 1991, Father Brooks asked us to bring the mission statement to a vote. After a year of discussion and minor revision, the faculty meeting (which includes professional staff and a few students) approved the statement by a nearly unanimous vote. A few weeks later it received formal and official approval by the college's board of trustees.

Mission Statement

The College of the Holy Cross is, by tradition and choice, a Jesuit liberal arts college serving the Catholic community, American society and the wider world. To participate in the life of Holy Cross is to accept an invitation to join in dialogue about basic human questions: What is the moral character of learning and teaching? How do we find meaning in life and history? What are our obligations to one another? What is our special responsibility to the world's poor and powerless?

As a liberal arts college, Holy Cross pursues excellence in teaching, learning and research. All who share its life are challenged to be open to new ideas, to be patient with ambiguity and uncertainty, to combine a passion for truth with respect for the views of others. Informed by the presence of diverse interpretations of the human experience, Holy Cross seeks to build a community marked by freedom, mutual respect and civility. Because the search for meaning and value is at the heart of the intellectual life, critical examination of fundamental religious and philosophical questions is integral to liberal arts education. Dialogue about these questions among people from diverse academic disciplines and religious traditions requires everyone to acknowledge and respect differences. Dialogue also requires us to remain open to that sense of the whole which calls us to transcend ourselves and challenges us to seek that which might constitute our common humanity.

The faculty and staff of Holy Cross, now primarily lay and religiously and culturally diverse, also affirm the mission of Holy Cross as a Jesuit college. As such, Holy Cross seeks to exemplify the longstanding dedication of the Society of Jesus to intellectual life and its commitment to the service of faith and promotion of justice. The College is dedicated to forming a community which supports the intellectual growth of all its members while offering them opportunities for spiritual and moral development. In a special way, the College must enable all who choose to do so to encounter the intellectual heritage of Catholicism, to form an active worshipping community and to become engaged in the life and work of the contemporary church.

Since 1843, Holy Cross has sought to educate students who, as leaders in business, professional and civic life, would live by the highest intellectual and ethical standards. In service of the ideal, Holy Cross endeavors to create an environment in which integrated learning is a shared responsibility, pursued in classroom and laboratory, studio and theater, residence and chapel. Shared responsibility for the life and governance of the College should lead all its members to make the best of their own talents, to work together, to be sensitive to one another, to serve others and to seek justice within and beyond the Holy Cross community.

A more detailed consideration of the process that led to this statement at one small and more or less prosperous Catholic college might serve as something of a case study, although Holy Cross is representative of American Catholic higher education only in its uniqueness; there are no typical schools. So the claims for this story are minimal: here is how one faculty committee tried to work it out.

BACKGROUND

The College of the Holy Cross was founded in 1843 by Jesuit priests at the request of Bishop Benedict Joseph Fenwick of Boston. Located in Worcester, Massachusetts, Holy Cross educated young men of all ages until defining itself as a liberal arts college in the early twentieth century. When other Jesuit schools added programs in business, the professions, and adult and continuing education, Holy Cross stayed with its commitment to undergraduate and strict liberal arts education, winning a reputation by its preparation of young men for further studies in professional schools and seminaries. Holy Cross was for many years best known for its strong athletic teams, its passionately loyal alumni, and its classical curriculum, heavy with requirements in math, Greek and Latin, and, especially, philosophy. While the classical core is gone, replaced by distribution requirements, the college's classics department remains one of the largest and strongest in the United States. Holy Cross has remained rather small, with enrollment now around 2,600, almost all of whom live on campus.

When change finally came to Holy Cross, it exploded. Under the leadership of Raymond Swords from 1960 to 1970, Holy Cross dramatically changed its curriculum, for a time abandoning core requirements altogether. The college added lay faculty, established new departments in the social sciences (one Jesuit referred to professors in these departments as "the second team") and the arts, and worked hard to upgrade the quality of instruction, particularly by insisting on a remarkably high level of scholarly production from the faculty. In 1969 the Jesuits transferred the charter and property of the college to an independent board of trustees, composed of a majority of laypeople, and shaped a set of statutes that guaranteed academic freedom and gave faculty and professional staff a voice in governance. Most important was coeducation; the first women students arrived in 1972.

Change did not come easy. Older Jesuits and many alumni opposed all these moves. Swords and Father Brooks, his successor, made a strong commitment to recruiting African-American students, but those students sometimes found the atmosphere and attitudes at Holy Cross difficult. In December 1969 the college was brought to a halt by a student strike occasioned by the dramatic withdrawal from school of all its black students, including future Supreme Court Justice Clarence Thomas. Only a few months later, students again closed the school, this time to protest escalation of the Vietnam War. Anti-war protester Philip Berrigan and socialist leader Michael Harrington were Holy Cross graduates; when the college awarded honorary degrees to Harrington and Jesuit peace leader Daniel Berrigan, S.J. and devoted an issue of its alumni publication to the Berrigan brothers, *Time* magazine dubbed Holy Cross "the cradle of the Catholic left."

Campus activism declined rapidly after Father Brooks became president in 1970. Before long, however, conflicts rooted in the rapid changes of the last decade put new distance between the faculty and the Jesuit-dominated administration. In 1976, the trustees, under presidential guidance, decided to overturn a number of faculty decisions on tenure, leading to a long, angry dispute. The faculty, following standard American academic practice, insisted on their primary responsibility for making academic policy, including personnel decisions; their decisions should be overridden only in extraordinary circumstances. The administration and inexperienced trustees insisted on their ultimate authority, required to protect the college's Jesuit and Catholic character. Because the faculty had no stomach for decisive action, the dispute had no decisive resolution, which meant victory for the trustees and administration.

In the aftermath, I wrote a public commentary emphasizing the contrast between the vision of Holy Cross as a potential "Catholic Amherst" held by a small group of faculty leaders and the defensive posture of the Jesuit administration. The latter agreed with the goal of making Holy Cross an excellent liberal arts college, comparable to the best in the nation; indeed, that was their most important objective. But they also insisted that Holy Cross remain visibly Catholic and Jesuit. Yet those words had little positive content beyond a strong theology department and campus ministry and retention of the presidency for the Jesuits. Most striking was the all but total absence in Jesuit arguments of references to the dramatic changes that were taking place in the Society of Jesus, particularly its collective commitment to the "service of faith and promotion of justice" in the context of a "preferential option for the poor." Later the president would often refer to these terms and to Jesuit General Pedro Arrupe's statement that the goal of Jesuit education was to form "men [and women] for others." But those terms were not used, during the dispute or later, to offer an alternative vision to the faculty leadership's image of a gradually improving liberal arts college whose Catholic and Jesuit connections would be increasingly marginal to its fundamental work.

The other interesting outcome of the mid-1970s dispute was a small committee of Jesuit and lay faculty who explored the meaning of Jesuit and Catholic identity and eventually produced a report that was discussed but not acted upon. This descriptive report emphasized the impact on Holy Cross of the professionalization of the faculty. In the mid 1960s, the faculty was predominantly composed of Jesuit priests. A decade later, they constituted only 20 percent of the teaching faculty; by the time our committee began its work in 1988, that number was less than 10 percent, though Jesuits still occupied dominant roles in administration and campus ministry. For many years, people spoke of such changes in terms of laypeople replacing priests and sisters, but the Holy Cross committee recognized that it was even more significant that the new faculty, including younger Jesuits, were academic professionals. Trained in the country's best graduate schools, they identified strongly with their discipline. They had received specialized training, written dissertations on tightly defined research topics, and then sought employment through the networks in their field. When they arrived at Holy Cross, they expected to continue research, and the college used its own funds and impressive foundation grants to help them do so.

The older Jesuits and many of the laypeople who had arrived at the college in the 1950s and early 1960s were dedicated teachers, intensely loyal to Holy Cross. The newer faculty, understandably, found their greatest personal satisfaction in publications and public presentations within their discipline. Their sense of themselves as academic professionals was affirmed by the college, which increasingly made research potential a criteria in hiring and research production a major element in promotion and tenure decisions. Of course, their presence at Holy Cross, a liberal arts college, showed their commitment to undergraduate teaching, and teaching remained a major factor in personnel decisions. But faculty and administrators alike agreed that research and publication held the key to the excellence that was the college's most important goal, a goal to which everyone seemed committed.

As the committee saw it, events at Holy Cross demonstrated that two clusters of problems came with this professionalization—one dealt with governance, the other with institutional mission and identity.

One element of academic professionalism is academic freedom, and, as we have seen, Catholic colleges moved quickly in the 1960s to adopt AAUP standards and incorporate their protections into their procedures. National disputes about Catholic theology made some Catholic faculty nervous, and from time to time non-Catholic faculty would speak of an atmospheric resistance to discussion of controversial subjects like abortion and birth control. The latter issues also posed serious problems among students and student life personnel, but most faculty usually felt at ease about their freedom to speak their mind, in the classroom and elsewhere.

But the less noticed and in many ways far more problematic area of academic professionalism was that which had led to the 1976 conflict at Holy Cross—governance. American professors do not see themselves as employees, a salaried staff, but as a community of scholars who in some fundamental way constitute the university; other offices and agencies should serve and support their work of teaching and research. At a minimum, professors consider it part of their professional responsibility to formulate academic policy, including curriculum, hiring, tenure, and promotion. They also believe that they should share responsibility with others for overall institutional policy. The trustees should accept the faculty's judgement in academic matters unless they have grave reasons to do otherwise, and they should give careful consideration to faculty views on all other matters. In the 1960s and 1970s, Holy Cross incorporated these ideas into its statutes and faculty handbook; the conflict that arose in 1976 reflected faculty conviction that they exercised primary responsibility for tenure decisions and the trustees' determination to insure their power to protect what they took to be the college's essential mission and identity.

The incident demonstrated that construction of institutions and procedures to embody shared responsibility was no simple matter. The overrides showed a lack of trust on the part of Jesuit and Catholic lay trustees about the faculty they had hired. The faculty, in turn, wanted the trustees to reduce emphasis on intercollegiate athletics, upgrade the college's academic profile, and allow the increasingly talented faculty to define academic policy. The Jesuits, for their part, controlled the major levers of power, but they were unable to articulate a compelling vision, beyond protecting the Catholic identity of the school.

What neither side had noticed, the committee argued, was that the growing professionalization of the faculty, with its emphasis on disciplinary research, endangered any notion of institutional mission. This problem became more acute after the passions of the tenure fight cooled. Trustees and administrators retained ultimate power, but they generally left departments alone. And departments at Holy Cross, as elsewhere, dominated the hiring process, looking for the best available person in the field for which an opening existed. In 1986, then Dean Raymond Schroth, S.J., after consulting with the president, directed the economics department to fill one of its two open slots with an economist interested in Catholic social teaching, then prominent because of the writing of the U.S. bishops' highly publicized pastoral letter on the U.S. economy. Schroth's request sparked resistance, first in the department and then among the faculty as a whole. A majority of the tenured faculty signed a letter of protest and Schroth submitted his resignation. Later, Schroth cited the fight as an example of the erosion of Catholic identity, at Holy Cross and at other schools.

Finally, the dispute of the 1970s had left a residue of hard feelings between Jesuit administrators and the lay faculty. The earlier mission committee helped ease the tension by inviting dialogue among Jesuit and lay faculty, one result of which was the discovery that the more academically engaged Jesuit faculty shared their lay colleagues' concern about academic freedom and self-governance. Equally important, Jesuit rectors, acting on behalf of the now distinct Jesuit community, reached out to the faculty at Holy Cross by hosting a series of dinners, preceded by talks on Jesuit life and work, over a period of several years. By the time our committee began its work, the faculty was more lay and far more professionally committed and successful, but, thanks to the rectors and chaplains, there was far better mutual understanding than had existed a decade earlier.

INCLUSION

Our committee decided to develop a mission statement that would reflect the experience and aspirations of people at Holy Cross, to take the bottom-up rather than top-down approach discussed earlier. We were aware of the major statements of the Vatican, the U.S. bishops, and other Catholic and Jesuit schools, and we sought advice from experienced leaders in Catholic higher education. But we made a conscious choice to be inclusive, to try to insure that, when the word "we" was used, it included, as much as possible, everyone. We wanted non-Catholic faculty, who sometimes saw themselves as outsiders or, as one put it, as nonfamily executives in "a family firm," to receive the same invitation to share in the life and work of Holy Cross as anyone else. And we hoped that they would want to extend the same invitation to the shrinking community of Jesuit faculty and to the mostly Catholic trustees, students, parents, and benefactors of our school. Most important, we wanted to produce a mission statement that would actually connect with the aspirations of the people who devoted themselves to the college and with the day-to-day work of teaching and research that in some fundamental way constituted the college's essential identity.

At the start we made a second set of assumptions about the words most often used to describe Holy Cross: liberal arts, Jesuit, and Catholic. We assumed as a committee that each of those words lacked authoritative definition — that, in fact, people deeply committed to each disagreed about what the words meant. Our experience proved that we were right: everyone, without exception, wanted Holy Cross to remain a liberal arts college and a Jesuit college, and almost everyone agreed that Holy Cross has special responsibilities as a Catholic institution. But there was and there remains very wide disagreement about what each of those terms means.

Yet, again without exception, people welcomed conversation about these terms and about the deeper questions they often mask. The liberal arts question was at heart a question about learning and teaching and what that means in the late twentieth century. Jesuit opened up questions about classical liberal arts — the legendary ratio studiorum — but also about religious faith and social justice. And the word Catholic posed questions about the role of religion in contemporary intellectual life and education and the relationship between that broad question and the specifically Catholic commitments of the college, all this in a bewildering world at once conscious of its interdependence and filled with multiple diversities. In short, the small group process uncovered large questions behind the practical problems of Catholic and Jesuit identity, core curriculum, and social responsibility. Recognizing the questions and faced with wide differences, participants affirmed the importance of their work but spoke of issues with humility and careful attention to the concerns of others.

Our draft mission statement, then, had three crucial elements.

First, the now quite diverse faculty and professional staff affirm with near unanimity their commitment to Holy Cross as a Jesuit, undergraduate, liberal arts college. No one suggested the introduction of graduate, professional, or vocationally oriented programs. But they immediately defined the essential meaning of that commitment as "an invitation to participate in conversation" about three essential questions: how do people find meaning in life and in history (the religion question); what is the moral dimension of learning and teaching (the liberal arts question); and what are our obligations to one another, and, in particular, what are our obligations regarding the poor (the Jesuit question). Dialogue about such matters, more than anything else, constitutes the identity of Holy Cross. It shares elements of this identity with other liberal arts colleges, but each is given a special flavor by Jesuit and Catholic traditions and commitments.

Second, as students, teachers, and staff in a liberal arts college, we at Holy Cross affirm that we, all of us, in our work together of teaching and research, must give serious consideration to "fundamental religious and philosophical questions" and remain open to "the sense of the whole that always confronts us as a question." Religion, the search for meaning and value, has a central role in the intellectual life and in undergraduate education. We make that contention as a liberal arts college and as a pluralistic community, quite apart from our Jesuit sponsorship and Catholic affiliation. A liberal arts college has an obligation to make it possible for students to explore basic questions of meaning and value—fundamental theology if you will—and to do so as a central and even integrating part of education. Because such questions are dealt with by "communities of meaning and value," a degree of religious diversity is valuable, even essential, but only if the faculty become more articulate about their own response to these fundamental matters.

Third, within that framework, we affirm that the Holy Cross community—that is, all of us who adopt the mission statement—has a special responsibility to provide opportunities to all who wish to do so to encounter the intellectual heritage of Catholicism and to engage in the life and work of the contemporary Catholic church. This community-wide responsibility is grounded in the history of Holy Cross, its Jesuit sponsorship, and the support of so many Catholic students, parents, alumni, and benefactors. The phrase "Catholic college" is deliberately omitted as ambiguous and misleading, but its substance is included in a way that would enable Holy Cross, if it chose to do so, to fulfill its specifically Catholic responsibilities to serve the church and evangelize culture. This commitment, made by the community as a whole, is not the responsibility of and cannot be fulfilled by some combination of the chaplaincy, or the religious studies department, or the Jesuit community. Like all other elements of the mission statement, it requires programs to carry it into effect. They include the presence of Catholic theology and a strong campus ministry, but also include the presence of scholars and teachers familiar with the Catholic faith and able to bring it to bear on their disciplines (as Dean Schroth had requested), as well as programs designed to educate people regarding the current life and work of the church. In short, Holy Cross has a responsibility to serve the church, and it does that best when it makes it possible for its participants to become intelligent Catholics engaged with their church and its mission. If Holy Cross wants to be Catholic, the mission statement provides a unique mandate.

Finally, we would contend that the intellectual life and liberal arts education are not ends in themselves, but are always carried on within a specific community at a particular time and place in history. The late Michael Harrington, a Holy Cross alumnus, claimed that the most lasting legacy of his Jesuit education was that ideas have consequences and that one is then responsible. Nowhere is that more clear than in the contemporary

Catholic and Jesuit commitment to faith, justice, and the poor. Must not research and education, teaching and learning, be carried on with attention to contexts? And the context of our times is marked, among other things, by the presence of poverty and unmerited suffering, by victims. Thus we believe that liberal arts education, as much as Catholic or Jesuit education, must take account of historical responsibility. But the "faith" part of the faith and justice motto is important: attention to ethics is not enough. Values are linked to fundamental commitments, so that justice and peace ought to be integrated with the fundamental religious and philosophical questions at the heart of liberal arts education. But here, once again, there are no blueprints, nor even agreement on the terms, and conversation among faculty must accompany curricular experimentation.

The community wished very much to affirm its Jesuit and Catholic commitments without in any way marginalizing its non-Catholic faculty and staff. This can seem like a weakness to avowedly dedicated Catholics concerned with academic secularization. But it takes on a different tone when dedicated professors of many years service wonder if they are really equal participants in the life of the school. The image of the family firm describes that experience of benign alienation. Too often there is the anomaly of attempting to define the essential elements of a school in terms not accessible to a substantial portion of its participants. Then there is the problem that a majority of faculty and staff may well be very religious, but religious with all the diversity, even eccentricity, that marks American religion. In civil society and in churches that are more than sects or ethnic enclaves, we have learned that the only solution is dialogue. So, the essence of the project lies in that word that recurs so often throughout this book and initiates the Holy Cross definition of mission — conversation.

THE POLITICS OF MISSION

The process of preparing the statement was a positive experience for the committee. We had numerous unusual chances to discuss serious issues with our colleagues. We found that there were fewer "religious exclusivists" and "secular exclusivists" than we had expected. The more or less secular faculty and those with a concern about the religious heritage of the school lowered their voices. We listened to each other and were more open to change than seemed to be true a decade earlier. Lacking clear agreement on the meaning of liberal arts, Catholic, and Jesuit, anxious not to exclude anyone unnecessarily, we opted for the "inclusive conversationalist" term of the debate.

The draft of this statement first arrived on faculty desks at the end of the 1988–1989 academic year. With it came three other reports, two dealing with curriculum and student life, prepared for reaccreditation, and a long-awaited report on faculty resources. The latter was occasioned by faculty concern about staffing valuable new programs. A fine committee did exhaustive research, comparing Holy Cross resources and experience to those of comparable institutions. The committee recommended a reduced teaching load for faculty, from six courses a year to the five now standard at the best liberal arts colleges, along with other reforms aimed at enhancing instructional quality. The heart of the matter was the need for additional faculty: Holy Cross's effective student-teacher ratios had not changed significantly in twenty years, despite the increasing demands made on the now professional faculty. More faculty would allow the college to improve the quality of instruction, multiply opportunities for independent study and research, initiate a new first-year program to provide students with a common learning experience and stimulate the intellectual and cultural atmosphere of the college, and initiate programs stemming from the mission statement's affirmation of Catholic studies and social justice, as well as to maintain the momentum of research.

In the fall of 1989, the president and the educational policy committee (EPC) (the executive committee of the faculty meeting) decided to spend a year studying all these reports with all constituencies of the college and preparing an integrated set of recommendations for the board of trustees.

The first major event, following a semester of hearings and small group discussions, was an all-day workshop during the January break, when faculty and staff were invited to join together to discuss the college's mission. As the basis for discussion, the EPC wrote a lengthy summary analysis of the recommendations of the four reports. Claiming to echo the voices heard during the semester, the EPC offered two interpretive models—one it called the professional model, the other the community model. People oriented toward the first model were anchored in their disciplines and valued working with bright students interested in the subject, especially those who might go on to graduate school. They were less interested in issues of general education and student life. The community model, on the other hand, was strong among the college staff and among professors whose priority interest was teaching and who regularly partici-pated in collegewide programs.

The committee believed that these two models were not two parties within the college, though issues often broke down around this division, but contending values within most individuals. Of course, most people who chose to work at a liberal arts college wanted to be both good scholars and effective teachers as well as participants in a community of learning. But choices had to be made: should resources be put into reduced teaching loads or new programs, research leaves or student life projects, improved computer systems or additional public space? The EPC thought it important for people on each side to hear people on the other. They also thought it important to emphasize that institutional mission — both statement and policy — could not reflect only the aspirations of the community-oriented faculty and staff. If a research-oriented faculty was valued and if Holy Cross wanted to enter the top ranks of liberal arts colleges, resources would have to be devoted to supporting that faculty and making the conversations highlighted by the mission statement possible.

Faculty and staff commitment to the college was evident in the near total turnout for the January workshop. Participants disliked the dualistic framework of the position paper, fearing that it posed a false either-or set of options for the school. Nevertheless, the dialogues sparked by the report, especially when it got down to specific choices regarding curriculum and faculty resources, supported its argument.

Later in the year, debate centered on whether to propose to the trustees the across the board reduced teaching load initially favored by the faculty or, in light of the student life and curriculum reports, growing interest in a first-year program, and surprising interest in projects reflective of Jesuit and Catholic mission, to recommend that additional faculty be allocated among these projects, with the enhancement of the already strong program of faculty research leaves. The latter choice, in short, meant offering a reduced teaching load to some, but not all, faculty. Remarkably, the faculty in the end chose the latter course, significant evidence that professionalization had not reduced the faculty's commitment to the community and its overall mission. At the end of the year, a final report containing these recommendations went to the trustees with a near unanimous vote of the faculty meeting.

Unfortunately, the trustees did not appreciate the significance of the report, its near unanimity, its programmatic endorsement of the mission statement, and its sacrifice of faculty interest in reduced teaching load in favor of projects to energize campus intellectual life and promote Jesuit and Catholic mission. They responded by establishing a first-ever trustee-faculty-administration committee on planning and priorities. That committee's meetings took place during a downturn in the economy that challenged the college's ability to persist in its "need-blind" admissions and financial aid policies. Shaken by financial forecasts, the committee eventually recommended three priorities: student financial aid, faculty and staff salaries, and library resources. This quickly became a "growth through substitution" policy; there would be no new resources, and, if new programs were initiated, they would have to draw on the people and money already available.

After that disappointing outcome, the president in the fall of 1991 reconstituted our mission committee and asked us to bring the mission statement to a vote. Once again a series of meetings were held to solicit faculty, staff, and student views. There was vigorous debate about the opening questions, about words that suggested exclusion to some, and about the meaning of "shared responsibility." Most notable was the absence of a strong voice calling for a clearer commitment to Catholic identity, which had risen to fever pitch elsewhere. In the end only a few minor changes were made in the initial draft. The text was adopted by the faculty with only two or three negative votes; there was no count. A few weeks later, after a brief flurry of discussion about the absent phrase "Catholic college," the trustees adopted the statement.

One final episode. After the faculty vote, the mission statement was sent to the board of trustees for their consideration. A few days after materials were mailed for the May meeting, our committee was informed that some trustees had expressed concern that the statement did not use the phrase "Catholic college." In order to explain why, our committee was asked to appear before the board. The administration seemed somewhat nervous about the meeting, and the committee caught that anxiety as we prepared our responses to the Catholic college question: almost no one had raised the issue, there was consensus to retain a clear Jesuit identity, and there was a practical commitment to provide concrete service to Catholic students and to the church, which could easily provide the foundation for programs and for hiring faculty interested in Catholicism. When the day of the board meeting arrived, we were kept waiting, a bit nervous, before the chairman of the board finally emerged to invite us in. As we walked across the hall, he whispered that the board had just unanimously approved the Mission Statement. I did not have time to ask, if that were the case, why were we there?

After we were seated, I gave a brief history of the process that had produced the statement. When I was done, one board member immediately raised his hand, and I braced for the Catholic challenge. "To get faculty approval, you must have watered this down," he said. "For example, I find no reference to God here. Why is that?" My first reaction, which almost slipped out, was "I never thought of God." But I caught myself, and Dean James Kee responded by explaining the origin and development of the sense of the whole section of the text dealing with "fundamental religious and philosophical questions."

A short time later, I submitted a proposal for a project to mark the college's 150th anniversary in 1993-1994. The proposal was based on a number of principles drawn from the experience of developing the mission statement. They were:

1. Creative and responsible liberal arts education requires persistent, public attention on the part of the community to the three questions posed in the first paragraph of the Mission Statement.
2. Meaning and value, faith and justice are integrally connected, both theoretically and practically, and their separation should be resisted.
3. Religion—that is, fundamental questions of meaning and value (in Jesuit terms faith and justice)—is (should be) at the heart of liberal arts education. A college with a Jesuit and Catholic heritage and commitment has a particular responsibility to translate this principle into practice.
4. A Jesuit and Catholic college also has a responsibility to enable all students who wish to do so to enter into the life and mission of the Catholic church. To carry out this responsibility, the college needs personnel trained for this job, in all areas, not just in campus ministry and religious studies.
5. No one has the answer to the interrelated problems of liberal arts integration, socially responsible education, or Catholic intellectual life. What is needed is a willingness to experiment on the basis of ongoing engagement with the underlying cultural problems.

The project suggested a number of faculty seminars and planning workshops designed 1) to develop educational strategies and pilot projects to make the study of fundamental religious questions the integrating element of undergraduate education; 2) to multiply opportunities for faculty and students to examine the relationship between their research and teaching and the contemporary search and the Jesuit concern for social justice and world peace; 3) to develop and implement a program of Catholic studies aimed at enabling those students who wish to do so to enter into the intellectual life of Roman Catholicism and to understand the role of the Catholic church in contemporary culture; and 4) to prepare for a major conference in 1994 on Jesuit undergraduate education, with these three areas as an agenda, to mark the sesquicentennial of the college. The proposal was not adopted; it remains, I think, a good idea.

COMMENTARY

The mission statement as adopted has some strengths and some weaknesses. Its greatest strength is that, unlike many statements of this sort, it was actually approved by a vote of the faculty (actually by the faculty meeting, which includes a few students, all academic administrators, chaplains, and professional staff). At Holy Cross College the faculty have agreed that they wish their school to remain a Jesuit, liberal arts college. They are committed to working to integrate fundamental religious and philosophical questions into the curriculum (and at some sacrifice have taken a step toward doing so since by initiating a first-year program on the theme "how then shall we live?"). The faculty also recognize a community-wide institutional responsibility to make available the intellectual heritage of Catholicism and enable interested people to form an active worshipping community and to participate in the life and work of the church. Given the frequent and not always good-spirited and unmerited criticism of Holy Cross as being far advanced on the "slippery path" to secularization, this agreement is a major achievement.

Secondly, the statement is honest, facing up to the very real lack of agreement about liberal arts education. So the mission statement makes conversation a central theme of the community's life, a theme strongly affirmed in much of the best literature about higher education. Making those conversations happen, however, is as big a challenge as providing a more integrated learning experience.

The text sounds themes drawn from the recent history of higher education: diversity, toleration, conversation, and dialogue. But it also preserves the theme of integration: Holy Cross remains committed to the integrating ideal of the liberal arts tradition.

And there is the theme of shared responsibility, a theme much heard but little practiced in the postconciliar church, but practiced a great deal in Catholic higher education. Remember that the religious orders gave the schools to independent boards and hired religiously diverse professors to carry on the work: think what would have happened if similar risks had been taken elsewhere, say in elementary education or diocesan administration. Again, shared responsibility is not a specifically Catholic theme, but it is one that reflects the changing contours of American Catholic life. In Holy Cross's remarkable campus ministry program, shared responsibility has become a reality: students and staff shape the program, and graduates who have been active could easily take charge of any parish's liturgical committee, staff its religious education program, implement its RCIA, or participate competently in its pastoral and social ministries. Recently shared responsibility provided the framework for a major reform of college governance approved by the board of trustees. From now on, all sectors of the college community will have the opportunity to participate in its most basic decisions.

For those who care about tradition, the outcome at Holy Cross is promising. Despite the diversity and sophistication of the faculty, almost no one has surrendered to what philosopher Louis Dupre calls the twin temptations of unrestricted freedom of choice or practical vocational education. According to Dupre, "humanist education has from its inception consisted in conversation" with three central purposes: first, to transmit "the spiritual legacy in which our culture has found its identity"; second, to respond to the critical examination of "those questions which every thoughtful person spontaneously asks"; and, finally, to provide moral education. Dupre says that the object of religious instruction consists not only in communicating the essentials of a doctrinal tradition, but, "even more, in assisting the student in extending the religious attitude based on that tradition into all areas of existence." That goal requires contemplation as well as study and liberation from "the manifold concerns and petty desires that obstruct the way to the other." We are not there yet, but I believe there is respect for that vision and gratitude that it is still alive at a place like Holy Cross.[1]

Other areas are more problematic. Those who raised the Catholic college question (to say nothing of the God question) were not without reason for their concern. In the discussions that took place, there were few strong interventions on behalf of the Catholic ecclesial (as distinct from the intellectual and cultural) elements of the college's life, especially in the last year when we were without a head chaplain. Despite efforts to circulate key texts, we had the impression that very few people were informed about the Catholic higher education debate and even fewer were worried about strengthening the college's Catholic connections.

Most important, at Holy Cross as elsewhere, there is probably too much complacency about the departmental/disciplinary structure that dominates higher education. High-quality interdisciplinary programs exist, but they must constantly struggle for resources. Almost all hiring is done within departments, and almost all departments regard publication in peer-reviewed professional journals as the measure of quality. And here, as elsewhere, even theology and religious studies generally agree. That system shortchanges general education, including education for effective citizenship. In religion it contributes to an a-intellectual pietism, in politics to a culture of complaint and irresponsibility. Yet, within the academy, it is almost unchallenged.

Our experience suggests that Holy Cross will never again be an unequivocally Catholic school marked by attentiveness to the teachings of the church as the central element of its life; it probably never was. Nor will Holy Cross become a confessional school, deliberately choosing Catholic faculty and staff, serving mostly Catholic students, or constituting an authentic Christian community comparable to a parish, as James Burtchaell seemed to require. On the other hand, Holy Cross will not become a multi-university. Its earlier decision to remain an exclusively undergraduate liberal arts college enjoys the total support of all its constituents. Can it achieve its goal of authentic excellence by winning recognition as one of the nation's best liberal arts colleges? New financial constraints appear to mean perpetuation of the resource problem, while a declining applicant pool suggests the need for strategies to attract more non-Catholic students. More money, more applicants, and more diversity will all help, but I believe the question will be answered by new programs, especially programs emphasizing what the Jesuits call "faith and justice" and I would translate into Catholic studies and a new civics. But that position enjoys little support at the moment. Whatever happens, morale is high, there are fine professional people at work here, they give far beyond what is required of them, the students are bright and have strong values, and the college enjoys amazing support from its alumni. In short, Holy Cross is one of the more promising of the 238 Catholic colleges and universities, all of which have enormous potential, if we learn how to tap it.

CHAPTER 8

Another Case Study: Catholic Higher Education and Abortion[1]

INTRODUCTION

In 1981 Holy Cross completed a three-year curriculum project, the Interdisciplinary Humanities Program, funded by the National Endowment for the Humanities. That spring, the NEH consultant, Professor Francis L. Broderick of the University of Massachusetts at Boston, discussed the program at an alumni education day. Broderick suggested that the college move beyond the linked courses of IHP to authentic interdisciplinary education. In response to a question, he cited abortion as an issue that required open, candid, and interdisciplinary discussion. As I recall, a number of alumni strongly disagreed. Several argued that the abortion issue was settled, there was no need for further inquiry, and Holy Cross should be teaching the church's teaching, not criticizing or reformulating it. Broderick's response was that neither Catholics nor the American public seemed entirely convinced by official arguments; the Catholic scholar and school could assist the church by helping it think through its position and articulate it more persuasively.

In 1992, faced with a proposal from the student government association to recognize a student-initiated pro-choice group at Holy Cross, the president and the board of trustees took the occasion to clarify college policy on abortion. Their statement affirmed the need for "self examination . . . carried out in a context where differences are honestly acknowledged and genuine dialogue between peoples with different points of view is fostered." And, while "the individual has the responsibility to make her or his own conscientious judgement" on the issue, the college "as a community has a right and responsibility to profess that, in the light of revelation, abortion is morally wrong." Thus, the trustees would not allow college funds or facilities to be used to support any organization "that seeks or is perceived to advance a right to abortion."

At almost the same time that this abortion statement was released, the college's faculty meeting was considering and adopting a mission statement that emphasized open inquiry on critical questions facing contemporary culture. The statement, developed through a process of shared responsibility and broad participation, affirms Holy Cross as a Jesuit, liberal arts college, but the term "Catholic college" is not used. Instead, the statement insists on the college's responsibility to make consideration of "fundamental religious and philosophical questions" integral to research and teaching, and it declares that Holy Cross has a particular responsibility to "enable all who choose to do so to encounter the intellectual heritage of Catholicism . . . and to become engaged in the life and work of the contemporary church."

At Holy Cross, then, as in many other Catholic colleges and universities, real problems have arisen from pro-choice initiatives. In other schools, many students, faculty, administrators, trustees, alumni, and benefactors have made it clear, sometimes painfully clear, that they will regard any formal recognition of pro-choice groups as compromising institutional integrity. In some instances, they have appealed to ecclesiastical authorities for support.[2] Others, including some who strongly oppose abortion, view the rejection of such groups as a violation of one of the essential terms of their relationship with the school: their freedom to express their views without fear of exclusion or retaliation. It is less a matter of academic freedom, well established at Holy Cross and the majority of Catholic institutions, than of student rights and responsibilities and definitions of institutional responsibility that, at least by implication, marginalize some ideas and those who hold them and place a chill on the very open debate that these institutions clearly value.

I feel that the problem stems in part from the chronic absence of the open, serious, and public debate called for by Broderick and affirmed by the Holy Cross statement on abortion and by its mission statement. As Broderick suggested, open and honest dialogue, including (perhaps especially) on issues of sexuality, is a requirement arising from the Catholic as well as the academic responsibilities of the college. If anyone doubts this, just talk to campus student leaders, at Holy Cross and elsewhere, many as committed to the faith of the Catholic church as any students who ever attended these institutions, who nevertheless see the issue in terms of free discussion, respect for the dignity and freedom of women, and acknowledgement of the demands of pluralism—perspectives seemingly in some tension with those informing official actions on this subject.

A working paper on the registration of controversial student organizations that was prepared by a committee of the Jesuit Association of Student Personnel Administrators in August 1991 and circulated widely among Catholic college leaders supports this view. It offers a balanced assessment of both sides of this debate, points to the criteria that should guide decisions, and insists on the importance of open public debate on controversial issues as a service that the institution owes both to its students and its supportive constituencies.[3] The presence of such debate, and not merely its rhetorical endorsement, is fundamental; in its absence, a decision to deny recognition to a pro-choice group or to any other controversial organization can only seem to violate the essential terms of academic discourse and to deny the most basic service that such an institution owes to the Catholic community—the service of identifying and refining the intellectual claims of Christian faith.[4]

ABORTION AS A PUBLIC ISSUE

An ever expanding and ever more sophisticated body of literature faces anyone who would try to make sense of the abortion debate. Nowhere in this literature is there a formula for resolution; everywhere there are signals of what Harvard law professor Lawrence Tribe calls "a clash of absolutes."[5] A decade ago, pro-life forces were on the march, fueled by New Right money, aroused by the unusual militance of conservative evangelical Christians, soon joined by the tactically ingenious Operation Rescue, and encouraged by an apparently sympathetic Republican leadership. Today, the pro-choice movement has new momentum and militance, arising from reaction to a perceived "backlash" against feminism that is evident throughout society and that exploded with the Clarence Thomas hearings. This movement is given added urgency by the prospect of judicial revision of the legal status of abortion.[6]

The worldwide situation is staggering: estimates run as high as 50 million abortions a year, perhaps half of them illegal. The World Health Organization estimates that 500,000 women die annually from pregnancy-related causes, perhaps 200,000 of them from illegal and unsafe abortions. Many countries in Western and Eastern Europe have kept abortion rates low by effective contraceptive and public health services, but in Poland and Russia abortion is a favored method of birth control. In the United States, there are 1.5 million abortions a year, 25 percent of all pregnancies and 50 percent of all unwanted pregnancies. Of those experiencing abortion, 81 percent are single women, 25 percent are under 20, and 10 percent are under 18. Of the abortions being performed, 90 percent take place during the first trimester, 47 percent in the first eight weeks, and less than 1 percent after the twentieth week. In 1989 it was estimated that 16 million American women had undergone an abortion. Only a small proportion of American women do not use contraceptives, but they produce half the abortions. 60 percent are unmarried, and 25 percent are poor enough to receive medicaid benefits. Catholics receive abortions in numbers equal to their share of the population; evangelical Protestants only at half their proportion.[7] The United States has liberal abortion laws and too many abortions, but access to abortion is not always easy: cost, distance from a clinic or hospital offering services, harassment, and an increasing number of legal restrictions present obstacles.[8] Moreover, the United States has the Western world's weakest support services for pregnant women and children and the most notable absence of easily available public health and contraceptive services.

For almost twenty years, Americans, asked whether they support unrestricted access to first trimester abortions, have divided almost equally; in 1973 45 to 50 percent supported access, 43 to 46 percent opposed it. In 1988 they divided 46 to 45 percent against a constitutional amendment to ban all abortions except those in the limit cases of rape, incest, and maternal survival. About 40 percent of Americans feel strongly committed on the issue. Since *Roe v. Wade*, most Americans have favored access to abortion services in the limit cases, and the extreme positions which dominate the debate have been far smaller, with about 25 percent favoring unlimited access and a smaller minority, under 20 percent, a complete ban.[9] Recent polls by pro-life groups suggest the persistence of majority sentiment against abortion, except in the limit cases, and support for a variety of abortion limits (such as parental or spousal notification, waiting periods, and required communication of information), combined with continuing resistance to criminalization.

So Americans are conflicted on the issue, the more extreme voices have been reenergized, and the middle remains mushy and unmobilized. Finding alternatives and building an effective and convergent middle ground is hard, but there are signs of hope. In a few cities, pro-choice and pro-life activists have been able to unite to support provision of pre- and postnatal care, financial and personal support for women with unwanted pregnancies, improved child and maternal health projects, and programs in sex education.[10] There is also a variety of new viewpoints from ecological, radical feminist, pro-choice Catholic, and nonviolence perspectives.[11] One can regard abortion as a tragic form of violence and yet be strongly against criminalization, with its utilization of the coercive power of the state. One can be pro-choice and yet recognize the hollowness of arguments about freedom in the context of poverty, racism, and patriarchal hegemony that distort the context and sometimes the self-awareness of so many of us. But constructive voices from the margins are muffled (how many have even heard of Juli Loesch and pro-lifers for survival, feminists for life, or Catholics for a Free Choice), in part because of media hype, in part because such voices are often very threatening. Pro-life feminists contest feminist orthodoxies as much as pro-choice Catholics undercut the bishops' moral authority by highlighting the exclusion of women from the process of discernment.[12] New voices can open up the dialogue, but they are rarely heard, especially on Catholic campuses, because public discussion is more affirmed than practiced.

Another sign of the potential of the middle is seen in the widespread popularity of former Surgeon General C. Everett Koop. Writing to President Reagan, Koop refused to release a report on the effect of abortion on the health of women who underwent the procedure, because the existing studies yielded no clear result. But Koop did tell the President that everyone, from all camps in the abortion battle, agreed that the large number of abortions "represented a failure in some part of society's support system, individual, family, church, public health, economic or social." The United States has failed, Koop wrote, "to deal responsibly and honestly with individual and societal sexuality." In the report, eventually released to the public, Koop outlined the principles that should govern a national public health policy:

> men and women should be helped and encouraged to conceive children only when they are ready and able to welcome and care for them; when children are conceived unintentionally, we must remove the stigma attached to this very human event; we must support those parents who bear their children and either keep them, or place them for adoption, just as our laws support those who resort to abortion as the only feasible personal alternative. To realize these goals, we as a Nation must provide better choices. How can we be less resourceful in supporting parents who decide to bear children than we are in protecting other parents' freedom not to bear unwanted children?
>
> This would require a serious national commitment to education, health and contraceptive services, and social reform.[13]

Koop's arguments are reinforced by the experience of European countries, whose laws often register disapproval of abortion, although first trimester abortion services are in most countries readily available, as are a wide range of educational, health, and contraceptive services. Further, there is little correlation between laws and abortion rates. The message is that unintended pregnancies should be avoided, and advocating abstinence as a way to achieve that goal can coexist with sex education, easy access to contraceptives, and, in some cases, far more permissive attitudes toward pre- and extramarital sexual activity than are common in the United States.[14]

The situation in the United States contrasts sharply with Europe and with the realism of the Koop report. For one thing, amid the dynamics of mobilization, pro-life and pro-choice movements become more, not less, sectarian. It would seem that, in the earlier stages of the debate, there was a consensus that at some point the fetus had moral status. Since Operation Rescue, with its blunt language, confrontation tactics, and unconditional opposition, appeared on the scene in 1985 and since the Webster case removed the viability limit on potential state regulation, advocates of both positions have become more absolute. A pro-life advocate who expresses reservations about criminalizing abortion risks excommunication for compromising essential doctrine of the inviolability of the fetus. In 1989, concerned about an apparent erosion of Catholic support, bishops cracked down on campus dissent and on Catholic politicians who took a pro-choice position.

Orthodoxy grew at the other end as well. To its opponents, pro-life quickly becomes antiabortion and, increasingly, antifeminism, while pro-choice is defined by the media as support for "a right to abortion" or even as simply "favoring abortion." A pro-choice advocate who suggests limits on abortion risks the charge of betraying the movement and lacking sympathy for women facing unwanted pregnancies. Pro-choice advocate Daniel Callahan, concerned about the growth of unnuanced arguments, asked whether it was possible to hold simultaneously two positions: first, that abortion should be left to the private choice of a woman and her doctor, and, second, "that each decision should be understood as a genuine moral choice that can be good or bad, right or wrong." The response of the leader of Catholics for a Free Choice was "absolutely," but she went on to admit that "the pro-choice movement has been inadequate in the pursuit of that message." Many feminists, she said, "have a deep seated fear of moral language" that has so often been used as a weapon against them.[15]

Matters would be easier if polarization was the result simply of oversimplification. But, in fact, for significant numbers of Americans, very important moral principles are at stake. Pro-life advocates are convinced that fetal life is human life, that human persons are involved, and that abortion is therefore a direct and intentional taking of innocent human life, an act obviously unacceptable in any community that claims to value human beings. Pro-choice advocates are committed with equal intensity and conviction to human freedom: whatever the status of the fetus, human persons become pregnant and human persons must determine their responsibilities and make their own decisions. What is more precious than human life? asks one. What is more precious than human freedom? asks the other. Pro-life advocates stress the moral weight of the private decision on abortion, but give less weight to the demands of pluralism. Their opponents take the disciplines of pluralism seriously, but tend to downplay the significance of the abortion choice itself. Each thus seems to trivialize the value held most dearly by the other side.

This language leaves almost no room for compromise, and it easily incorporates a whole range of other values and symbols, as the work of Kristin Luker has made so clear.[16] People in the middle want to affirm both life and freedom, and they want to add words like responsibility and community. Dr. Koop hopes to see programs of sex education engaging the help of families, churches, and community groups to reinvigorate "communal values" and a sense of love for one's self and for others, but the erosion of communities — and with them the disciplines that nurture a sense of responsibility — perhaps helped create this problem in the first place.

If we are to find common ground, reduce the number of unintended pregnancies, provide the services that can make both freedom and life living realities, we will have to energize movements of political and cultural renewal that might mobilize large numbers of people. For that to happen, we need to find a new set of meanings and convictions, with communities to sustain them. We will not awaken such an alternative by concern with orthodoxies, but by critical invitations to consider the costs of division, the attractions of dialogue, and the responsibilities of the common life. As with so many other issues, no common ground gets occupied perhaps because no common ground exists, perhaps because too few care for the commons.

It is perhaps the responsibility of institutions of higher education to insist on shared responsibility for the common life. If there is truth in this, then the open discussion called for by Broderick, affirmed by the Holy Cross abortion statement, but all too rarely present, represents the indispensable condition for building authentic alternatives.[17]

CATHOLICISM AND ABORTION

The abortion debate and its limits suggest the need for attention to the common life, for an ethic of responsibility as compelling as the sectarian righteousness of existing discourse. So does the debate (and its absence) in the church. There are theological issues behind the moral dispute. As Bernard Cooke pointed out in a series of lectures at Holy Cross, the Vatican Council reintroduced an understanding of the divine-human relationship that was more horizontal than vertical. God is less above the people, sending down messages through delegates, than abiding with them. The older, now resurgent position leads to a moral teaching that, however skilled its intellectual rationalization, remains in essence an articulation of truths handed down from above. We might refine our understanding of these truths and we might make them more credible by our actions, but they have no need for critical examination in terms of the human sciences or historical experience. The more communitarian view leads to an ethical method that is anchored in the scriptures and in the experience of Christians, who necessarily must be consulted in moral formulations. The vertical position generally seeks to strengthen Catholic faith and institutions, regarding the church and its spiritual and sacramental services as the ordinary means of human salvation. The more horizontal understanding fastens the vision of the church beyond itself, in the historic liberation of the human family.

The contrast relates directly to the abortion issue. In their impressive pastoral letter on peace, the bishops engaged in two forms of discourse — one within the church as it shaped its conscience in light of its faith, another in the larger community as they shared with others in forming a public moral consensus. The bishops clearly recognized the "political folly" and prospect of "mutual suicide" present in the nuclear arms race, but they admitted that "it is much less clear how we translate a 'no' to nuclear war into personal and policy choices which can move us in a new direction."[18] Recognizing the attraction of evangelical pacifism and affirming it as sometimes appropriate for individuals, the bishops themselves adopted a careful realism respectful of the complex and limited options available to decision makers and citizens. They explicitly distinguished between broad principles, such as noncombatant immunity, on which they teach with authentic authority, and the application of these principles to concrete cases, where there is room for disagreement. Their goal was to form Catholics into "a community of conscience" capable of making those applications.

On abortion, in contrast, the bishops have not made these distinctions.[19] In January 1973, the hierarchy condemned the Supreme Court's *Roe v. Wade* decision and then launched a national program of education to make church teaching known to all Catholics. In some places the bishops initiated forms of political mobilization that came close to overstepping traditional church-state boundaries. Since then they have remained committed to ending abortion, they have continued their political activism, and they have from time to time acted to discipline dissenters within the church. They have also modified their demand for an immediate and complete ban on abortion to support legislation limiting abortions, which remains open to further restrictions in the future.

Despite enormous effort, there is little evidence that the bishops have made a significant impact on public opinion within or beyond the American Catholic community.[20] In 1984, Catholics by a margin of 59–38 favored a constitutional amendment to ban abortion in all save the limit cases. In 1988 non-Hispanic Catholics favored such an amendment by 46–44, Hispanics by 51–37, an overall drop of 10 percent. In October 1988, 77 percent favored access to abortion to save the mother's life, about the same proportion as 1979; 71 percent to protect maternal health, up from 46 percent; 71 percent in the case of rape or incest, up from 57 percent; and, in the case of birth defects, 57 percent, up from 40 percent. 28 percent of Catholics even would allow abortion for economic reasons, up from 15 percent in a decade. Now white evangelical Protestants, not Catholics, are the backbone of the pro-life movement.[21]

Gaps between church teaching and Catholic opinion on birth control have been much noted; most Catholic people and priests do not agree with the fundamental teaching that every act of intercourse must be open to the transmission of life. The growing disagreement on abortion is particularly remarkable, however, in light of the fact that most Catholics, almost all in fact, agree with the basic principle on which the church rests its position: that the direct and intentional taking of innocent human life can never be justified and that abortion is the taking of life. In the past, theologians, canonists, and bishops were often unsure of the point at which life begins and "ensoulment" takes place, but for over a century the official church has held that this takes place at the moment of conception. In 1973 there was still a vigorous argument about the point at which life begins; technological advances and the breakdown of almost all efforts to define a specific moment when personhood is present have all but ended that debate. Catholics do not differ with their bishops on this point, that life begins at conception, but on its applicability to concrete cases, such as rape, incest, maternal health, and fetal deformity, and on the translation of that principle into law.[22]

At this point, three divisions emerge. First, the bishops argue that abortion can never be permitted and that civil law must make suitable provision for the protection of fetal life at all stages of development. This is the position of the Pope, it is affirmed by the hierarchy and enforced as orthodoxy on theologians and religious, and it enjoys considerable popular support. From this perspective, pro-choice is pro-abortion, a point made explicitly by Boston's Cardinal Bernard Law and by Jesuits at Georgetown who charged that recognition of a pro-choice group on that campus "would be seen as pro-abortion no matter what distinctions the university makes."[23] Those who dissent must be publicly corrected and, when appropriate, visited with ecclesiastical sanctions.[24] Advocacy of this position has a sectarian tone, with less attention paid to the persuasiveness of arguments than to the integrity of witness. It blends easily with other church teaching on sexual and private or personal morality. In both substance and method, it differs markedly from the church's social teaching. While there is room for debate about how to make peace, secure justice, or defend human rights, there can be no real debate about this issue.

The second position is that of dissent, which is greatly misunderstood. Some who are charged with dissent are far less concerned with taking the proper position than with accompanying women through the agonizing process of decision and, in that setting, wish to affirm as strongly as possible the dignity, freedom, and responsibility of the person involved. There are various forms of dissent, but almost none challenge basic pro-life principles or deny the significance and value of fetal life.[25] Most center on the limit cases, on the method used to formulate a position (particularly the exclusion of women from that process), and, most commonly, on the direct move from antiabortion teaching to public policy prescriptions. No serious person can deny that there is merit in each of these arguments. Refusing to face them, whether by exclusion or by acquiescing in the general chill on debate that exists in the church, is to deprive the church of the refinement of argument and the larger and more inclusive consensus it needs for the integrity of its witness and the effectiveness of its public actions.

Here, as happened with birth control, aquiescing in the silencing of debate is the worst contribution that scholars and schools can make to the life of the church. The church's credibility on matters of human sexuality is very low, and it reached this low in part because too many responsible leaders who knew better failed to pick up on Vatican II teaching on love and marriage, dealt with attacks on theologians only in terms of academic freedom, and willy-nilly surrendered to self-serving ecclesiastical definitions of the issues at stake. While most academics admire Archbishop Rembert Weakland for his willingness to engage women, including so-called dissenters, in conversation about the experience of pregnancy and abortion, few have vigorously protested the actions taken against him by the Holy See. Accepting prevailing definitions of dissent, even before listening to dissenters, harms both the church and the communities that the church and its scholars and schools are called to serve.

The third option, associated with Chicago's Joseph Cardinal Bernardin, is the so-called "seamless garment" or consistent ethic of life.[26] Bernardin first articulated this position when he took charge of the bishops' pro-life activities in November 1983, immediately after guiding to completion their work on nuclear arms. He was determined to overcome the tension between the peace and antiabortion movements and to present a more consistent, integrated, and positive approach than had so far characterized antiabortion activism. It is important to recognize that this position in itself rarely challenges unequivocal opposition, but instead places that condemnation of abortion in the context of a wide-ranging commitment to human life and human dignity. Church teaching and action on abortion, to be persuasive, compelling, and honest, needs to become integrated with other pro-life teaching on war and peace, capital punishment, and economic justice. And it must become more positive, with attention to the needs of women, children, and families.

The strength of this position is that it draws upon a century of rich papal and American social teaching, it insists that the church continue its active support for social justice legislation and community action, and it avoids the apparent hypocrisy associated with the image of a church that cares about life before but not after birth. Its logic has persuaded almost all bishops to lend at least rhetorical support to other church positions about which they may feel less strongly. It has undoubtedly helped broaden the base and deepen the arguments of antiabortion activism within the church and contributed to strengthening its credibility by dramatic commitments of resources to assist women with unintended pregnancies.[27] Recently, the bishops have issued very strong statements on the needs of children, and they tried to persuade voters to make children and their needs a central criterion for their 1992 political decisions.

But the seamless garment has its weaknesses. For one thing it can appear opportunistic. Attempting to overcome the stigma of single-issue politics, the Bernardin camp insists on listing all the public positions taken by the bishops in alphabetical order; conveniently, abortion is usually listed first. When pro-life activists asks about priorities, seamless garment people often respond by insisting on the whole package. That may seem to be a convenient way of finessing the moral demands made by a particular issue, and it offers little guidance to people who often must choose between parties and candidates who support many peace and justice positions, but affirm free choice on abortion, and others who are in the reverse position.

When New York's John Cardinal O'Connor, for example, made his single-issue assaults on Governor Mario Cuomo and vice presidential candidate Geraldine Ferraro, in 1984, the multi-issue response seemed to lack both moral and political force. Once again, in the absence of a more compelling commitment to citizenship and the common good, the judicious balancing act of conflicting claims ends up seeming simply mushy and irrelevant or, worse, a way to finesse the tensions between liberal Catholics and their non-Catholic pro-choice associates. Thus the dilemma of Mario Cuomo.

The Bernardin position rests on an ethic of broad civic responsibility, and as such it sometimes seems to blur the church's authority by leaving room for dialogue about concrete cases. It also depends in part upon a deeper emotional commitment to the common good and a deeper sense of responsibility for the common life than most Catholics and most Americans seem to feel. The single-issue emphasis, in contrast, is essentially sectarian, concerned with validating church principles, integrating the claims of discipleship and citizenship, setting boundaries to community life, and making demands on Catholics, with less concern to in fact translate universal principles into effective action. The Bernardin position, resting on the assumptions of American pluralism, wrestles with the obviously conflicting demands of discipleship and citizenship, recognizes that they involve two different, and often conflicting, forms of discourse.

It is the position that fits integrally into the Catholic college and university's function of bridging the gaps between faith and culture, church and society, most importantly by organizing and structuring systematic reflection on such matters. That is what the open discussions called for by Broderick and the abortion statement are about: if they don't happen here, they will never happen in the church. But for them to happen, we need conversation partners, and we need—once again, right here, among us— authentic commitment to the common life of the church and society.

ABORTION AND CATHOLIC HIGHER EDUCATION

We have seen that, amid the crosscurrents of religious and cultural changes washing across the church, colleges and universities share in the ferment of what Andrew Greeley calls "do it yourself Catholicism." As in the church, on campus there are advocates of both subcultural restorationism, who want the schools to be visibly and structurally Catholic, and evangelical radicalism, who think it would be nice if they were recognizably Christian. Some, still pursuing full membership in American academic life, are comfortable with the diversity and secularity that accompany academic professionalization. Here, as elsewhere, the natural American dynamics confine religion to personal choice and private life, to chapel and voluntary religious associations, with little bite on the daily work or public life of the institution. Many schools, Holy Cross among them, continue to struggle to be in the fullest sense both institutions of higher learning and in some sense authentically Catholic. And this is no easy matter, as is made clear by persisting conflicts over academic freedom, ecclesiastical authority, and theological teaching.[28] As these conflicts show, ambiguity still exists about the relationship between those two terms: Catholic and university (or college).

What, after all, does it mean to refer to these institutions as Catholic? Does it mean that they are part of the institutional church? When Bernard Cardinal Law denounced Boston College for hosting a talk by Planned Parenthood's Fay Wattleton and when Washington's Cardinal James Hickey said that Georgetown's recognition to a pro-choice group was "inconsistent with the aim of an institution of higher learning that has a Catholic identity," they reflected this position, as do almost all the documents defining recognition of student groups.[29]

According to Pope John Paul II's *Ex Corde Ecclesiae*, all Catholic institutions should be marked by theological reflection and "an institutional commitment" to serve the church and the human family, but also by "a Christian inspiration not only of individuals but of the university community as such" and by "fidelity to the Christian message as it comes to us through the Church."[30] American Catholic academics have naturally wished to avoid conflict with the hierarchy, as we have seen; when challenged, they adopt a pragmatic approach, pointing to who they are and what they do. But, in recent years, they have also insisted that their accountability to the hierarchy is voluntary and conditioned by their nature as academic institutions. In short, the institution will call itself Catholic, but, like most individuals, it will more or less decide what it will say and do to express that identity.

For a variety of reasons, I think it better to avoid attaching the word Catholic to the word college. The combination inevitably creates confusion about institutional relationships that inhibits rather than encourages projects that forward its central function — building bridges between faith and culture. There are other ways in which the word Catholic can be understood. After Vatican II, the church speaks of itself first of all as a community, a people, who together constitute the very presence of Christ at any particular time and place. In that sense, these institutions have arisen from the church, they continue to draw students, administrators, trustees, parents, benefactors, and many faculty from that church, and they almost always profess a commitment to serve that church. This service is conditioned by their nature as academic institutions: they do teaching and research and provide a place where the church can do its thinking. To the extent that service is a vital part of the college or university, it is assisting in forwarding the mission of the church as servant to the larger human family.

And how does such an institution serve the church on abortion? The Jesuit task force mentioned earlier suggested that our schools hope to create an environment in which students (and the rest of us) can gather the information and develop the skills to make sound ethical judgements. But, they admitted, "too often Catholic colleges have shied away from dialogue, debate, discussion and educational forums on controversial issues" and especially on issues related to sexuality. They, their students, and their alumni have paid a price for avoiding those subjects, and so has the church. But "dialogue is the best way for a Catholic college to promote pro-life positions and help pro-choice advocates see and hopefully come to believe that pro-life is the better way." The authors must deal with the fact that authentic dialogue requires self-criticism and a willingness to admit the possibility of error, which is why it is so threatening. They continue: "Critical inquiry can help foster a respect for those with whom one may be in profound disagreement." So dialogue, premised on mutual respect, seriousness of purpose, and concern for the common life of school, church, and society, remains the most basic responsibility of the Catholic college and university in dealing with abortion.

This leaves us with three questions in need of further examination.

First, the Catholic problem. The college or university that wishes to serve the Catholic community as an academic institution must continually examine the role of other persons and communities both on campus and beyond, especially those others who truly disagree. Pluralism as a theological issue is a question of how to think about Catholic Christianity in a world in which others live, and those others are equally members of the human family and equally loved by God. In light of the tragedies of this century, for all of which the church somehow shares responsibility, how are we to think of mission, evangelization, education and the intellectual life? Should we think in terms of conversion or toleration or dialogue? And do we who care for the church take seriously enough the shift to dialogue, with all it implies about our own commitment, the presence of God outside the church, the need to be open to change, the discipline of mutual respect and shared responsibility? And, if dialogue is the word, is a community Catholic, is a college or university Catholic, can it serve the community of faith, if it exists apart from rather than within the larger, pluralistic community? But how can any organization—church or college—retain its identity as Catholic if the boundaries between faith and reason, between the full participants in a Catholic institution and the others, are removed or become blurred? Is the only answer a chronic contest between boundaries set by authority and a purely voluntarist democratization of discipleship? There are answers to such questions, I think, but they will require harder thought than has taken place so far.[31]

Second, the liberal arts problem. Do we invite one another to dialogue about ethical and moral issues among people of authentic conviction? Would one want a group committed to peace who would only discuss peace and not try to make it? In the larger community, there are people of passionate intensity at both ends of the abortion debate and a wishy-washy middle, which includes many of us most of the time, who would like them both to be quiet. The middle's problem is not intellectual but emotional, not logical but symbolic; it has too little care for or commitment to the common good. An energetic middle at Georgetown or Holy Cross would not need to ban pro-choicers or belittle pro-lifers, but could hope to enlist the energies of both in a shared effort to renew our society and culture so that ordinary and free men and women could build lives and a common life worth living. The danger at Holy Cross is to think that the alternative to pro-life and pro-choice fundamentalism is a soft and sentimental commitment to openness, critical learning, and diversity, which usually means the reservation of decision and postponement of commitment. "How then are we to live?" is the thematic question for a new first-year program at Holy Cross. It is a question answered for most people within communities of meaning and value, including churches and social movements. It requires people who speak within and from such communities and who speak with passion and intensity about belief, meaning, and action. In this setting, communities of the committed become resources for the debate, not to be marginalized, as religious and social idealists were for so long at Holy Cross, nor excluded, as with the religiously or politically unorthodox.

It may be hard for Holy Cross alumni and trustees to accept pro-choice advocates as full members of the community. But is it any easier for a professionalized and specialized faculty to allow religion, serious religion, a place at the table where academics gather? One wonders. A 1992 letter writer in the *New York Times* caught the problem: "Editorial writers on right and left call for a return to religion," this person wrote. "Well, Iran has returned to religious values: intolerance, cruelty, discrimination, hatred, torture, murder and mayhem. I thank God no one takes religion seriously in America."[32]

Third, both the political and the Catholic argument converge around the theme of open and honest dialogue. From thirty years of academic experience, I would argue that almost nothing is more celebrated in words and less present in fact than open conversation about serious issues on our campuses. If it were not for student initiatives, there would have been at Holy Cross almost no attention to the Gulf War, only a little more to the death of the Jesuits in El Salvador, and none to abortion. The mission statement commits us to an ongoing conversation as essential to our work as scholars and teachers. Making those conversations happen is now the challenge. Will trustees and administrators take that seriously? Will we? Only, I suspect, if we scholars and teachers, Catholics and others, break out of our largely self-imposed isolation and locate the horizon of our work, personally and collectively, out there in the struggles of women and men for life and for freedom. In that setting, and that setting alone, will we find the inspiration to share responsibility for abortion and the host of issues in which it is embedded.[33]

CHAPTER 9

Catholics as Intellectuals

MAKING SENSE OF AMBIVALENCE

I once gave an informal talk about the relationship between the church and the academic vocation to a group of Catholic graduate students. All of them had experienced the conflict between a church that at times seems to have little use for independent, critical thinkers and an academic community with little respect for religion or religious people. Several spoke of the ambivalence they felt about the church: Catholic faith was woven into the very fabric of their lives, yet they often felt distanced from the church as they found it, distanced enough to wonder if they were really Catholics.

I tried to explain that their difficulty in integrating their faith with their passionate commitment to their work was a common lay Catholic experience. Many voices in the church would tell them, as they tell all laypeople, that ambivalence is their fault, that it results from the weakness of their faith. Academic colleagues, even the professed Christians among them, like coworkers everywhere, would probably tell them they were taking religion too seriously. Pastors and fervent believers, convinced that a vast chasm divides the church and the secular world, can only regard commitments and deep engagements outside the religious sphere as disloyal and spiritually dangerous. Persons deeply invested in worldly activities, for their part, necessarily view powerful convictions rooted in particular faith communities as sectarian, divisive, and intellectually indefensible.

So religious people always feel a bit torn—Catholics a bit more because of their history. Despite its sacramental heritage, modern Catholicism in practice assigned religious value only to specifically religious activities, an umbrella large enough to embrace intimate relationships and family values, but not so-called "secular" activities, like politics or work. The Americanists, or some at least, thought that God was active outside the church, so that economic progress and social mobility might be liberating steps toward fuller participation in the very life of God. But the Americanists were

157

defeated and their message about meaning in work was lost, and with it the possibility of giving religious meaning to the experience of family and group progress. Religion was confined to church and private life, and American Catholicism never developed an effective theology or spirituality of work, of citizenship, or of the intellectual life. Popes, like John XXIII, and a few theologians occasionally noted with regret the deep gap between faith and professional life, but almost everyone blamed "secularism" and its devilish advocates, and almost no one suggested that Catholic activities and ideologies might also have something to do with the problem.

At one level, as Americanists from Isaac Hecker to John Courtney Murray understood, it is a problem of the laity. For some the church is most the church when people are gathered *as* the church, most often *at* church. Once that was because of clericalism; later it was the altogether natural product of the need to organize one's own people because of competitive pressures from dissenters, other churches, or secular alternatives. But of course the church is also *the church* — the Body of Christ and the people of God — all the time, including that great block of time when people are not *in* church. Thus work, including intellectual work, might well be itself a form of piety.

In the past, including the recent past, as William Leahy argues persuasively, Catholic colleges and universities failed to achieve intellectual distinction in part because of the pervasive localism of Catholic institutional and clerical life and the resulting subordination of academic to pastoral considerations that came with the dominant role of the founding religious groups. Separate incorporation, with its remarkable trust in lay leadership, represented an instinctive realization that the path to excellence required formal and structural affirmation of those elements of life that exist apart from and independent of the formal church. Perhaps that is what Cardinal Newman meant when he pleaded: "You will be doing the greatest possible benefit to the Catholic cause all over the world if you succeed in making the university a middle station at which the clergy and laity can meet, so as to learn to understand and to yield to each other and from which, as from common ground, they may act together in unison upon an age which is running headlong into infidelity."[1] If we could take clergy and laity here as metaphors pointing toward the now separate spheres of religion and secular life — a separation inside each of us and in our institutions — Newman's plea points us toward an understanding of the Catholic vocation focused, as we are told by Vatican II that it should, on "the joys and hopes of the men and women of this age."

The split between faith and work, and the resulting ambivalence, still infects Catholic institutions. Father Donald Monan, S.J., president of

Boston College, in a speech to the International Federation of Catholic Universities in Toulouse in 1991, noted the widespread satisfaction with improvements in academic quality and managerial effectiveness in U.S. Catholic colleges and universities and the equally widespread uneasiness about Catholic identity. This "dualistic view" made the ordinary work of research, teaching, and administering, excellent or otherwise, altogether distinct from and irrelevant to whatever it is that makes the Catholic university Catholic. "The professional excellence we have achieved is too often seen as, at best, irrelevant to our Catholic character, at worst, at odds with it." Even the much vaunted interdisciplinary work with theology, by suggesting that it is only through contact with theology that the other disciplines make contact with the schools' specifically Catholic mission, serves to "further marginalize the role of disinterested pursuit of academic or managerial excellence."[2]

So, apparently there is no real role in shaping "the distinctively Catholic character of the university for the large majority of our faculty, and especially our non-Catholic faculty, in their fundamental commitment to research and scholarship and teaching in specialized academic disciplines." This point Monan thought crucial for the "institutional culture" of Catholic universities. "If the bulk of the finest scholarship is being conducted by faculty who regard themselves, or are regarded by church figures, as marginal to the Catholic character of the university, the resulting fragility becomes a genuine peril."

Yet, Monan noted, Vatican II had affirmed human work as a share in God's ongoing creation and warned against the separation of religion from professional activity. In its "Pastoral Constitution on the Church and the Modern World," according to Monan, the Council made "a mighty act of faith—in the secular, human world as the arena of God's unceasing activity." So it should be possible to think of "rigorous professionalism as religiously meaningful—to consider a university meaningfully Catholic, precisely in its culturally autonomous endeavors." But, Monan admitted, sharing with and deepening among the faculty (one might add even among the Catholic faculty, perhaps even among members of sponsoring religious communities) "an incarnational view that transcends the simplistic dichotomy of sacred and secular" is an imposing challenge. Somehow, Monan believes, all who work together should come to see that their "apparently secular endeavors that constitute the lifeblood of university activities are valued more, not less," because the school is Catholic.

At first glance this seems a peculiarly lay problem, but it is not. It is a problem for any person of faith who undertakes serious work outside Catholic institutional boundaries. Evidence for this comes from another

Boston College source. In June 1991, a group of Jesuit scholars gathered there to discuss the intellectual apostolate of the Society of Jesus, but without the usual immediate reference to Jesuit institutions. Each participant was asked to name a key problem that defined his current research project, how that project reflected his larger intellectual interests, and how it engaged the Society. At the end of the first day, a participant reported: "we were able to recognize that we spent a significant amount of time talking to one another about things that are often left unspoken." The group's enthusiasm about the fact of conversation about their work might shock non-Jesuits, who think they spend their time doing just this. But the most positive feature of this small conference was "the very fact that these questions" about their basic research interests "were raised and taken seriously."[3]

That uncovered a deeper problem, for "neither our home institutions nor individual disciplinary commitments comprise fully coherent frameworks within which we can articulate our intellectual commitment as Jesuit scholars." The answer was conversation with other Jesuits, but they were afraid that this would end with their individual work as scholars being submerged within Jesuit structures. In short, there was a real conflict between Jesuit institutional commitments, with their need for Jesuits to influence and in most cases lead their colleges and universities, and the commitment of some Jesuits to scholarship. "We wish to recreate the Jesuit intellectual apostolate," they concluded, but "a clearly delineated intellectual apostolate . . . is irreducible to institutional commitments." In short, Jesuit scholars have the same unmet need to relate their work to their larger intellectual interests and personal commitments as do laypeople.

So Monan's challenge to relate faith and work, even in an institutional setting influenced by people of faith, presses faculty and administrators, lay or religious. It is a challenge that the church is dealing with in other settings. Contemporary pastoral theology encourages people — married people, poor people, people of all sorts — to search for God in their everyday experience. There is no reason why middle-class people, including professors and other academic personnel, cannot do the same. And if married people come to think about God as the love they experience and if poor people come to locate God in the experience of overcoming oppression and injustice, perhaps middle-class Christians will find God in their experience of ambivalence, their often unacknowledged care for their Catholic heritage and their often unspoken love for their work and for their country. Contrary to the integrism of what my friend called "religious exclusivists" and "secular exclusivists," it is once again a case of "inclusive conversationalism" — both/and, not either/or.

In perhaps the most widely quoted passage in the literature of African-Americans, the great W.E.B. DuBois once wrote: "One ever feels his two-ness, an American, a negro; two souls, two thoughts, two unreconciled strivings; two warring ideals in one dark body, whose dogged strength alone keeps it from being torn asunder." Later he told his fellow citizens: "This is as much our country as yours, and as much the world's as ours. We Americans, black and white, are the servants of all mankind and minister to a greater, fairer heaven." The American dilemma—and tragedy—is our failure to grasp that reconciliation and make our own the Americanism that DuBois, Martin Luther King, and other of our African-American prophets called us to, an Americanism built on the struggle for integrity and responsibility. For people of serious religious faith in this American land, "two-ness, two unreconciled strivings" may always mark their vocation.[4]

VATICAN II AND INTELLECTUAL LIFE

The Catholic church has only rarely been a comfortable home for intellectuals. In the post-Reformation church, scholars were expected to provide ammunition for religious wars, and the critical, imaginative temperament of artists and intellectuals seemed dangerous, even disloyal. Enlightenment rationality, whether in the guise of scientific method or historical criticism, seemed even more dangerous. In the nineteenth century, ultramontane Catholicism reduced scholarship to apologetics and drove restless spirits out of the church or into a sort of Catholic underground. More common than such frustrated dissenters were institutional intellectuals who subordinated truth to ecclesiastical power. The world crises of the twentieth century, from World War I to the Cold War, eventually undermined the legitimacy of Catholicism's anti-modernist ideology, but its organizational legacy of surveillance and fear remained intact until Vatican II.

At the Council, institutional controls over Catholic intellectual life appeared to collapse. The Council's deliberations encouraged self-criticism on such subjects as church-state separation, religious liberty, relations among Christians and with non-Christian religions, anti-Semitism, and the misuse of power by such agencies as the Congregation on the Inquisition, or the Holy Office, delicately renamed the Congregation on the Doctrine of the Faith. Honesty, openness, and dialogue replaced loyalty, solidarity, and orthodoxy as key values. When they were violated, as they were very publicly several times in the United States during and after the Council, there was usually a public outcry. Suddenly, the words Catholic and intellectual did not automatically seem a contradiction.

In the United States, a growing number of young Catholics followed intellectual careers. Many joined the faculties of non-Catholic colleges and universities, and, as we have seen, Catholic higher education pursued academic excellence with almost unseemly enthusiasm. As church leaders called for renewal based on personal and communal reconsideration of Christian commitment, significant efforts were made to improve the intellectual level of Catholic life. Bishops provided opportunities for serious continuing education for their priests. They sent religious educators and other specialized personnel to summer schools and training institutes. They and the superiors of religious orders relocated many seminaries and houses for religious formation near university centers. Despite Pope Paul VI's public worries about overly venturesome speculation, it seemed that intellectuals had finally found a secure place with the Roman Catholic church.

Yet it was less secure than it appeared. There were at least three problems that should have been self-evident.

First, there were dangers in the methods of historical criticism informing much popularization of Vatican II reforms, which seemingly moved Catholicism away from a nonhistorical orthodoxy toward a more flexible and adaptive understanding of faith and life. The history of Protestant theology, Scripture studies, and ethics over the previous century forecast the way in which modern consciousness could erode the historical foundations of Christian faith and render problematic the whole structure of institutional Catholicism. Like nineteenth-century Protestant advocates of historical criticism or Darwinian science, Catholic reformers were not always anxious to spell out the full implications of their methods.

This was evident, to take only one example, in Thomas Sheehan's iconoclastic essay on "The End of Catholicism," published in 1984 before a wide academic and literary audience in the *New York Review of Books*.[5] A philosopher of Catholic background, an admirer of Heidegger and Rahner, and an apparently appreciative observer of post–Vatican II "liberal" scholarship, Sheehan argued that the best contemporary Catholic theologians had undermined the foundational doctrine of the Resurrection and that it was now time to acknowledge that fact. Sheehan rather innocently followed where the truth seemed to lead—to a religionless Christianity of the type advocated some years earlier by secular theology and echoing liberal Protestantism of the nineteenth century.

Although Sheehan's views were sharply challenged by many of those he claimed to be interpreting, one suspects that not a few Catholic intellectuals, affected as much by the spirit of the times as by Sheehan's precise argument, assumed with him that this was the logical outcome of the Council's dispensation. In this, ironically, they were in agreement with Catholic reactionaries, such as the Thomistic philosophers in Catholics United for the Faith and some of the diehards in the Vatican curia. But neither the latter nor the pope and the bishops could be expected to accept such a prescription lying down. Indeed, liberal scholars failed to understand the political implications of their position: threatening as it was to institutional church interests, it could only be upheld if there were organized and successful efforts to influence centers of power within the ecclesiastical organization. In the postconciliar period, as in the nineteenth century, conservatives better understood this fairly obvious truth. Under their influence Pope Paul VI in his later days lashed out at liberal scholarship and his successor launched a counterattack that divided the scholarly community, put theological renewal on the defensive, and legitimated some extremely conservative ecclesiastical policies. Amid this counterrevolution came the series of efforts to regain control over Catholic colleges and universities that climaxed with *Ex Corde Ecclesiae.* None of this happened by accident. There is a politics of Catholic intellectual life.

Second, the post–Vatican II easing, perhaps temporarily, of repression within the church was widely believed to open the door to a more intelligent understanding of Christian faith among the people of God. The call to renewal was in part at least a summons to responsibility, inviting Catholics to think about what they believed, to renew their personal commitment to Christ and the church, and to examine themselves, their church, and their world on the basis of that commitment. This had to be, at least in part, a critical intellectual project.

In the United States, initial renewal strategies following Vatican II often involved a combination of academic training for church personnel and "adult education" for the laity. Again, familiarity with Protestant history might have enabled reformers to anticipate that not everyone would jump at the chance to learn, even in domesticated doses, about historical criticism of the Bible, symbolic interpretations of doctrine, or the social and cultural contextualization of morality. In fact, that history suggests that, when intellectuals take charge of the interpretation of Scripture and ministers become convinced of the need to reinterpret doctrine and morality, the people might turn to the Bible and rely on their own experience to understand it, in what Nathan Hatch has called a "democratic hermeneutic."[6]

Charismatic renewal, scriptural and a peculiarly Catholic doctrinal fundamentalism, and stubborn, unreflective loyalty to "traditional morality" have plagued modernizing reformers, echoing previous Protestant experiences in the United States and raising within the Catholic church the chronic American problem of anti-intellectualism, more accurately described as the alienation of intellectuals from popular support. Theologians might claim to be transferring their loyalty from the institutional church to the people of God, but more than one has been shocked, if not repulsed, by the experience that at least some of God's people are less than appreciative of their work. While Catholic theologians, usually quite removed from pastoral care, worry about fundamentalisms, that is probably less of a problem than the wider currents of evangelicalism that mark all American Christianity. If the Catholic intellectual feels caught between doctrinaire ecclesiastical authorities and a fluid, romantic religious populism, the feeling reflects the social reality. Add to the mix the sharp drop in religious vocations and the bishop-led retreat of seminary education from university centers, and the gap between theology after "the critical turn" and popular piety becomes enormous.

The tension between theology and pastoral ministry exists on campus as well. Cardinal Bernardin told campus ministry personnel in 1989 that the bishops understood the challenges they confronted in dealing with a great diversity of religious experience and interests on campus. Unable to draw on "the general social support" once available in parishes and ethnic groups, people were religiously "on their own" and the church had to respond by helping them develop their inner spiritual resources. A sensitive and appreciative pastoral letter on campus ministry was published by the bishops that same year.[7] Still, one well-informed observer notes that campus ministry does a fine job with liturgy, community building, and pastoral counselling, but he gives them much lower marks for communicating the idea that Catholicism makes intellectual claims. Leaders of campus ministry acknowledge that young people usually do not see much connection between their intellectual and spiritual lives. And on Catholic campuses they rank strained relations with theology or religious studies departments, which often look upon pastoral ministers as second-class citizens within the university, as among their biggest problems.[8]

Third, intellectuals—freed from roles defined by the church—had to relocate themselves. Formerly, most had been clerics; now many were laypeople, including laywomen, for whom there was no obvious ecclesiastical home. They naturally located in the university, contributing enormously to the improved quality of undergraduate instruction. But they could as easily become captive of the university as their predecessors may have been of the institutional church. This danger is particularly acute because knowledge has become so specialized, professionalized, and collaborative. The obvious example would be the Catholic sociologists who, having welcomed the recognition accorded to the discipline of sociology in Catholic institutions, no longer felt the need for their own organization. They replaced one set of institutional relationships with another, assuming both different opportunities and constraints. From the point of view of Catholic intellectual life, such a step suggested that Catholics did not need to engage each other in reflection on the relationship between faith and scholarly work; religion, for sociologists as for physicians and bricklayers, was a matter for church and family. And, increasingly, it seemed that it made little difference whether that sociologist worked in a Catholic or non-Catholic institution. The supposed secularization of the schools had its counterpart in the apparent secularization of scholarship. In the absence of organization and strategy, most would accommodate to the segmentation of modern academic culture; ambivalence would hardly be noticed, save in the test cases when the church spoke clearly, as on abortion. Serious Christian and Catholic scholarship would arise only from individual initiatives, and for persons ambivalence is built in.

THEOLOGY AND RELIGIOUS STUDIES

When American Protestant theology left the university, it made its home in the seminaries. Until very recently, that was also the exclusive home of Catholic theology. Father Hesburgh regularly tells Vatican authorities that theology was forced out of the universities and into seminaries during the French Revolution and as a result lost its public influence.[9] In 1966 Andrew Greeley said it was an "iron rule" that, at a Catholic college or university, chemistry would be the strongest department, theology the weakest.[10] Now, however, just as Catholic schools are claiming their place as true universities, they are also building up strong departments of theology. A 1977 report found that, of 103 Catholic colleges and universities reporting, 61 had religious studies departments and 37 had departments of theology. In a later study of 154 schools, all had departments, 140 offered a major, 36 offered graduate degrees, and 88 played a role in training deacons or lay ministers. In 1977, 11 schools required one course in religion, 42 required two, and 25 required three or four (the rest did not report). While most said that their requirement did not specify a course in the Roman Catholic tradition, they felt that the courses they did offer adequately addressed Catholic theological teaching. Half the schools reported that their administration emphasized the central role of their department in maintaining institutional identity; 51 of 96 said that their budgets compared favorably with those of other departments. The majority felt that in fact their department should not have special responsibility for the Catholic character of the institution. In 56 schools, a little more than half, 90 percent or more of the department staff were Catholics, but less than half that number were priests or religious. [11]

This strong commitment to theological and religious studies presumably reflects attentiveness to Catholic identity and enhances the church's ability to influence culture, as *Ex Corde Ecclesiae* demands. Yet, oddly, many theologians are critical of the policies governing university theology, and Rome, in attempting to assert control over the teaching of Catholic theology, places the whole enterprise in jeopardy.

How can one account for this paradox? For one thing, church authorities think that theologians are supposed to carry out what the bishops call the "principal task" of the Catholic university: "to make theology relevant to all human knowledge and all human knowledge relevant to theology." In practice, however, these departments labor under multiple and often conflicting assignments. They are supposed to provide access to Catholic theology, establish theology as a respectable academic discipline, offer an intellectually coherent approach to fundamental religious and moral questions, encourage diversity by offering courses on world religions, and engage in various forms of interdisciplinary research and teaching. When they attempt to meet the need of today's students for an honest examination of fundamental religious and moral questions, they are attacked by Catholic conservatives; when they try to provide opportunities for serious study of Catholic history, doctrine, and moral teaching, they get hit from the other side for "privileging" Catholicism.

In addition, theology had no sooner found a home in the Catholic university than it was challenged by the more inclusive and, apparently, academically respectable and popular, religious studies. As Philip Gleason noted, new methods of studying religion brought an "academic neutralization" of the older "sacred theology." Major battles took place over the naming of departments theology, religious studies, or, in some cases, theology and religious studies. But, even when religious studies lost out to theology, the latter became an academic subject "just like any other subject in the sense that competence to teach it had nothing to do with the personal religious commitment of the teacher."[12] So one battle was between theology and religious studies, another was between advocates of Catholic theology (understood as integrally related to the faith of the church) and those who placed the priority on securing theology's academic credentials.

Surely, from the outside, academic religion seems remarkably diverse. Professors might join one or more of the broad organizations for teacher-scholars in religion (in addition to organizations in their subspecialty, such as biblical studies or ethics):

- The Catholic Theological Society of America, where priests and seminary professors have gradually shared control with laypeople and women. Its journal, *Theological Studies*, is the most prestigious among professors in Catholic institutions.
- The somewhat eclectic, definitely ecumenical, but Catholic-dominated College Theology Society, an interdisciplinary environment friendly to laypeople, women, and undergraduate teachers. Here theologians rub shoulders with philosophers, historians, and social scientists, with a sense of good fellowship amid "blurred genres" that in fact characterizes most departments most of the time.
- The wildly diverse American Academy of Religion, a vast and prosperous umbrella organization for everyone with even the dimmest interest in things religious. In 1993, 7,200 people attended the AAR convention to listen in on 1,500 panels listed in a 348-page catalogue.[13]

At most schools the faculty are so busy offering core courses and fending off critics that they have little time for intramural disputes. Yet the gaps are very real. A recent AAR study indicated that scholars of religion find their discipline "marked above all by flux" with a marked diversity of subject matter and methods: "Nearly all aspire to study plural traditions pluralistically." Graduate study in particular is seen as "troubled and unsatisfactory." Research is overly specialized, and students are compelled to concentrate too heavily in their specialized subfield, resulting in ever greater "Balkanization" of the discipline and leaving graduates unprepared to teach popular courses for undergraduates.

Faculty in non-Catholic research universities, where many of the professors at Catholic schools are trained, express serious disdain for theology, which they still regard as confessional, a subject appropriate for seminaries but not universities. Rejecting "essentialist" understandings of religion, they all but unanimously identify with religious studies. Faculty in private and church-related schools are more sympathetic to theology and often speak of themselves as related to both religious studies and theological studies, but even there many favor an approach to religious studies modeled on the sciences, being descriptive and explanatory, except in ethics, where moral advocacy is not only allowed but encouraged. "In most segments of American higher education," Ray Hart concluded, " 'religious studies' is a largely unambiguous and unproblematic designator referring to the scholarly neutral and non-advocative study of multiple religious traditions.

'Theological studies' as a term, is intrinsically ambiguous and comprises an academic enterprise about which many are ambivalent and to which some are hostile." Whatever and however done, most believe that it privileges Christianity or at least western categories for interpreting religion.[14] That is why George Marsden refers to the "normatively non-Christian stance among practicioners of religious studies."[15]

But theology has its defenders in secular schools. William Scott Green of the University of Rochester, editor of the *Journal of the American Academy of Religion,* agrees that the "naturalistic paradigm," with its denial of theology, dominates the academy. Most professors think that "religion should be taught in the university, theology in the seminary." As one student told him: "If theologians came to the academy's party, they would sit in a corner by themselves, talk only to one another, and have nothing to say to anyone else." So one can complete a religion degree without reading Barth, Bonhoeffer, or Tillich, even Augustine and Aquinas. Yet, as Green sees it, theology — the intellectual elaboration of a religion, "thinking emerging from within the religion itself" — is weakened when confined to a community of assent, so for its own sake it needs life in the university. As for students, Green believes that they should study theology for three reasons: so they will recognize it when they see it, because it is a natural part of religion and it misrepresents the subject to exclude it, and because otherwise religion may appear to students as only private and parochial, a kind of curiosity, lacking intellectual content.[16]

Green seems to be an exception; academic religion is usually hostile to theology as traditionally understood. Theologians in general do not return the animosity of the religious studies professors, but a growing number of Catholic theologians are worried. They are especially disturbed by the tendency of Catholic schools to hire faculty from the secular universities and interdenominational seminaries. Graduates of these institutions, they claim, even when they do not question theology as an academic discipline, have little knowledge of "the Catholic tradition," classical languages, patristics, church history, and Christian theology before — and even after — the Reformation. Some of these critics even claim that methodological pluralism, ecumenical latitudinarianism, and hospitality to fads, all of which new professors bring from graduate school, make systematic theology all but impossible. So Catholic theologians — those scholars operating from a position of faith and commitment — feel beleaguered, even on many Catholic campuses. It is a setting hospitable to arguments about secularization and the need to reaffirm Catholic identity.[17]

Still, the evidence is clear that Catholic theology still dominates the teaching of religion at most Catholic schools. Faculty are well trained, conversant with modern thought, and critically engaged with the larger church. For over a century, religious instruction on campus was largely catechetical. When theology did appear before Vatican II, it was intended to affirm and inspire the lay apostolate. In the last generation, theology has made the critical turn; it is now seeking critical reflection on faith. In addition, departments and the 1,500 or so people who compose the body of Catholic theologians are more lay, more professional in research and teaching, and more democratic in governance. Finally, theology, like other disciplines, is passing through a "hermenutical explosion" as new voices — African-American, feminist, environmentalist, liberationist — bring new resources and an altogether new diversity to the enterprise.[18]

The dark side is that, despite two decades or more of hard work to professionalize religious and theological studies, there remains a vast chasm separating Catholic religious scholarship from the academic mainstream. A clue to the problem is found in the AAR study's report on the journals most valued by academics in religious and theological studies. When major university professors were asked to list the five most important journals in their field, *Theological Studies* does not make the top 15, while it is in first place among professors in Catholic schools. *The Journal of the American Academy of Religion,* tops among the secular school faculty, does not make the Catholic list.[19]

PUBLIC THEOLOGY

This distance between Catholic theologians and the mainstream of religious studies may not worry advocates of stronger Catholic theology if their goal is simply to make Catholics more Catholic. But it is disturbing to those who hoped that Catholic teaching could have an impact on American culture and, within the academy, on interdisciplinary research and teaching. The same is true of the professionalization of scholarship which requires Catholic academics to leave their religion at home. In the past, the phrase "Catholic intellectual," according to historian James Turner, "if not downright oxymoronic to non-Catholics, connoted a strong person who read Thomas Aquinas and papal encyclicals while harboring deep suspicions of Sigmund Freud and John Locke. This character might be bright, even interesting as a curiosity, but certainly was not someone to engage in debate about contemporary sociology or recent literary criticism." Vatican II may have "exploded the cosy nest within which this odd bird was hatched," Turner continued, in the essay discussed in chapter 6, but from the debris few recognizable Catholic intellectuals, as distinct from intellectuals who happen to be Catholic, have arisen.

Nor has a lively intellectual life developed among Catholics. Turner, a friend of the Catholic university, is not surprised, because "Catholic universities have rarely fostered scholarship that plunges Catholicism into the pluralistic intellectual life of our times . . . and Catholic colleges have seldom encouraged their students to think seriously and flexibly about the relationship of their faith to the novels they are reading or the chemistry they are studying." But none of this is inevitable: "No Christian people has a richer intellectual tradition. But to activate that tradition in the lives of Catholics, to fulfill its mission to the church, Catholic higher education needs to make a dual move: back to the intellectual resources of Catholicism and out into the larger world of modern knowledge, so as to bring each to bear upon the other."[20]

Turner is not the only friendly critic. In 1991 Michael Lacey, director of American Programs at the Woodrow Wilson International Center for Scholars, gave similar bad news directly to Catholic theologians. Theology in general, not just Catholic theology, enjoys "very little standing at all in this vast scholarly enterprise" of American higher education, Lacey reported. "Theology is simply absent from the ongoing discussions and arguments that drive the disciplines to their topmost level. . . . Beyond the reservation, if I can put it that way, you can generally expect to find that your subject is regarded at best as part of the maintenance machinery of a sectarian subculture, and thus of no great general interest."[21]

To those who were worried that the schools were becoming too much like others, Lacey reminded them that those "other" schools now sustain the most powerful, difficult, and fruitful inquiry in the world, whereas Catholic institutions had still not entered the first rank of academic achievement. Instead, they appeared to remain part of "a clerically led, denominational subculture, perceived by outsiders and by many insiders as less concerned with the increase of knowledge than the maintenance of tradition and the preservation of the faith." Those might be valid objectives, but Lacey questioned whether they could be achieved "without more confident address to the challenge of free inquiry in all the modern arts and sciences," and on this issue he admitted to doubts.

Lacey noted with regret the absence of any formal organization of Catholic intellectuals and academics. Did that mean that they, like some of their clergymen, perceive no relationship between the life of inquiry and their ecclesial life, Lacey asked? Equally important, continuing attacks by Catholic theologians on non-Catholic intellectuals and some Catholics, as secularists, reinforced the suspicion that for Catholic scholars, "their loyalty to the church is stronger than their commitment to the life of the mind." Outsiders suspected that Catholic intellectuals did not "really understand the depth and intensity of the struggle that modern secular scholarship at its best has been engaged in, the heroic side of it, and just how hard won its victories have been." Lacey feared that "a certain element of strenuousness is felt to be missing in Catholic intellectual life, and outsiders suspect that rather than wrestling with the real demons of modernity, too often Catholics have been wrestling with strawmen, under the approving gaze of ecclesiastical superiors."

This is doubly unfortunate, both Turner and Lacey believe, because they detect a new openness to religion among some academics. After two decades of close association with American scholars and scholarship, Lacey admitted that a philosophical naturalism that is hostile to the supernatural and transcendent remains "the predominant common sense working philosophy on the secular campuses." But he also reported the growth of a more open and ambiguous religious modernism, affirming the existence of a supernatural or transcendent realm and convinced that knowledge of that realm is of fundamental importance for human living. Its advocates, many of them Catholics or former Catholics in fields other than theology, are generally ashamed of the performance of the mainline churches and had distanced themselves from organized religion. In fact, little is known of the personal religious beliefs of American scholars, but Lacey is convinced that there is a large number of people, neither secular nor religious in any formal sense, but making up a potential constituency for dialogue with an intellectually serious Christianity. They constitute a potential audience for such theologians as Rahner, Lonergan, and David Tracy and for such Catholic intellectuals as Alasdaire MacIntyre, Nicholas Lash, and Charles Taylor.

Certainly, if one looked for a renewed dialogue between serious Catholic scholarship and the secular academic world, one might start with the Jesuits. While they captained the countercultural Catholicism of the past, they also provided much of the intellectual leadership for Catholic renewal. John Courtney Murray, Karl Rahner, Bernard Lonergan—the list of Jesuits who helped shape renewal is long and distinguished. And to a man they were intellectuals who engaged both the Catholic tradition and contemporary scholarly life. Speaking at the Jesuit Theological School in Cambridge in 1988, General Peter Hans Kolvenbach said that Jesuit scholarship "tries to communicate the Church to the modern world and the modern world to the Church. This is a scholarship . . . that takes its place in the intellectual marketplace. It is a scholarship that grows from faith, that seeks to articulate the Church's Gospel tradition intelligently for today's world and to integrate that Gospel into the broader context of human knowledge and inquiry."[22]

But Jesuit John Coleman noted a short time later that American Jesuits were deeply divided and uncertain about the intellectual apostolate.[23] Fathers Arrupe and Kolvenbach insist on the importance of serious intellectual work; they want each Jesuit to be trained in philosophy, theology, and at least one specialized study, be adept in at least one modern language, and have an international outlook and the capacity for critical analysis of society. No wonder people occasionally remark of a newly arrived Jesuit: "he's studied everything everywhere." Why then the uncertainty?

Coleman reports that there is chronic disagreement about, even resentment of, the Jesuit commitment to "a faith that does justice." Coleman believes that the thirty-second General Congregation (GC 32) gave "a new and pressing apostolic direction to Jesuit intellectual life." "The service of faith through the promotion of justice remains the Society's major apostolic focus," Coleman insists. It illumines studies, raising questions almost impossible to ask in secular schools: "knowledge for what? service in whose interests? including and leaving out which groups?"

But Coleman and most serious observers know that these questions have yet to penetrate Jesuit colleges and universities. And the reason once again is the inability or unwillingness of people who believe in a position to organize in such a way as to promote that position in the politics of institutional life. Coleman thinks that Jesuits who believe in the faith and justice idea should take the lead. "Only a concerted Jesuit *conspiracy* (I use the term consciously) to tilt our educational institutions in the direction of GC 32 will allow a serious collective conversation within them about the structural prerequisites for an intellectual life in service of the faith which does justice. Almost nothing in American culture or structures of academic life will naturally impel us in that direction." Acknowledging the need for lay collaboration, Coleman nevertheless insists that "only a cadre of committed Jesuits" can see to it that the values of "faith and justice" become "more than a mere 'extracurricular' work of social outreach or a public relations appendage to our schools."

Of course, the need for strategic thinking and concerted action goes beyond particular colleges and universities. Jesuit General Pedro Arrupe never encouraged the Jesuits to turn their back on their connections with the powerful. He believed that contemporary culture and social structures are formed by leaders who draw their ideas from "the knowledge industry at the heart of which we find the university."[24] On the basis of this conviction, he strongly reaffirmed Jesuit educational apostolates. Jesuit provincials in the United States also have tried to keep the justice commitment before the attention of their academic leaders, with some success at the level of secondary education. But institutional autonomy limits their ability to influence the colleges and universities, whose natural dynamics have little to do with transformative idealism.

Still, while rejecting many aspects of older Jesuit elitism, Coleman hopes the Society will not forget its concern for the value of culture-forming elites. He argues that family of origin, the educational climate of the school, the interests of bodies that control and shape institutions, and "opportunities to become occupationally and politically tied to a variety of social groups during and after their formal education" influence people to take the claims of social justice seriously. So, "society is the horizon for our schools" that "cannot succeed in their formative purposes unless society itself becomes an object and horizon of their apostolic outreach."[25]

Coleman, Lacey, and Turner all agree that the problem of theology, and by extension Catholic intellectual life, requires a double move: attention to the Catholic tradition and engagement with the problems of the age, the Americanist agenda. I suspect that it is the latter, deep engagement with contemporary culture that will motivate the former, rather than the reverse. The approach that says first concentrate on the Catholic retrieval and then engage society is premised on assumptions about faith, church, and culture that will inevitably short-circuit public theology in favor of mild denominationalism or passionate sectarianism.

STRATEGIES

It is the height of folly to think that any organization, including the church, will act intelligently or that the quality of its cultural life will be adequate to the scope of its mission, unless intelligent people are dedicated to it, devoting to it at least some of their time and talent. There is a direct connection between the quality of church life, the vigor of its evangelical proclamation, and the strength and vitality of its colleges and universities, publications, and learned societies. The issues facing Catholic higher education, particularly the relationship between institutional commitment and mission on the one hand and the professionalism of the faculty on the other — with all that means for undergraduate curriculum, for research priorities, for faculty development — are of obvious and crucial importance for those who take the intellectual life seriously. There are no easy solutions; the perils of ecclesiastical control and confessional exclusiveness as well as the perils of uncritical secularization are real. Trustees, administrators, faculty, and benefactors all share responsibility; for the most part they pass the buck, blame each other, and settle in practice for policies that allow them to muddle through.

But some strategies for invigorating Christian intellectual life have emerged. They provide hope for the future, if conspiracies like that suggested by John Coleman begin to take shape at individual schools.

Jesuit Institute, Boston College

In an effort to "preserve and deepen the Catholic and Jesuit character" of Boston College by developing a more fruitful collaboration between Jesuits and lay faculty, the Boston College Jesuit community organized a series of retreats. Participants in these "Cohasset Weekends" soon discovered that, before they could have a strategic discussion, they needed to talk together about their experience of teaching at Boston College and their sense of the meaning of their work. That led the organizers over several years to acknowledge the diversity of meanings and the absence of a common language for discussing religion. They concluded that the conversation itself was an important contribution to the goal they were seeking. "Nothing should be more characteristic of a university than the presence of people of widely different backgrounds and quite specialized expertises and ways of talking about them," wrote Joseph Appleyard, S.J. "So perhaps what is most distinctive of a university with a religious identity today is not that it represents the doctrines of a particular religious group, but that it sponsors and values precisely the kind of discussion where all religious experience is brought into dialogue with 'secular' knowledge, faith with critical inquiry, not as one of many things that might go on in a university, but as the central activity which the university community thinks of as its characteristic interest. Rather than be a matter of private concern, or the business of a few specialists, the dialogue of religion and culture should stand in the foreground of our attention. Clearly this does not mean that everyone need be preoccupied with it. A university is not a church. All sorts of inquiry go on there which do not need authenticating from a religious point of view. But perhaps it is not a bad shorthand formula to say that in a pluralist and overtly secular culture, a religious university is one which keeps open the lines of communication about the meaning of faith, keeps finding better languages in which to carry on the discussion. . . . The challenge for Jesuits today may be to . . . bring the perspective of our distinctive spirituality to the task of inventing a new language in which authentic religious experience can be brought into real dialogue with the forms of experience and knowledge which the secular world offers and the university studies." In that case the role of the Jesuit community may be to sponsor discussion on the identity of the college. No one else so visibly embodies the tradition, has a pastoral motive to care for and build community, and is as detached about protecting its own version of what the university should be.[26]

To forward that approach, the Jesuit community at Boston College, with the help of numerous lay colleagues, launched the Jesuit Institute, jointly funded with the university. The Institute is designed to stimulate and support interdisciplinary research and conversations about issues in which faith and academic inquiry intersect. It is based on the realization that Western academic life is separated from religion and that even church-related universities have been organized around this separation. To explore the possibility of mutual enrichment and forms of reintegration, it is necessary to "avoid denigrating the impressive achievements of modern academic life, and to find ways that will capture the imagination and win the allegiance of the academic community." The Institute thus seeks to build on rather than oppose established methods of research and to encourage research in areas that university structures and funding patterns tend to neglect. Activities include faculty seminars, visiting scholars, weekend retreats, and interdisciplinary research projects. The seminars engage scholars in dialogue on interdisciplinary issues. There, as on the informal weekends discussed earlier, people sometimes struggle to find a common language. Philosopher Stephen Pope reported that in a seminar on "God and Science" participants had to find common ground as they went along. Pope provided further evidence for the priority of dialogue: "these are conversations that typically don't take place in the University."[27]

Catholic Studies

James Hennessy, S.J. asked a few years ago whether the Catholic college and university had provided a "Hospitable Home" for Catholic scholarship.[28] To do so, they would need to value scholarship and find strategies to attract scholars interested in Catholic subjects—easy enough perhaps in theology, less easy in other departments, remembering, as commentators rarely do not, that the faculty dominates the hiring process. Holy Cross, as we have seen, lost a dean over this issue. Then its mission statement, by acknowledging a community-wide responsibility to provide opportunities to appropriate the Catholic tradition and participate in the life and work of the church, laid the basis for programs to achieve that goal. Such programs would require qualified faculty, so that, if the college wishes to do so, it now has the basis to hire scholars interested in Catholic culture in all disciplines.

The question then arises: what kind of programs? One answer increasingly heard is interdisciplinary programs in Catholic studies. Here Georgetown University, sometimes regarded as among the more secularized schools, is leading the way. There a committee, including Catholic and non-Catholic faculty from history, literature, philosophy, and political science as well as theology, has proposed a Catholic studies program with an affiliated John Carroll Institute of Catholic Studies. Organizers value the pastoral and spiritual work of the Jesuit community and campus ministry, but they worry that campus religious life lacks a strong intellectual component. Georgetown also has its problems with hiring, and the academic as opposed to confessional approach might help. But the focus is on Catholic intellectual life, both for the faculty and the students, rather than on institutional identity. "Catholicism is a living religion based upon a complex system of ideas and beliefs," the committee states. "Through the centuries, the Church and its members, acting on the basis of both thought and faith, have had an incalculable impact upon world history and culture. Catholic Studies examines what the Church and its members have said and done, and the consequences of their action, for the world at large. Catholicism has also, from its inception, considered and evaluated the world around it from a uniquely Christian perspective. Catholic Studies continues this critique." In addition to offering an undergraduate minor, leading eventually to a major, the program looks forward to financing for faculty release from departmental responsibilities to teach in the program, small grants for new course development, a visiting scholar program, seminars and symposia to "create and evolve ways to introduce into the intellectual life of the faculty current significant issues in Catholic studies and in Catholic intellectual life," a new *Georgetown Review of Catholic Studies,* and a monograph series at the Georgetown University Press.[29]

The University of St. Thomas, Boston College, and several other schools are studying similar initiatives.

Collegium

The Lilly Endowment has made an impressive grant to Jesuit Thomas Landy to organize a series of two-week summer institutes for graduate students and new faculty in Catholic colleges and universities that enroll as members. The program is intended to offer participants an invitation to Catholic intellectual life. This may mean thinking about one's work in light of faith and, for those who work in Catholic schools or are considering that option, a renewed sense of a constructive relationship between their own work and the school's Catholic mission. The program includes dialogue with mentor faculty (experienced scholars who are people of faith), talks by major Catholic scholars, and a variety of spiritual and liturgical activities. The first program took place in the summer of 1993.[30]

Lilly Fellows Program in Humanities and the Arts, Valpariaso University

The Lilly Endowment supports two postdoctoral fellowships in the humanities and arts "for teacher-scholars who seek to renew and enrich their intellectual and spiritual lives while preparing for leadership roles in teaching and administration in institutions of Christian higher education." The fellows are in residence for two years at Valpariaso, where they are mentored by local faculty and a senior research fellow funded by the program. This is coupled with a national network of twenty-six church-related colleges and universities "interested in exploring Christian under-standings of the nature of the academic vocation." These schools gather for an annual conference on this subject, while the network serves as a referral system for Christian scholars seeking academic positions.

The Values Program

LeMoyne University, a Jesuit institution in Syracuse, has concentrated on faculty development. Organizers raised enough money to offer twenty to thirty professors and professional staff an opportunity to participate in a two-week interdisciplinary summer seminar on "values." Participants take a theme each summer (e.g., peace, economic justice, family, diversity), read and discuss a series of texts, and then explore ways in which the theme can be brought into their teaching. The following year, through the "academic forum," the seminar members design new courses, lecture in each other's classes, and develop modules for use in several classes. They meet regularly during the year and work together with students to incorporate the year's theme into cocurricular and extracurricular events, such as plays, poetry readings, and film series. While critics worry about the values focus, experience demonstrates that participants cannot separate values from the meanings in which they are embedded. Religion invariably becomes central to the conversations. It is a fine example of making the religious commit-ments of the school and the sponsoring religious community a positive factor in the actual work that people do. The program brings scholars and teachers to reflect on their work, it builds community, it enriches teaching, and it enlivens the intellectual and moral climate of the campus.[31]

Non-Catholic schools and scholars have been thinking more strategically than most Catholics.

The Christian College Coalition (CCC)

This is an association of "Christ-centered colleges and universities of the liberal arts and sciences . . . committed to cultivating communities of academic excellence in which the Lordship of Jesus Christ is central." These schools expect their faculty to witness to Christian faith, and many incorporate into hiring, evaluation, and faculty development systematic reflection on the relationship between faith, research, and teaching. Many of these schools work very hard to insure "an unfettered pursuit of truth" and avoid the "highly sheltered and perhaps sectarian environment" long associated with such schools.[32] To assist that process, the CCC offers a variety of programs, including orientation seminars on subjects like "Christianity and the Liberal Arts" and seminars for more senior faculty on topics of current interest, from "Moslem Culture" and "Reunited Germany" to "Multiculturalism." Even presidents of member institutions attend think tanks with outstanding Christian intellectuals. The Harvey Fellowships assist graduates attending first-rate graduate schools, and the Carl F.H. Henry Scholarships are awarded to students who publish in secular media articles reflecting the biblical point of view on contemporary issues.[33]

In 1983 the CCC sponsored a series of summer institutes for faculty, funded by the National Endowment for the Humanities, each examining the relationship between Christianity and an individual discipline. Since then they have produced seven volumes of a supplemental text series by outstanding scholars, with titles like *Sociology* (or Music or Economics) *Through the Eyes of Faith*. These focus on the presuppositions of the discipline and offer Christian commentary on its central questions.

The CCC has been active in arranging programs for its own students and faculty to Russia, Eastern Europe, the Caribbean, and the Middle East. Thinking strategically of penetrating key sectors of American culture, they maintain centers for undergraduate experiential learning in Washington (government) and Los Angeles (film) as well as overseas.

The Evangelical Scholars Initiative

In order "to strengthen intellectual activity among evangelical Christians in North America," this project was established with the help of the Pew Memorial Trust. It provides three fellowships for senior faculty and six for junior scholars to support specific research and writing projects designed to bring Christian voices to bear on important scholarly problems in the humanities, social sciences, and theological disciplines. The Initiative "hopes to identify evangelical scholars who have the potential to make a lasting impact on their disciplines and support them at critical stages of their research careers." Applicants should be "willing to identify themselves as evangelical Christians and should be able to demonstrate how their Christian faith informs the assumptions and methods with which they approach their scholarly work." Headquartered at Notre Dame, where evangelical historian Nathan Hatch serves as dean of the graduate school, the Initiative hopes to build enduring networks among evangelical scholars by bringing fellowship recipients together for summer seminars.

Recently, the Initiative received a $1.8 million grant from Pew to hold annual summer seminars with outstanding Christian scholars for forty-two promising undergraduates from Christian colleges. This project is intended to encourage them to seek entry to the nation's best graduate schools, to support their applications, and to assist them with fellowships. The hope is that they will bring a Christian voice to their disciplines and that some among them will return as faculty to raise the intellectual level of the faith-related colleges. Small grants are also available to the schools to encourage their students to consider graduate study.[34]

Hatch and Michael Hamilton won these grants by arguing 1) that a pervasive secularism dominated American intellectual and especially academic life, a secularism hostile to religion in general and to evangelicals in particular; 2) that evangelicals did little to offer counterarguments to secularists or in fact to take responsibility for the major issues of meaning in society at large; and 3) that evangelical religious culture, in parishes and on campuses, was less anti-intellectual than it was indifferent to intellectual concerns. The low state of evangelical intellectual achievement could be attributed to the democratic religious culture, which trusts in popular judgement, and to the sharp separation of the late nineteenth century when the makers of modern universities rejected religion and many evangelicals rejected modern intellectual life as dangerous. They concluded: "If evangelicals are to help preserve even the possibility of Christian thinking for their children and grandchildren, they must begin to nurture first-order Christian scholarship, which means of course freeing Christian scholars to undertake" that work.[35]

ORGANIZATIONS

The Association for Religion and the Intellectual Life, which publishes the quarterly *Cross Currents,* and the Society for Values in Higher

Education are two national interfaith networks of scholars concerned about the role of religion in modern intellectual life. Through summer conferences, annual symposia, special projects, and a variety of publications, they seek to put academics interested in religion in touch with each other, encourage cross-disciplinary and interfaith dialogue and research, and eventually influence the climate of higher education and American intellectual life.

There are many comparable organizations among evangelical Christians, and a few Catholic learned societies survive. The two theological organizations mentioned above are vigorous, and there are occasional efforts to bring them together with organizations of biblical scholars and canon lawyers for reflection and action. The only organization that seeks to enlist a wide variety of Catholics in dialogue is the Catholic Commission on Intellectual and Cultural Affairs, a by-invitation organization of people in and out of academic life that sponsors an annual conference on a subject of current interest.

UNDERGRADUATE PROGRAMS

One unfortunate result of the abstract and institutional focus of debates about Catholic identity is that emphasis is given to policies and projects that involve the entire institution. Thus the language of *Ex Corde Ecclesiae* and of much response to it focuses on institutional commitment and implies educational strategies that touch all students. In some places that is done without apology. At Mount Saint Mary's in Maryland, for example, the rationale for the core curriculum states quite frankly that it offers "a Catholic perspective on the humanist tradition of Western European culture." As a central tenet of that perspective, the college "views individuals as free moral agents, created by God, redeemed in Christ, responsible for their choices and their acts." While valuing the academic disciplines, "in view of the College's mission and historic identity, we can never be satisfied with disciplinary pluralism." Among the various frameworks for integration, "the Christian humanist tradition occupies a position of privilege and the Catholic contribution to that tradition receives special attention."[36]

But at many schools, changing the core curriculum is a massive project; a diverse faculty can debate endlessly the terms used at St. Mary's, and no one is really sure what the core should include. Smaller projects might be a better way to make religion a more vital part of the undergraduate experience. Catholic studies might be one way to do that; first-year programs with a moral theme, like the program at Holy Cross, would be another, as would "capstone" courses at the end of the student's education.

Several Jesuit schools have "faith and justice" programs that offer students opportunities for serious theological study and spiritual growth alongside their normal program.

Sometimes, special programs serve as "research and development centers" for the curriculum. Seattle University's Matteo Ricci College, a joint project with Seattle Prep and several other area high schools, provides a six-year integrated high school/college program anchored in the humanities. Its goals include providing an integrated, values-centered education, an experience of community and interactive forms of instruction that emphasize the responsibilities of students.

GRADUATE PROGRAMS

Undergraduate teaching, of course, reflects graduate education. To their credit, theology chairs in Catholic schools are questioning the fragmentation and incoherence of non-Catholic graduate programs and are exploring the possibility of a Catholic alternative, though one that, in my judgement, seems too defensive and parochial. But they recognize the link between graduate school and undergraduate teaching and between graduate schools and Catholic intellectual life, and they are trying to do something about it.

No element of American higher education is more striking or more puzzling than the dramatic contrast between the remarkable diversity of undergraduate, vocational, and professional education, from community colleges through small faith-related schools to technical institutes to research centers and multi-universities, and the equally remarkable uniformity of graduate instruction. The "Balkanization" that marked the self-description of academics in religion could be repeated in almost every discipline. So could the experience of so many graduate students who were inspired to undertake graduate education by the example of humane, broadly educated undergraduate teachers and then forgot their motivation under the pressure toward specialization and narrow research in graduate school. Questions of value only rarely find their way into the classroom or comprehensive exam. Questions of meaning, religious or philosophical, never do. Here, in graduate education, research and disciplinary self-definition is the real battleground of modern higher education (at least for its theory; for its practice the battleground will be federal and state legislatures). Unless Catholic intellectuals confront this reality, there really will be no available third choice between confessional restoration and all-out integration into the seamless web of academic culture. Yet, oddly, critics concentrate almost entirely on theology, giving almost no attention to other disciplines, except for complaints about the absence of religion, and make almost no suggestion about alternative graduate programs or faculty development. Unless we do better here, we may decry sectarianism and secularism, but will end up with sophisticated but isolated theology departments, whose professors can communicate with their colleagues only on intimate weekends. And the hope for a Catholic higher education that forms disciples and citizens will pass to the realm of fantasy.

CONVERSATION

When Jesuit provincials and college and university presidents decided to launch a project to rekindle an awareness of Jesuit and Catholic identity on the twenty-eight Jesuit campuses, they formed a national seminar of professors, administrators, rectors, and trustees to discuss these matters. They in turn launched a publication to assist local communities to initiate similar discussion on the individual campuses. They named the publication *Conversations,* a title reflected as well in such projects as the Jesuit Institute, noted above, and the many informal efforts to engage faculty and administrators with institutional mission. But initiating and sustaining such conversations, much less making them central to college life and fruitful sources of research and teaching projects, has proven to be enormously difficult.

Why is it so difficult to discuss these matters? Some answers to that question are obvious. For one thing, the word Catholic immediately suggests "The Church," and the conflict between Rome and the American universities is for the moment literally insoluble. In addition, the religious diversity of self-governing faculties has developed in the absence of an adequate theory: as Philip Gleason regularly insists, Catholic higher education remains in an "ideological crisis." But the difficulty also resides in the fabric of contemporary American culture and, in particular, in the problem of pluralism. Talking about religion, especially about religious differences, is no easy matter.

The basic dilemma of pluralism is always the same: how to create a society in which people "who espouse widely different and incompatible conceptions of the good life" can "live together peaceably . . . enjoying the same political status and engaging in the same economic relationships." To sustain the American experiment, a number of idea clusters were once widely believed: social contract theory; the "inalienable rights" of autonomous individuals; reason as a source of principles to govern the common life; and the common good served by relegating nonrational beliefs to private life. None of those idea systems has been rejected, but each is now in doubt. John Courtney Murray forty years ago found wide agreement on the formula "we hold these truths." Today, consensus is harder to locate.

The last idea — that the common good requires a secular, neutral public space — arouses deep concern among Christians:

> While a religious understanding of life naturally seeks cultural wholeness and expression in the public realm, the ideology of modern liberalism relegates religion to the private domain in an attempt to construct a public square devoid of religious conviction and independent of any particular conception of the good. In a liberal society, all "sectarian" beliefs will be tolerated of course — but only if those who hold them agree that all such beliefs are equally valid and equally irrelevant to matters of public concern. The common life is to be conducted on essentially secular principles to which we will all subscribe and agree by virtue of our common share in reason.[37]

Three options then arise, all of them evident in contemporary Catholic higher education. One is to reaffirm the particular values of particular groups: the church must be the church, the sectarian option that informs explicitly confessional schools. The second, a denominational option, is to live and let live and allow various marketplaces to adjudicate all claims; the church should concentrate on religion and heal the pains of personal and family life, leaving public and academic life alone. Theology and pastoral ministry may be welcome on campus, but they are options for individuals with little purchase on the real business of the university.

The third option, what some now call the public church, would be to take up the shared work of reconstructing the foundations of public discourse and thus the common life, recognizing that to do so one must at the same time attend to the distinctive resources of one's own community and nourish its inner life. This latter, *American* Catholic option, was the goal of the Americanists, from Isaac Hecker to John Courtney Murray. As an aspiration it had much to do with why Catholic higher education changed after World War II. Its present weakness and defensiveness accounts for the difficulty of so many conversations about Catholic identity. In those conversations, invariably, the voices of Catholic restoration and religious integrity are heard, contending with the voices of professional autonomy and academic integrity. The third voice — the voice of Murray and Hesburgh and *Gaudium et Spes* and the pastoral letters on war and economics — is muted, its advocates fewer and unsure of themselves and its place in the debate shrinking.

What is at stake here is not so much Catholic identity as religion's role in intellectual life and American culture. Both denominational and sectarian options, alert in their criticism of liberalism, surrender to its demands by abandoning the public task. Liberal Catholics have always insisted on the importance of that task and would read recent history as providing new resources and thus new responsibilities for that work. Christian critics (though not only Christian critics) rarely challenge the structures of liberalism: the creation of religiously neutral institutions within which the concrete demands of the common life must be negotiated. What they do object to is liberalism's resolution of the religious question. By excluding particular religious views and thus particular views of the good that are at all contested, liberalism restricts religious concerns to private life. In doing so it drains public life of meaning and undermines its own need for civic virtue. This resolution depended more than was recognized in the past on a liberal ideology, perhaps even a liberal religion, rooted in the Enlightenment faith in reason. Thus, what was common — reason — could provide the foundation for truly common enterprises like education and, though the critics say this less often, war and preparation for war.

More and more, the secular, neutral resolution of the problem of pluralism seems inadequate. Mark Schwehn, for example, revives the idea that the virtues of public life are nurtured best in communities sustained by a common narrative about life and history, so that society should nurture, not marginalize, such communities. As many of the foundations of the scientific domination of the academy come into question, the notion returns that all learning is a "generically human enterprise," often carried out best within communities. Communities of conversation are an asset for the educational enterprise as well, in part because recent work suggests the communal character of human inquiry, but also because such virtues as faith, humility, self-denial, and charity make a positive contribution to the advancement of knowledge. They help make us the kind of people who can learn with and from others. "I believe that the most promising argument for an integral relationship between religion and higher education can be made through a demonstration that the practice of certain spiritual values is and always has been essential to the process of learning, even within the secular academy," Schwehn argues.[38] Connecting faith and work, religion and real life, is the unfinished and usually unmentioned agenda.

THE RENEWAL OF CATHOLIC INTELLECTUAL LIFE

Thirty years after the publication of John Tracy Ellis's famous essay on "American Catholics and the Intellectual Life," the challenge of Catholic intellectual life remains unresolved. It is true that there are now plenty of Catholics who are intellectuals. They have access to the public culture and to opportunities for shaping the public consensus beyond anything the earlier generations could have hoped for. Against numerous predictions, the church still has a thriving network of colleges and universities.

But the problematic element today, even more than in 1955 when Ellis presented his famous paper, is how distinctly and deeply "Catholic" are these intellectuals, these universities, and the very public presence of Catholic laypeople? If people stumble over this, if they are unsure whether "Catholic" adds anything to their work, if they are uncomfortable with the very idea of adding that modifier to a school or to themselves, then we must conclude that the project Monsignor Ellis called attention to thirty years ago has been a failure. But if Catholic scholars, writers, thinkers, and artists today wish to share and reinvigorate such a project, they will best do so not by lengthy arguments about the precise meaning of the word Catholic, but by reentering the public life of the modern church: seeking out the issues and the problems people confront; responding to the numerous invitations coming from popes and bishops; and rebuilding communities of conversation, so as to shape the quality of public discourse and help their people form their consciences on public issues.

How can Catholic scholars, writers, and artists be persuaded to participate more energetically and constructively in the church's public life and ministry and thereby develop a network of Catholic intellectuals in many fields and disciplines who will share in the task of making the church's contribution to American culture more creative and effective? Surely one answer to this pressing question is for ecclesiastical leaders to recognize the need to affirm and support Catholic thinkers and creators. Another is for academic leaders to cooperate with bishops in reforming seminary education and ministry training, emphasizing high academic standards, serious study, and research. Surely, too, the leaders in Catholic higher education must translate their high-sounding words about Catholic identity into effective strategies for attracting, supporting, and rewarding scholars who seek to work within the Catholic tradition and define their research and teaching, at least in part, in response to the needs of the American church. Finally, organizations of Catholic scholars and intellectuals should try to make their hitherto modest efforts at cooperation both strategic and programmatic.

There is plenty about today's church that inspires hope: its turn toward the poor, its defense of human rights, the rich pluralism of its theological scholarship, and the challenge of the recent pastoral letters of the American bishops. Yet these promising movements will bear fruit in the United States only if serious people, mature enough to ride out the tensions and ambiguities present in our moment in history, decide to devote a portion of their talent and energy to the church, specifically to the intellectual life of the church, its cultural enrichment, and its dialogue with the larger society. The pastoral letters represented an effort to avoid the twin shoals of the sectarian isolation championed by radicals of left and right and the final accommodation to contemporary culture that would be the outcome of the sharp separation of religion from secular life championed by some Catholic neoconservatives. If the experiment represented by the pastorals is to work, if the middle way of Cardinal Newman and Monsignor Ellis is to remain a viable option, Catholic scholars must decide to make it so.

CHAPTER 10

Disciples and Citizens

"MEN AND WOMEN FOR OTHERS"

In 1989, the murder of six Jesuit priests and two women coworkers at the University of Central America in El Salvador shocked the world. On Catholic and particularly Jesuit campuses in the United States, the event sparked outrage, expressions of solidarity, and renewed attention to academic responsibility for poverty, violence, and injustice. The slain Jesuit scholar-educators embodied ideas about "the service of faith and promotion of justice" much discussed on Jesuit campuses, particularly the idea of former Jesuit General Pedro Arrupe that the task of the educational apostolate is to form "men and women for others." "We have to be the voice of those who have no voice," Arrupe once told his fellow Jesuits. "We have to strive to transform the mentality of society."[1] The El Salvador Jesuits took up that challenge, and they were murdered by soldiers trained by Americans and bearing American arms.

For me, that event stirred memories of a day a few years earlier, in 1978, when Holy Cross awarded an honorary degree to Cesar Jerez Garcia, S.J., at that time provincial of the Jesuits in Central America. Jerez Garcia, a Chicago-trained social scientist, and his fellow Jesuits in Guatemala had been threatened with death if they did not leave that country. The honorary degree was a small sign of support. Canisius College in Buffalo invited Jerez Garcia to deliver the commencement address a few days after the Holy Cross graduation. There he told the assembled graduates, teachers, and families that he wondered whether Jesuit education was helping to ease their path into what he obviously regarded as an unjust and repressive economic system. He became very specific.

Do you plan to use your degree for your own profit, be it profit in the form of money or power, status or respect? Will you end up with

187

General Motors or Morgan Trust, with Chase Manhattan or Abbot Laboratories, with Goodyear or Boeing. . . . Will you become people who use your knowledge for the furtherance of justice . . . or live the good life of manipulated, unconcerned people in suburbia who grant honorary degrees to people from the Third World but refuse to join them in the fight for justice and liberty for the poor of the world.[2]

This was a strong message, familiar to most Jesuits and to people informed about contemporary Catholic life in Latin America, but undoubtedly shocking to the graduates and their families. That surprise constitutes a far more serious and justified indictment of Catholic higher education than the more prominent arguments about secularization.

EDUCATION FOR JUSTICE

At its thirty-second General Congregation in 1974, the Society of Jesus defined "the service of faith, of which the promotion of justice is an absolute requirement" as definitive of all Jesuit ministries, a commitment made within the framework of what the Jesuits called an option for the poor.[3] The Jesuits are not alone. At every level the institutional church has become ever more insistent that its educational mission cannot be confined to matters of personal morality and eternal salvation, but must be tested by its contribution to peace, justice, and human liberation. Pope John XXIII issued a powerful appeal for a Christian education appropriate to the magnitude of the church's mission in the modern world and the new potential of an educated laity:

Indeed, it happens in many quarters and too often that there is no proportion between scientific training and religious instruction: the former continues and is extended until it reaches higher degrees, while the latter remains at an elementary level. It is indispensable, therefore, that in the training of youth, education should be complete and without interruption; namely, that in the minds of the young, religious values should be cultivated and the moral conscience refined, in a manner to keep pace with the continuous and ever more abundant assimilation of scientific and technical knowledge. And it is indispensable too that they be instructed regarding the proper way to carry out their actual tasks.[4]

This plea is repeated again and again in the major documents of the modern church, from Vatican II through the speeches and encyclicals of John Paul II. The American bishops, for example, argued in 1972 that:

> The success of the Church's educational mission will also be judged by how well it helps the Catholic community to see the dignity of human life with the vision of Jesus and involve itself in the search for solutions to the pressing problems of society. Christians are obliged to seek justice and peace in the world. Catholics individually and collectively should join wherever possible with all persons of good will in the effort to solve social problems in ways which consistently reflect Gospel values.[5]

In their much discussed pastoral letters of the 1980s, the U.S. bishops repeatedly called upon Catholic colleges and universities to incorporate peacemaking and justice seeking into their teaching and research. "Those who enjoy the benefits of Catholic higher education have the obligation to provide our society with leadership on matters of justice and human rights,"[6] the bishops wrote at one point.

The goal of Catholic education, then, should not be far from what Cesar Jerez called for that day—not comfortable accommodation to society, nor even limited public spiritedness, but formation of what the Vatican Council called "those great souled persons who are so desperately required by our times."[7]

But education is done by educators, and educators are always learners themselves. There can be no education for justice and peace without scholars so committed. And the church has spoken to them as directly as possible. At Hiroshima in 1981, to take but one example, John Paul II did not hesitate to tell a largely non-Christian audience of scholars and scientists that all of us together have to try to transform the social order and that we will do it only if we recognize the imperatives of love:

> From now on, it is only through conscious choice and through a deliberate policy that humanity can survive. . . . The task is enormous, some will call it a utopian one. . . . The building of a more just humanity or of a more united international community is not just a dream or a vain ideal. It is a moral imperative, a sacred duty [requiring] a fresh mobilization of everybody's talents and energies. . . . The construction of a new social order presupposes over and above the essential technological skills a lofty inspiration, a coura-

geous motivation, belief in man's future, his dignity, his destiny. . . .
In a word, man must be loved for his own sake.[8]

Theologian Jon Sobrino of the Central American University in San
Salvador, who is alive only because he was traveling when his colleagues
were assassinated, argues that, from the point of view of the poor, most
Christian universities have been working in opposition to the Kingdom of
God because they have not questioned unjust social structures but have
instead educated professionals to "shore them up." But he argues as well
that the question of the poor arises from within any university, Christian or
not. "In the face of injustice, oppression and repression, there can be no
institutional neutrality. The entire university should be in accord, at least
morally, on a minimum standard of living for the poor." But a Christian
university above all must "seek its center outside itself; de-centering is a
Christian demand not only on individuals but also on institutions, in order
that they place themselves at the service of the Kingdom of God." In this
context, the "option for the poor" is first of all "a hermeneutical principle"
rather than a political project. Catholic intellectuals and institutions are not
to abandon their work for social and political action, but to renew their
work in light of the universal obligation to "do the truth."[9]

So far, these arguments have captured only a few U.S. Catholic
academics. One thinks again of the Jesuits, because of their size and
influence and because their rhetorical commitment is so unequivocal.
Before there had been any serious effort to incorporate Jesuit social ideals
into research and teaching, much less into graduate or professional
education, resistance developed. This led to innumerable reassuring statements from Jesuit authorities confirming the Society's continued commitment to education and to the intellectual apostolate. But no amount of
reassurance seemed enough. When Jesuit personnel in higher education
gathered in 1989 to celebrate the 450th anniversary of the Society, Avery
Dulles expressed the feelings of many when he questioned the commitments
of the 32nd General Congregation. Many Jesuits believed, according to
Dulles, that the Congregation had taught that each of them had to be
involved in the social apostolate "under pain of doing nothing for the
Kingdom of God" and that they and the Society as a whole had to be
committed to the "dismantling of unjust social structures, conscientization
and the building of a new and better society." This work apparently had a
higher priority than converting "individuals in their interiority," the heart of
Ignatian spirituality. Scholars in the arts, sciences and classics, Dulles
contended, felt they had no place in such efforts and either left the Society
or refused to join it. Fortunately, Dulles added, Pope John Paul II had

made "a necessary correction of course," presumably not in his social teaching, which remains very demanding, and by criticizing liberation theology and intervening in Jesuit affairs.[10]

So the notion of an intellectual life lived in terms of justice remains controversial and threatening to many in the academy and in the church. Jesuit schools continue to use the phrases "faith and justice," "option for the poor," and "men and women for others," and most Catholic schools join them in insisting that care for the poor and a general concern for justice are part of their educational mission. Indeed, the integration of such terms into mission statements and publicity materials is almost universal. But developing programs to implement these ideals remains unfinished business.

"PRAXIS"

Of course a few substantial programs have developed which reflect these commitments. There are new departments and curricula in peace studies and international studies, a variety of volunteer and service programs, and institutes and centers that feature lectures, films, discussions, and reflection on war, the arms race, hunger, economic justice, and racial and sexual discrimination. Creative theologians and philosophers develop "ethics across the curriculum" programs to enable faculty to raise critical moral issues in diverse disciplines. Small groups of faculty and students, often identifying with the expressed goals of the sponsoring religious community, provide a variety of outlets for the impressive generosity and idealism of the larger campus community, raise current issues, and serve as a critical presence challenging more conventional elements of college and university life.[11]

A few examples include the following. St. Joseph's University has a Faith and Justice certification program that involves ongoing participation in a faith and justice studies seminar, six upper division courses (the last of which is an independent study project designed as a capstone for the program), and consistent participation in some form of social action. Boston College, Fairfield, and a number of other schools have similar "Faith and Justice" programs for small numbers of interested students. Boston College also is the home of the PULSE program, a national model for community service that allows students to fulfill two requirements in philosophy in a course that combines a full year of service, working directly with people in need, with philosophical study and reflection. At DePaul University, the Vincentians have endowed scholarships for students who provide leadership in service-learning programs, and presidents from Catholic schools have taken leadership roles in Campus Compact, a national support organization for community service programs.

Community service programs flourish on Catholic campuses, including postgraduate service in such groups as the Peace Corps and the Jesuit Volunteer Corps (JVC). In 1993, 57 Holy Cross graduates joined JVC and at least a dozen more joined other volunteer service programs, a total of well over 10 percent of the graduating class. At Notre Dame, student projects find a home in a building, the Center for Social Concerns, backed by a professional staff and located outside the library, at the heart of the campus. The Center supports domestic and overseas programs of community service and experiential education, including a program of summer internships with poverty agencies supported by local alumni clubs. Loyola of Chicago, working with several other Chicago area schools, supports a Policy Research Action Group funded by the MacArthur Foundation to enable faculty and students to conduct research in cooperation with community-based organizations. This is a particularly interesting effort at partnership, with the research agenda and interpretation of results fully shared with the organizations. Sociologist Philip Nyden says: "We recognize that many research projects occur within disciplines and involve primarily conversations among academics with only sporadic input from the community. We are trying to change a little part of that."[12]

According to Sr. Loretta Carey of Fordham University, some 155 Catholic colleges and universities have a coordinator for peace and justice, and 105 have some kind of program, either directed by campus ministry or incorporated into the academic program. Also, 37 have a faculty committee and 26 a sequence or concentration, of which 30 offer a minor and 5 a major in peace and justice studies.[13] So there has been "intense activity" in this area. Beyond the curriculum and student service programs, of course, many schools are institutional good citizens. In the past, some of the large urban schools received criticism for aloofness from their local neighborhoods, but that is rare today. Schools like DePaul and Loyola in Chicago, Santa Clara and Loyola-Marymount and St. Mary's in California, Fordham University, and Marquette University have all received national attention for their engagement with urban problems. The University of St. Thomas, with a long history of service in St. Paul, Minnesota, has recently opened a large downtown campus in Minneapolis, where it is developing a wide range of programs in cooperation with local government, business, and civic organizations. So there can be little question that, however much Catholic colleges and universities struggle with their theory, perhaps with undue emphasis on their Catholic identity, they are in practice alert to their public as well as their academic responsibilities.

Yet there is only limited success in translating all this into creative programs of research and teaching focused on discipleship and citizenship. And the programs that do exist, centered on community service, have some serious weaknesses, which their leaders readily acknowledge. The Loyola program is unique; in few places are local academic communities reaching beyond helping services to assist local groups working to overcome injustice, such as the local grantees of the church's own Campaign for Human Development. There is no national student movement as there is in so many other countries to connect students with one another and with students abroad, giving them a sense of their specific vocation and strengthening their determination to find life work that is oriented toward social justice. While Catholic learned societies in theology, canon law, and biblical studies devote considerable scholarly attention to peace and justice issues, there are few networks of Catholic scholars and teachers in the humanities, social sciences, sciences, engineering, or business to connect them with one another for professional and personal growth in faith or to enable them to more effectively serve the social, public mission of the church.

Most important, few of the many good programs touch directly the heart of the academic enterprise of teaching and research. All seem somewhat marginal to academic life: few offer courses for credit, almost none do research, and, while they may have the support of individual faculty members, they are rarely seen as integral elements of the overall educational mission of the college or university.[14] Research centers at some of the larger schools, like Notre Dame's Kellogg Center, which does important work on development, especially in Latin America, and its Kroc Center for International Peace Studies, make only limited impact on undergraduates. At most places, most of the time, the language of social responsibility is used uncritically: rarely is it the basis for self-examination and programmatic innovation.

DISCIPLESHIP, YES; CITIZENSHIP, NOT SO SURE

One reason may be the style of advocacy adopted by proponents of justice and peace education. Many speak more passionately of Christian discipleship than of responsible citizenship. There is a tendency to short-circuit the persuasion and politics of campus academic policy making by recourse to authority, including that of the sponsoring religious community: "this is a Catholic school, this is what the church teaches, therefore we should have a program." At times, too, advocates pick up the radical language of the new evangelicalism, applying Gospel mandates directly to complex economic and political questions without filtering them through hard-headed social and economic analysis and assessment of political options. This direct move from faith to social judgement also limits their ability to find common ground with non-Christians or less fervent Christians. Too many advocates, and I include myself here, seem at times to confine social responsibility to countercultural Christianity.

Grounded in scripture, emphasizing personal commitment and interior spirituality, forming relatively intense communities, this explicitly religious, even Christological, approach reflects a powerful and probably permanent element in the emerging Catholic community. In matters of social justice and world peace, its central questions are posed not in terms of natural law or papal teaching, but in terms of scripture: "What would Jesus do?" This leads to a stance of advocacy on behalf of the poor and of pacifism and nonviolent resistance to the arms race and nuclear weapons. In education it seeks through a combination of experimental consciousness raising and theological reflection to bring about what the Synod of 1971 described as "a renewal of heart . . . based on recognition of sin in its individual and social manifestations." Its great strength lies in its ability to generate what the Synod called "a critical sense which will lead us to reflect on the society in which we live and on its values; it will make men ready to renounce those values when they cease to promote justice for all men."[15]

This approach, which I have termed evangelical,[16] is deeply rooted in the dynamics of American religious culture, with its emphasis on personal decisions, voluntary communities, and interior contact with the divine. Catholicism cannot avoid the impact of religious individualism and evangelical piety, in both its soft and prophetic forms. It reflects as well the weakness of constructive political movements and the absence of vigorous political debate in the country at large. After all, Catholic social activists have always been more comfortable building bridges to movements that originated outside the church (the labor, peace, and civil rights movements) than initiating politically oriented movements themselves. What David Bromwich says correctly, speaking of secular ideological extremism, applies equally well when addressing evangelical radicalism: "there will be no end of the unreal politics of the academy until we begin again to have real politics outside the academy."[17]

Echoes of this evangelical, at times sectarian, radicalism can be found in a Jesuit study team's conclusion that the United States may be "the least favorable context for our ministry of preaching the Gospel."[18] Even Dulles, no friend of liberation theology or the faith and justice theme, finds little of worth in contemporary culture and calls for a smaller, more committed church composed of people who have made personal decisions of faith over and against an increasingly "pagan" society. We have noted earlier the bishops' appropriation of Dulles's language of a "secularized, neo-pagan society" in which Christians must "regard as normal the path of persecution and the possibility of martyrdom." Similar themes of withdrawal can be found in a number of works by Catholic novelists, from Walker Percy's *Love in the Ruins* to Morris West's *The Clowns of God*.

THE CLAIMS OF CITIZENSHIP

Yet if advocates of education for justice and peace, the promoters of social concerns on campus, often find themselves isolated from the mainstream of campus life, it is not mainly their fault. For elsewhere in the Catholic university community, there is, as Jerez Garcia suspected, a scandalous gap between pretense and practice, between warm affirmations of Catholic identity and the absence of programs designed to make the relationship between the university and church creative and compelling, between rhetorical affirmations of the responsibilities of citizenship and the absence of serious political study, and between the sponsoring religious community's powerful commitment to justice and peace and its more or less passive accommodation to academic culture and the pursuit of an excellence defined largely in terms of specialized research within present disciplinary boundaries. Too often the college or university has allowed a segregation of academic and religious matters that goes far beyond the authentic respect for the autonomy of the secular recognized by Vatican II. It marginalizes religion, as we have noticed, but it also institutionalizes political and civic irresponsibility. Here, far more than in the area of supposed secularization, lies the real failure of nerve.

Of course, one test for Catholic higher education would be whether it provides an education appropriate to the lives of modern Catholics. In the past, the colleges and universities took pride in graduates who became successful laypeople, with success defined in terms of social and economic mobility, both for men and women. Naturally, they also took special pride in those graduates who became priests and sisters. And, at least from 1900 to the 1960s, the roles of priests, religious, and laypeople were relatively clear.

Things are far less clear today. Most schools would still be pleased if a good number of graduates entered the priesthood and religious life, and the

American dream is intact: most try very hard to recruit students from poor and moderate income families and assist them in building better lives for themselves. But clerical and religious roles in the church are far less clear today. Jerez Garcia clearly hoped for citizen-disciples who would serve as allies in North America for liberation movements in South America. Father Arrupe asked Jesuit schools to renew their educational apostolates around an option for the poor that would produce persons caring about "others," especially those in need. The critics of secularization we discussed earlier hope for graduates who have an intellectual understanding of the Catholic faith. Everyone, if one judges from speeches and brochures, sees the schools as nurturing faithful Christian disciplines and responsible American citizens. But the meaning of discipleship and citizenship is under dispute and so, especially, is the relationship between them.

As we have seen, many theologians speak of discipleship today in countercultural terms, and the American bishops picked up this language in the more religious sections of their pastoral letters. On the other hand, the bishops also spoke strongly of the need for a moral dimension to public policy, at least implicitly calling Catholics to active engagement with public life. The policy sections of the peace pastoral were realistic and carefully nuanced, even including acceptance under certain conditions of nuclear deterrence. The policy sections of the economics pastoral were similarly realistic, recognizing the complexity of issues, affirming markets and entrepreneurship, and offering modest proposals for reform. Part three of the peace pastoral outlines proposals for negotiations, international organization and conflict resolution, and peacemaking through the give-and-take of politics. In the case of the economy, the bishops called for a "new American experiment" in economic democracy based on collaboration between government and the private sector and within the private sector itself. Clearly, Catholics have an obligation to practice the virtues and arts of citizenship in the workplace, in the marketplace, and in electoral politics — all pluralistic, all in some sense secular, and all requiring competence and shared responsibility for society, even if it borders on the pagan.

It almost seems that the introductory and concluding sections, aimed at Catholics, were written in theology classrooms and churches, after prayer, while the middle sections on policy were written in social science classrooms and corporate or Pentagon offices, with no mention of Jesus. The letters mirror the dilemma of contemporary Catholicism become American: be responsible, but be very careful! On the one hand be disciples; on the other, not so fast!

Once again, the center is marked by ambivalence and "two-ness" — a hesitant, almost ashamed, both/and rather than either/or. In one draft of the economics letter, the bishops referred to the danger of the laity living a "spiritually schizophrenic existence," with the values of their faith bearing little relationship to their lives as workers, consumers, and citizens. Yet they themselves were unable to integrate the seemingly conflicting demands of citizenship and discipleship. Instead they honestly acknowledge the presence of "two styles of teaching." One style, addressed to members of the church, begins with the message of Jesus and explores the responsibility of Christians. The tone is radical and demanding, tending toward nonviolence and calling for a separation from social values and practices that contradict the Gospel. The second style, directed at the general public, which includes Catholics, is intended to contribute to the development of the public moral consensus, to influence public opinion, and to help shape the public debate about policy by clarifying its moral dimension. Here the language is that of natural law, human dignity, and human rights. Nothing could better mirror the ambivalence of the Catholic university, trying to be faithful to its Catholic heritage and responsible in its academic work. Perhaps the problem is built-in to the location of American Catholicism, as I have suggested.

Little has been done to build on this ambivalence rather than seize one pole or the other: evangelical radicalism or subordination of religious to secular claims. One reason is that educators and scholars give the problems of social responsibility so little attention; they simply don't talk about it. Thomas Landy, S.J., a young Jesuit scholastic who is the founder and director of the remarkable Collegium program mentioned earlier, recently studied the viewpoint of younger Jesuits toward the educational institutions where most of them work or plan to work. He found that many measure their institutions by the Jesuit commitment to the poor and to "faith and justice" and find them wanting. Landy points out that these criticisms often sound like criticisms of the government for not "doing something about" homelessness. Such complaints, blaming abstract government, avoid recognition of the fact that homelessness results from concrete choices we have made and that, even if "government" tried to do something about the problem, it is not at all clear what it should do. Similarly, he finds that Jesuits blame their schools for failing to embody Jesuit ideals when in fact "we do not know how to bring that about." Jesuits "do not talk enough about what it will take as a group to construct the kind of institutions we want." Few put the major share of their efforts into programs that could really shape institutions to embody faith and justice ideals, and few ask how well prepared they are to commit their institutions to these ideals. Only 8 percent of Jesuits in graduate studies are in fields related directly to social and political problems.

Landy's comments about the lack of conversation and the failure to translate rhetoric into personal commitments, intellectual and educational strategies, and concrete programs could be extended to the whole community of Catholic scholars, administrators, and teachers in Catholic higher education. We all can nod our heads at exhortations from liberation theologians and demand more of ourselves after tragedies like that in El Salvador, and we can criticize the church, the government, and the university. But in the end we are forced back to Landy's challenge: do we "blame our institutions for not embodying qualities which we do not know how to give them?"[19]

CHRISTIAN BILINGUALISM

Laypeople thus remain "citizens of two cities." John Courtney Murray argued that the church-state question had been transformed from an institutional question to a question of conscience, so that Christian influence on public life depends less on the institutional church and the hierarchy than on "the quality and credibility of Christian witness in secular society." Father Bryan Hehir argues that the church's ability to influence public policy depends on its "capacity for moral persuasion of its own community and of the civil community." The goal is to make the church "a community of conscience, a body of citizens with a commitment to human rights and a concept of social justice which allows them to make concrete judgements of where and how to stand on questions of legislation, social policy and specific choices facing their neighborhood and nation." For this to happen, Catholics must become convinced that public policy issues "are the business of the Christian community as part of [its] faith commitment."[20] The goal must be the nurturance of a body of laypeople who seek to live with integrity as Christians and responsibly as citizens.

Certainly, the United States needs committed citizens as much as the church needs faithful disciples. Derek Bok, former president of Harvard, speaks out regularly about the need to become more self-conscious and deliberate in educating for responsible citizenship, a message echoed in the widespread popularity of Clinton-era initiatives to encourage community service. In his farewell address at Harvard, Bok spoke of the need for "caring, active, enlightened citizens and civic leaders" and of the vast "work to be done to revitalize our nation." "We must work much harder to strengthen our efforts to prepare able people for professions, such as teaching, government service, ministry and public health, that grapple on a daily basis with the gravest challenges facing our society," Bok said. "And we must do our very best to work with each and every one of our students to deepen their concern for those who need help, to build with them a strong sense of ethical responsibility, to help them acknowledge that exceptional talent carries with it exceptional responsibility for the welfare of others." Yet he admitted that "education for humane citizenship remains a stunted enterprise while preparation for teaching and most of the other helping professions suffers from benign neglect."

Also, Bok implied that a religious issue is involved: "unless universities take their social responsibilities seriously—more seriously, I think—they will never inspire their students with a purpose large enough to fill their lives with meaning." Yet he also insisted that concern is not enough, that competence also matters. Even when the desire to help exists, he argues, people are often stymied by not knowing what to do, so the college and university has a special responsibility to "contribute the knowledge that will help society discover how to overcome its pressing problems."[21] Meaning and competence sounds like the defining terms for a mission statement for a church-related college or university. The fact that Catholic schools have this combination of commitments and great resources of teaching and experience makes this message particularly relevant for them.

Catholic higher education needs to attend both to discipleship (educating lay Catholics) and citizenship (educating responsible participants in public life), as well as to the research required to carry out those responsibilities. The next step, rarely taken, is to ask how.

Jesuit theologian John Coleman has given a lifetime to exploring strategies for translating the faith and justice ideals of the modern church into American terms. He has defended that commitment against Jesuit critics, insisting that society as a whole must provide the horizon for intellectual work and the educational apostolate. But several years ago Coleman noticed that Catholics and, perhaps, all Christians lacked an adequate theory of citizenship. Citing the insights of Alexis de Tocqueville, Coleman argued that Christians tended to make a direct move from faith to politics, the evangelical option mentioned above, judging situations and prescribing solutions on the basis of scripture or church teaching, with little reference to social science or to political reality. This leads to cycles of intense moralism—God's will must be done!—followed by other-worldly defeatism—the world is too sinful and corrupt to respond to God's call!

Active, responsible citizenship, seeking solutions to public problems amid multiple pluralisms, diverse interests, and varying perspectives is sometimes hard to justify on Christian grounds, for this work requires constant negotiation and compromise. Faith can provide vision and motivation and norms to guide judgement, but these work best when expressed negatively in prophetic judgements against prevailing sinfulness. Thus, many of the great Christian heroes are agitators, protestors, and conscientious objectors. As Karl Rahner noted, faith can name an evil and demand action, but it cannot of itself prescribe solutions and mandate choices.

Yet choices will be made. In a democratic society, everyone is responsible for those choices, especially when they have moved, as so many Catholics have, from the margins to the center of society. Peacemaking (as opposed to war avoidance), and justice creation (as distinct from protest and agitation), and political responsibility (as opposed to a religious "culture of complaint") all require precisely such choices—a never-ending process of dialogue, negotiation, coalition building, and reform, an ongoing "new American experiment."

So Coleman and his coworkers seek a pedagogy for citizenship and discipleship.[22] Politics is a dangerous route to the exercise of power, so that the vigilance of a community of conscience is required and a Christian church true to itself can never be incorporated fully into any political community. But the responsible exercise of de facto power is necessary in order to carry out human and Christian obligations of love and justice. Power corrupts, but so does powerlessness.

Thus, one must develop thicker concepts of politics involving the public work of making operative the moral consensus of the community reached through face-to-face discussion. Coleman agrees with Robert Bellah and his associates who follow de Tocqueville in regarding religion as crucially important for a democracy because it affirms "those mores which alone anchor a republic and make democracy possible." Given the necessary tensions between Christianity and the values of our highly individualistic culture, the church "must develop a distinctively Christian pedagogy of discipleship that approaches its bilingual conversation with citizenship in clear command of its own vocabulary." But politics is a realm where concrete human choices are made; to render present the reign of God, Christians have to read and act on the signs of the times. So the church that educates for discipleship must also educate for citizenship. And reading the signs of the times and making responsible choices require what Father Hesburgh and his generation knew it would require—academic excellence. To get Catholics to think and to think in responsible ways means working with others, equals and colleagues, and it means risks. But it is necessary, unless the only task is to build up the church.

Christian co-stewardship with fellow citizens turns the church away from such parochial introspection and keeps alive the important truth that the church exists for the world. Active citizenship adds to Christian discipleship a "taxing reality test." Christianity earns its ground for hope in the concrete experience of working to transform power. Christianity adds to citizenship the disciplines of conscientious reserve, imagination about the possibilities of forgiveness and of justice and utopian transformation, and the permanent reminder that the ultimate purpose of politics is the service of real human persons and their communities. Coleman concludes:

> Christians view their life as a vocation, a calling to construct — using the only political materials we human beings have at hand — at least an approximation of that undistorted communication in neighbor love envisioned by God's new community. Hence . . . beyond critical negativity, beyond eschatological reserve against every historical social achievement, and beyond countercultural refusals, discipleship must also unleash the constructive power of vocation to build, in and through the present structures, a more habitable commonwealth through what Bonhoeffer calls the "venture of responsibility."

If there is a challenge for Catholic higher education in this, it is once again to find religious meaning in the experience of ambivalence: Christian commitment and professional competence, active discipleship alert to violations of God's creation, and responsible citizenship ready to bear with others, all others, full responsibility for neighbor, nation, and world. There is a decisive division between the moral ideals of citizenship and discipleship, to be sure, so we need the church. But whatever their personal convictions, disciples can make their case as citizens "only in the discourse of secular warrants and public reason." Otherwise, as on abortion, they lose consistently and blame the others. This is why Coleman calls for "bilingualism," a capacity to help form the church as a community of conscience loyal to the Gospel and alert to the Catholic tradition, and able *at the same time* to share with others in shaping the public moral consensus that in the end governs the behavior of states, corporations, and other powerful institutions.

Christianity's great achievement was to form a human community beyond national societies, thus witnessing to the possibilities of a larger human family. But the duties of people to their country — the public virtues exercised daily — have been inadequately defined and considerably neglected. In John Coleman's words: "It is undeniable that Christianity lacks a coherent, fully developed Christian theory of citizenship, a specifically Christian sense of any sacredness or vocational meaning of membership in a particular nation, with its own national character type and historic goals and challenges." In classic political thought, no republic can withstand tyranny without virtuous citizens, and there can be no virtuous citizens without vital religion. But it is hard for Christians to see their public role as disciples in a society marked by pluralism and expressive individualism. Thus, the need for Coleman's "pedagogy for discipleship and for citizenship." And perhaps, as we have argued above, for the recovery of Americanism.

PURPOSE IN THE ACADEMY

Service to church and society by thinking and teaching about discipleship and citizenship sets the terms for understanding the purpose of the Catholic college and university. By these terms, not everyone need be in agreement when they hear a message like that of Father Jerez Garcia, but they need to engage the questions he raises. The fact that some regard such a focus on public responsibility as vaguely "political" and therefore inappropriate is worrisome. Laurence Veysey has pointed out that in its origin the American university was torn between three conflicting visions of its purpose: research for its own sake, the preservation of traditional culture, and public service. By World War I the rhetoric of service had won out, both in the universities and in the professions they spawned.[23] When the American Academy of Arts and Sciences surveyed American professional organizations regarding codes of ethics after World War I, all who responded included ringing affirmations of the service to society rendered by their professional group: lawyers helped to make America more just, doctors to make its people more healthy, businessmen to make society more productive, engineers to make it more efficient, and all to make it more democratic.

Yet beneath the rhetoric, as Veysey saw, were other impulses impelling the academic world and the professions toward an increasing emphasis on standards of entry, certification, internal modes of reward and status, intensified specialization, and the spawning of clienteles interested in their security and advancement. In the universities, even historical and literary studies, philosophy, and theology became specialized. The process brought about what Reisman and Jencks called "the academic revolution," with the triumph of the graduate school, the decline of general education, and an academic culture marked by the loss of a common language and a common set of goals and prospects—a set of problems so widely acknowledged that they hardly need elaboration.[24]

Catholic schools, as we have seen, are now so much a part of the academic community that they share its problems as well as its resources, but they have their own angle of vision. Today, the Catholic problem is to bring the vision and values grounded in faith to bear upon the problems of the larger public life we all share. It is a cultural problem of language and symbols; it is a political problem of power and its use; it is an economic problem of determining how to allocate scarce resources and share in needed sacrifices and prospective benefits; and it is a personal problem of overcoming the paralyzing gap between personal and public life, between the values of love and mutuality all of us try to express in our family and church and among our friends and the constraints of institutions and structures that mark our working life, our political life, and our participation in advanced industrial society. We in higher education can and unfortunately often do contribute to the problem, legitimating the gaps and affirming in practice if not in theory the self-serving conventional wisdom that things are pretty much as they have to be.

I have emphasized these broad requirements because I believe that the problems we confront in Catholic higher education are less problems of technique than of will. Deciding what to do is far less important at this stage than deciding that something has to be done. But the direction we might take is also fairly clear.

Discipleship

If it is true that work is a central means by which one defines one's personality and orients oneself toward the world and if it is also true that Christian faith must express itself in a concern for the poor, for social justice, and for peace made integral to the whole of one's life, then clearly Christian responsibility for the world is not adequately served by participation in the weekly meeting of one's parish social action committee or volunteer service in a social agency. Vocation, or calling, is the word we have used to describe the belief that each of us has abilities and talents that we are called upon to offer in the service of Christ and his people. We know this today in the internal life of the church, where we are elaborating various forms of lay ministry to enable persons to place their gifts at the service of the specifically Christian community. Yet, according to the teaching of the church, the laity's vocation is in the world — in marriage and family, neighborhood and community, work, politics, and culture. The People of God, the Body of Christ, is that all the time, including those times we are not in church.

Thus, we could argue that the most basic question that laypeople have to answer is "What shall we do?" "What shall I major in?" a student asks. "What courses shall I take?" I answer, "Well, what do you want to do?" Some respond quickly: law, medicine, education, engineering, business; others seem never to get an answer straight. In light of the social teaching of the church, we have several responsibilities in regard to such questions. We need to assist students to decide what they wish to do in a way that is intelligent and informed but is also self-consciously related to their faith, their values, and the kinds of people they wish to become. Secondly, we need to provide opportunities early in the college career for students to examine a department, discipline, or school in its concrete social location. What kind of knowledge is gained from this discipline and why is it available here? What is done and can be done with this kind of knowledge? What are the institutions through which careers are built on the basis of the knowledge thus obtained, and what purposes do those careers and institutions actually serve? What is the meaning of that discipline in light of religious faith, humane social values, and the actual conditions of modern life? Such questions need to be asked more than informally; they might be asked in general education courses, but only if practitioners of each discipline are participants in those courses. Needless to say, similar questions should be asked, formally, and with even more intensity and rigor, in graduate and professional programs.

Finally, we need to offer similar experiences at the end of the college or graduate school career. What have I learned and what does it mean to me in light of my faith, my values, and my goals and aspirations? What is the public role that people with my kind of knowledge play? If one element of my understanding of my specialty is public service, how is that public service offered? Who controls access to the knowledge of which we are custodians? Is the knowledge and power I have acquired available to the poor or only to the powerful? How do I conduct myself within the careers now open to me? At what points must I refuse certain kinds of work? What support and assistance can I expect in attempting to make my knowledge and the institutions through which I practice my skills just and peacemaking and socially responsible? How can I organize, with others, to make the institutions for which I will share responsibility work better?

In short, the quite natural concern of students with careers, the current emphasis on cooperation as the key to economic reform, the weakness of social values, and the current teaching of the church regarding the integral, constitutive role of justice and peace in the Christian life converge to make vocation a central symbol and theme for contemporary higher education and a useful and appropriate vehicle for building a more integrated, humanistic, and Christian education.

Everyone or almost everyone understands that all the questions we have raised are in some sense political. There is a politics of the arts, sciences, humanities, engineering, and business as well as of higher education as a whole. On the large scale, we know that we are responsible for the decisions of our government on issues of war and peace, world trade, social justice, taxation, and a thousand other questions. On the small scale, we know that our choices about allocating our time and talent affect the quality of local public life, the climate for business, the treatment of labor and minorities, and problems of crime, housing, and education.

Yet, while we all acknowledge political responsibility, we do little to teach it. Clearly, we need training for citizenship, and, like religion, that means not simply another course in the professional field of politics, but an encounter with the political issues that are present in and can be examined through all disciplines. Public responsibility means not only learning how to participate in politics, but learning also how to raise the political standards of the body politic in work, in cultural pursuits, in all those ways in which we interact with one another and shape a common life. In this society, where government is so important to all phases of life and where we profess to share responsibility for its actions, we can no more afford to leave political education to the politicians than to leave religious education to the clergy. Catholic colleges and universities, with a rich tradition of political theory, an exciting body of social and political thought emanating from every country in the world, and connections through the church with people involved in political struggles from Poland to the Philippines, have particular responsibilities in this regard as well as wonderful opportunities to make a significant contribution to American society, with its evident poverty of political conversation. Thus, political education — education that recognizes existing political involvement and seeks to make our public life richer and more intelligent — is indispensable to our efforts to renew Catholic higher education.

TOWARD THE THIRD STAGE

Jesuit historian William Leahy, concluding a series of provocative essays on the history of Catholic higher education, stated that before World War II people worked in these colleges and universities under the inspiration of a "clear and compelling sense of purpose." More than anything else, he argued, "Catholic higher education in the United States urgently requires a coherent, convincing theory of education and articulate, persuasive proponents of that theory."[25]

In its earliest stages, Catholic higher education in the United States was designed to help Catholics survive, in part by recruiting and training priests and sisters. In its second stage, it assisted Catholics to move up the social and economic ladder. In the first stage, people struggled to create and sustain colleges and universities. Later they worked hard to make them very good colleges and universities. The model for the first stage was the priest helping his people to build a church and root themselves in America and its local communities. During the second stage we continued to celebrate our priests and sisters, but there were some new models now: the talented, tough, ambitious veterans of the World War becoming doctors and lawyers and businessmen, carving out for themselves and their people a place at the center of American life: Democrat Bruce Babbitt and Republican John Sears, my classmates at Notre Dame; Abigail McCarthy from St. Catherine's and Mary McGrory from Emmanuel; Edward Bennett Williams, a symbol for Holy Cross—a dozen men and women come to our mind for each of these schools.

Today, in our work together, in church and on campus, we are defining a third stage. The models of the next generation? They are people who are as committed as those priests and as competent as those laypeople, more Christian, perhaps a shade less Catholic, still faithful to the Catholic people, but finding the boundaries of churches and nations more blurred. They are people now ready to ask some tough new questions about religion and church, patriotism and politics, and ready to build communities that are communities of conscience and to raise families that are authentic partnerships.

They are out there already: A nurse building a Catholic Worker hospice for terminal AIDS patients in Oakland. A doctor with the World Health Organization in east Africa. In Baltimore a community organizer developing affordable housing and another creating a new way to support high school students faced with the perils of urban poverty and violence. A graduate student studying ethics and arms control in hopes of improving the quality of public discourse and then working awhile in social services until his wife gets her law degree. Another young couple with several children who decide that she will work at a job she loves while he works at home with the children and provides leadership in ministry and religious education in their parish. A Catholic Worker facing jail for challenging the Trident submarine. A Hartford insurance executive helping other laypeople to discover opportunities to make the search for human dignity part of their everyday experience at work. Three young Fordham graduates, community organizers and youth outreach workers, driving across the United States to join the Congressional campaign of another Fordham graduate, a one-time Jesuit seminarian committed to helping his Latino people in San Diego fulfill their American dreams.

Once we celebrated those tough priests and tougher sisters, and we still must attend to the need for talented, educated leadership for our church.

Then we celebrated those successful business and professional people, and we still need to help people gain the knowledge and skills and access they need to make a life for themselves and to share responsibility for the common life. There are still a lot of people knocking at our doors, hoping for what we were given. But today we especially celebrate, in our speeches on and off campus, those women and men for whom the search for justice and the making of peace are personal commitments that provide vocational guidelines. We hope that our schools will be places where people, young and increasingly not so young, can form convictions, become confident about compassion, sharpen their wits, turn talent and knowledge to use for the world, and perhaps find some friends for their journey.

Almost forty years ago, in the second stage of our collective history, John Tracy Ellis worried that we were doing a good job penetrating business and the professions, but not as good influencing American culture. One reason, he thought, was that there were too many schools and there was too little cooperation among them. Recent history, especially in dealing with Rome and the American bishops, demonstrates that Catholic higher education has come a long way. Localism — the preoccupation of the pastor with his parish, the bishop with his diocese, the priest or nun president with his or her college or university — has been a great strength of the American church. But it has also been a weakness, one reason for low academic achievement for many years. Now some of that leadership needs to be given to national work, to raising money not for one school but for programs to benefit all schools and to help give new meaning to Catholic higher education. An honest look at our own situation and at the state of our culture, however, suggests the need for additional cooperative efforts if we are to successfully enter our third stage of service.

Briefly, let me mention three possibilities.

First, we need a national student movement. On each of our campuses there are men and women deeply and intelligently involved in the church and in the works of justice and mercy. In my experience, such people and the faculty and staff working with them often feel isolated, sometimes on campus, more often in the church. In the past, such apostolic young people found courage and hope in the visions awakened and friendships formed through national and international student action groups. Archbishop Jean Jadot, our former Apostolic Delegate, often remarked on the strange absence here of Catholic student organizations such as those he had worked with in Belgium. He thought they provided appropriate alternative ways for young people to share their faith and experience the church. Equally important, with a degree of autonomy and an apostolic orientation, they could serve as a goad to the more complacent parishes and chancery offices, they could form people with a sense of the lay vocation, and they could provide a way for people to experience the universal reach of the contemporary church, an international consciousness badly needed in our American religious culture.

I think we need to connect our pockets of dedicated students with one another and with their peers in other parts of the world. We might begin by supporting regional and cluster groups, such as the Catholic Student Leadership Conference, and the initiative of John Carroll students to gather people from Jesuit campuses or developments that reinforce student activism, like the growing interest in Taize and its distinctive spirituality. With relatively modest effort, we might animate an American Catholic student movement that would witness to our third stage vision, put flesh on our professions of service to the church, provide some ground for collaboration with local churches and bishops, encourage struggling young people in Africa, Latin America, Asia, and Eastern Europe, and repay with energetic, educated, and enthusiastic young adults the persistent support of our schools by the American Catholic people.

Second, we need a national center for Catholic scholarship. Several years ago, Archbishop Pilla of Cleveland headed up a committee charged with implementing the bishops' pastoral letter on the economy. That committee recommended the establishment of a national research center that would tackle economic issues from a moral perspective. A short while later, Father James Heft of Dayton called for a national research center, modeled on the Woodrow Wilson International Center for Scholars, as an engine to lift the quality of intellectual life on campus and in the church. Earlier I noted that Michael Lacey of that same Wilson Center made a similar proposal to the American Catholic Theological Society. Lacey agrees with William Shea that we have taken the plurality of modern culture into ourselves, at the risk to our identity as Catholic institutions, but that experiment offers us unique opportunities to explore with those others the religious meanings of our common life. But to do so we have to first of all "take responsibility for our convictions and exercise and argue those convictions in the political, academic and ecclesial arenas," in public, if you will — something that most of us, surprisingly, rarely do.

From Tracy Ellis to Heft, Lacey, and Shea, we have been told that we need to demonstrate our intellectual seriousness. For years we thought that this meant primarily the establishment of first-rate graduate programs. But Lacey, correctly, thinks otherwise: "I would recommend that rather than thinking simply in terms of gradually developing through marginal improvements a great, comprehensive Catholic university, we think instead about creating a more modest, more flexible, more specialized and altogether more modern institutional form . . . some kind of institute for advanced study to be devoted to the needs of Catholic scholars in all of the humanities and the social sciences."[26]

Such a center might awaken interest in Catholic ideas among American academics. It might catch the attention of Catholic scholars who are now not very interested in religion. After all, as Heft insists, no university can honestly claim Catholic identity unless a critical mass of the faculty is intellectually committed to Catholicism. But intellectually committed Catholic scholars will not automatically emerge from secular graduate schools; they need to be identified, recruited, and supported. Most of all, they need to be invited to share in a sustained dialogue on issues that matter, which such a center would initiate. Summer institutes and special seminars like those offered for Christian college faculty by their organizations could begin to build that "critical mass" of faculty scattered across the disciplines and interested in Catholic intellectual life.

Third, as I have indicated in this chapter, we have not thought seriously and systematically enough about how to integrate matters of faith and social responsibility into our undergraduate and graduate curriculum. In their economics letter of 1986, the bishops said that laypeople seek holiness by fighting for human dignity in the workplace. In short, we have to help each other bring our faith to life in our own work and help our students do the same. Campus ministry, religious studies, voluntary service projects, and small social justice or peace studies programs alone won't do it. So Catholic schools have a special responsibility to attempt to integrate religious questions into general education and to offer interested students, including those in professional and graduate programs, opportunities to engage the Catholic tradition and learn of the life and work of the contemporary church. They also share with all other schools an obligation to assist faculty and students in thinking through their social and civic responsibilities, especially in the context of the specific forms of learning that they pursue.

In colleges and universities, the justice imperative is usually connected with community service programs for students and courses in ethics in departments and schools. The limited impact of these programs after two decades of rhetorical commitment indicates that there are some problems. I have suggested some in discussing service programs above. But there are problems with ethics as well. For one thing, the ethics involved are usually personal and professional. They highlight the moral problems that people face when working in particular fields, and they locate the center of action in the person and his or her conscience. They speak less about the institutional settings within which such decision making takes place and rarely address the politics of decision making in business, law, medicine, or society at large. Unavoidably, there is often a negative character to the discussion, as it usually gives more attention to avoiding evil than to doing good. One learns how to draw the line over which one cannot step without losing integrity. Even when drawn further, to do good, the good is usually personal, involving legal or medical assistance or efforts to hire minorities and women. Less is learned about how to transform sinful social situations, such as a class-biased justice and medical system, so that it might become easier to be good. Still less is heard about the organizational and political commitments that might be required to make justice a reality.

A second problem is that ethics is philosophical, not theological; it tends to separate value questions from meaning or faith questions. In the process, decision makers (including professors and students) are abstracted from communities of meaning and value, churches, parties, and movements. The person who makes ethical evaluations is not a Protestant, a Catholic, or a Jew, a fundamentalist or a liberal, a Republican or a Democrat. Detached from communities of meaning, dropped into structures that are simply given, the abstract person finds that justice is a matter of choosing the best available option. Goodness becomes just another art of the possible, in an age of shrinking possibilities.

The world transforming goodness of a Gandhi, a John XXIII, or an Oscar Romero, in contrast, arises from faith, from powerful convictions about meaning. In the absence of serious reflection on such matters, one tends to adapt to changing historical circumstances. Perhaps that worked humanely when everyone believed that somehow things were always getting better. In light of the Holocaust and other human being–made tragedies, defeatist meanings (after all, what can I do?) easily fill the void left by the fragmentation of knowledge and the decline of public dialogue. The gap between the claims of education and the realities of culture is enlarged, and the chasm between sophisticated technical knowledge and helplessness in dealing with larger questions of life becomes all but impassable.

So what can be done to reintroduce matters of faith into research and teaching and to make meaning part of the agenda of Catholic higher education? A start is to insist that ideas have consequences; this was the late Michael Harrington's summary of his Jesuit education. In his undergraduate years at Holy Cross, the presence of Jesuit priests, their distinctive garb, their unusual celibate and communal lifestyle, bore living witness to this conviction. They believed; and because they believed what they did, life was different. They seemed convinced that those beliefs were completely reasonable and, therefore, that they should shape the lives of people and nations and not just their own. One could, then, study and come to some conclusions; those conclusions should influence how one lived one's life as spouse and parent, as worker and citizen. Thus, if educators speak of faith and justice, they have to show that these ideals make a difference for them and for their communities and institutions. If not, they make meaning (that is, religion) merely private, fit for chapel and voluntary discussion groups, but not for classroom, laboratory, or the streets.

With the decline of reason or, no better, of faith in reason, and with the refusal of religion (that is, its withdrawal from the center of culture), how does one address the question of whether the world makes sense? An artist produces a painting or a poem that asks: where do we come from? who are we? where are we going? Catholic and Jesuit colleges and universities have tried to present a variety of ways, from science to theology, of approaching those questions. Do we know now, in our own culture, what meaning means and how to deal with its questions? One thinks of Epiphany: the revelation of God in Christ is for everyone. The church, as Christ's presence in the world, must pronounce the word in ways that make sense and meaning for everyone, not just for professed Christians. Men and women will make liberating values their own, do justice, and love mercy in the setting, and only in the setting, of meanings about life and history. So one cannot and one should not detach faith from justice, religion from ethics, or, in this case, the university from its Catholic companion.

BEGINNING ANEW: A SUMMARY AND CONCLUSION

The history of the last thirty years is not adequately captured by the word secularization. A generation ago, most religious orders turned their schools over to lay-dominated Board of Trustees and simultaneously attempted to improve their academic programs by hiring more lay, professionally trained faculty and staff. Separate incorporation broke the link of juridical accountability through religious orders to the church hierarchy; despite persistent trustee expressions of loyalty, Rome has never accepted that. Academic professionalization required adoption of prevailing American standards of academic freedom (though not always for theologians, especially in schools which retained juridical ties to the hierarchy) and, less noticed, forms of academic government which gave the increasingly lay and diverse faculty and professional staffs predominant jurisdiction over matters of personnel and curriculum.

As critics note, with all this came the problems of modern American academic life, most notably the increasing power of departments and the emphasis on the disciplines, making general education, core curriculum and interdisciplinary work of all kinds more and more difficult. Most assuredly, then, the combination of separate incorporation and faculty-staff professionalization made formulation of an integrally Catholic mission statement and development of integrated Catholic academic programs difficult.

On the other hand, these changes were not primarily the result of passive accommodation to prevailing culture resulting from a desire to be accepted by secular elites or to gain government financial assistance. No, leaders of Catholic higher education made decisions to improve the quality of research and teaching by opening their institutions to contemporary culture and to the pluralisms which marked that culture, and increasingly marked the church as well. They took Vatican II's words on "The Church and the Modern World" seriously, and hoped that the church could become more intelligent and the nation, through the work of the laity, a bit more just and even a bit more religious. It was a rather Americanist agenda, to be sure, but one which reflected the new responsibilities of Catholics moving from the edge to the center of American society and culture. In one of the great moments of renewal, these priests and sisters took the risk of actually turning their schools over to lay people and sharing responsibility with them. Elsewhere in the church (except perhaps in hospitals) that was not done, and our church is paying a very heavy price for that refusal.

So, what are the options now? Critics, in the Vatican and among professional Catholics, see an integrity problem, so they want to restore a degree of truth in advertising; if the schools say they are Catholic, then they should be Catholic. But when you ask what that means, things get murky. Few want to take the route of the truly confessional schools, admirable as many of them may be. Almost no one mentions campus ministry, which in fact is well supported and thriving on many campuses. In fact, there is not much discussion about the faith of students, professors or staff; there are some negative undercurrents about student moral behavior, but that is hardly new. Most of all, there is the usual yearning for integrated liberal arts education, and the usual sentimentalizing of the old days: Catholic professors teaching Catholic students about Catholic things. But so far, Catholic restorationists offer few interesting ideas about how Catholic colleges might do better than others in overcoming the fragmentation of the disciplines or the exclusion of religion from most areas of academic research and teaching.

If there is a consensus, it is that schools return to theology, in fact to *Catholic* theology. Once that is in place, it seems, wonderful dialogues between these Catholic theologians and scholars in other schools and departments will begin, these conversations will reinvigorate the Catholic mission of the schools, and a really integrated curriculum and graduates articulate about the Catholic tradition will not be far behind. There is much to be said for reinvigorating Catholic theology, but for even a casual observer of contemporary Catholic theology this argument seems inadequate. To take it seriously as a program for restoring Catholicism in higher education requires one to ignore a great many things: that it is precisely theology's encounter with other faiths and disciplines that has led some serious people to take it seriously; that academic theology is as prone to superspecialization and methodological obsession as any other discipline, and shows no greater affinity for general education and core curriculum than history or English, for example; that much academic theology has lost almost all contact with the church's pastoral life, a chasm which on some campuses places the theologians at odds with the campus ministry staff.

Worst of all, it mirrors one of the most depressing aspects of American Catholic culture these days, the near universal conviction that the church and its constituent elements have become too American and need to pull back, presumably to church. Whether ordinary Catholics have become too secular, like those professors trying to get approval from the big shots at Harvard, or too mindlessly religious, like those students attracted to evangelical style piety or merely humanitarian service to poor people, they need to get back to church and get themselves properly instructed, or so they are told.

Catholic higher education, now with many structures of shared responsibility, more open to the cross currents of our culture than other Catholic institutions, located at the intersection of David Tracy's three publics: the academy, the church and society at large, has enormous potential to contribute to higher education, to American Christianity and to our country. Despite supposed secularization, there is great talent and amazing good will at these places. People who care about these schools and about the publics they serve need to develop creative, attractive proposals for curriculum, faculty development, interdisciplinary dialogue, professional and graduate education, and service to church and society. One thing is sure, the people who give their lives to these institutions will not — and should not — regard complaints about secularization and calls for Catholic restoration as serious proposals for renewal. Self-consciously Catholic theology, deeply versed in the church, is indispensable, but it is not close to the heart of the matter.

Twenty years ago, during an earlier controversy on this subject, one of the wisest leaders of Catholic higher education insisted that the problem of Catholic mission of colleges and universities was first of all pastoral. That has something to do with living the faith, and speaking about it, in such a way that the church and its traditions and ideas seem worth considering. In other words, inviting the people who give their lives to Catholic higher education to join in the great work of enriching human life and culture is probably a better route to renewal than complaints about selling out to secular gods.

The beginning of the next phase of the discussion of Catholic higher education may require more public attention to such matters. Attentive to the culture of pluralism, inviting persons from diverse communities to dialogue about important matters, and committed to a faith that is intellectually serious, Catholics can bring rich resources to contemporary culture. The effort to do so, to ask questions about faith and justice and frame the answers in the midst of contemporary history, alone makes the continuing effort to clarify the Catholic mission of Catholic colleges and universities helpful to the human community. Most of all, Catholic commitment brings to the Catholic university communities that should nourish the beliefs, and the virtues, that, often unrecognized, make the academic vocation personally rewarding and humanly fruitful. In that sense one hopes that the prediction of Mark Schwehn will be fulfilled: "the most authentic centers of knowledge in the future will have to be based upon a correlative conviction, namely, that there is a relationship between our love of learning and our love for one another, and that both of these loves are in turn, expressions of our desire for God."[27]

Notes

PREFACE

1. Alice Gallin, O.S.U., ed., *American Catholic Higher Education: Essential Documents, 1967-1990* (Notre Dame, 1992).

1. AUTOBIOGRAPHY AND CATHOLIC HIGHER EDUCATION

1. John Henry Newman, *On the Scope and Nature of University Education,* Everyman Edition (New York, 1958); John Paul II, *Ex Corde Ecclesiae,* in *Current Issues in Catholic Higher Education* (hereafter cited as *Current Issues*) (Winter, 1991), pp. 31–42.

2. Nathan Hatch, *The Democratization of American Christianity* (New Haven, Conn., 1989).

3. Daniel Berrigan, S.J. and Robert Coles, *The Geography of Faith* (Boston, 1971).

4. Typescript of speech by Bishop Walter Foery, no date, Foery Papers, Archives, Diocese of Syracuse, N.Y.

5. John Paul II, *Redemptor Hominis,* par. 13; text in *Catholic Free Press* (Worcester, Mass., March 16, 1979).

6. The following is a revised version of "Faith and Work: An Experience of Religion and Intellectual Life," a paper delivered to a conference of the Association for Religion and the Intellectual Life and published in *Cross Currents: Religion and Intellectual Life,* 40 (Summer, 1990), 194–206.

7. From the Society for Religion in Higher Education, now the Society for Values in Higher Education.

8. Michael Novak, *The Open Church* (London, 1964).

9. Pope John XXIII, Opening Speech, in Walter Abbott, ed., *The Documents of Vatican II* (New York, 1966), p. 715.

10. Michael Novak, *Confessions of a Catholic* (San Francisco, 1983).

11. Harry Emerson Fosdick, *The Living of These Days* (New York, 1956), p. 53.

12. David J. O'Brien, *The Renewal of American Catholicism* (New York, 1972).

13. Joseph Cardinal Bernardin, "Church Impact on Public Policy," *Origins,* 13 (February 1984), p. 567.

14. "X" [George Kennan], "The Sources of Soviet Conduct," in *The People Shall Judge: Readings in the Formation of American Policy,* II (Chicago, 1949), p. 829.

15. Page Smith, *Killing the Spirit: Higher Education in America* (New York, 1990), p. 5.

16. Daniel Callahan, "Religious Slum-Dwellers," *Commonweal* (August 19, 1966), pp. 530-533.

17. David J. O'Brien, *American Catholics and Social Reform: The New Deal Years* (New York, 1968).

18. The story of the Call to Action Conference has not been told in print. I have an unpublished manuscript about the project; unpublished probably because I was too close to the program.

19. John XXIII, *Pacem in Terris* in David J. O'Brien & Thomas Shannon, editors, *Renewing the Earth* (Garden City, NY, 1973), pp. 117-130; "The Pastoral Constitution on the Church and the Modern World," in Abbott, *Documents,* pp. 198-199.

20. "The Dogmatic Constitution on the Church," in Abbott, *Documents*, p. 58.

21. David Tracy, *The Analogical Imagination* (New York, 1981).

2. CATHOLICISM, AMERICAN STYLE

1. For an excellent statement of this approach, to be discussed later, see Michael Buckley, S.J., "The Catholic University and Its Inherent Promise," in *America* (May 29, 1993), pp. 14-16, and, in somewhat longer form, "The Catholic University and the Promise Inherent in Its Identity," in John Langan, S.J., ed., *Catholic Universities in Church and Society: A Dialogue on Ex Corde Ecclesiae* (Washington, 1993), pp. 74-89.

2. Mary Gordon, *Final Payments* (New York, 1978), p. 3.

3. Andrew Greeley, *American Catholics: A Social Portrait* (New York, 1977); *The Communal Catholic* (New York, 1976); *Crisis in the Church* (Chicago, 1979).

4. David J. O'Brien, *Public Catholicism* (New York, 1988), chapters 8-9.

5. I have examined the tripartite sources of change in the American church in "Some Reflections on the Catholic Experience in the United States" in Irene Woodward, ed., *The Catholic Church: The United States Experience* (New York, 1979), pp. 5-42, and in *Public Catholicism*. See also Sidney Ahlstrom, "National Trauma and Changing Religious Values," *Daedalus* 78 (1978), pp. 13-29.

6. John Coleman, S.J., "The Future of Ministry," *America* (March 28, 1981), pp. 243-49.

7. Andrew Greeley, "Going Their Own Way," *New York Times Magazine* (October 10, 1982).

8. Patrick M. McNamara, *Conscience First, Tradition Second: A Study of Young Catholics* (Albany, N.Y., 1992), especially pp. 158-162; and Michael Hunt, "All is Not Lost: An Early Look at the Class of '96," *Commonweal* (April 9, 1993), pp. 18-21, and *College Catholics* (Mahwah, N.J., 1993).

9. John Tracy Ellis, *American Catholicism* (rev. ed., Chicago, 1969); James Hennessy, S.J., *American Catholics* (New York, 1982); Jay P. Dolan, *The Catholic Experience* (New York, 1985).

10. Hennessy, *American Catholics*, p. 331.

11. Timothy L. Smith, "Religion and Ethnicity in America," *American Historical Review* 83 (1978), pp. 1155-85. See also Timothy L. Smith, "Lay Initiative in the Religious Life of American Immigrants, 1880-1950," in Tamara Harevan, ed.,

Anonymous Americans (Englewood Cliffs, N.J., 1971), pp. 214-49; Smith, "Immigrant Social Aspirations and American Education, 1880-1950," *American Quarterly* 21 (Fall 1969), pp. 534-36.

12. Hayden V. White, "The Burden of History," *History and Theory,* 5 (Spring 1966), pp. 29-33.

13. John XXIII, quoted in Giancarlo Zizola, *The Utopia of Pope John* (Maryknoll, N.Y., 1974), p. 246.

14. "Pastoral Constitution on the Church and the Modern World," in Abbott, *Documents,* p. 200.

15. Karl Rahner, "Towards a Fundamental Theological Interpretation of Vatican II," *Theological Studies,* 42 (1981), pp. 716-27.

16. Karl Rahner, *The Christian Commitment* (New York, 1963), p. 29.

17. Peter L. Berger and Richard John Newhaus, eds., *Against the World, For the World* (New York, 1976); Avery Dulles, *The Resilient Church* (Garden City, NY, 1977).

18. *New York Times,* May 1, 1991.

19. "The Challenge of Peace" (Washington, D.C., 1983), par. 276-277.

20. Thomas Merton, *The Nonviolent Alternative,* ed. by Gordon C. Zahn (New York, 1980), pp. 29, 33, 117, 209.

21. Joseph Cardinal Bernardin, "Church Impact on Public Policy," *Origins,* 13 (February 1984), p. 567.

22. Joseph Komonchak, "Clergy, Laity and the Church's Mission to the World," *The Jurist,* 41 (1981), pp. 425-47.

3. EX CORDE ECCLESIAE AMERICANA

1. Bernard Bailyn, *Education and the Forming of American Society* (New York, 1972); Thomas Bender, *Community and Social Change in America* (New Brunswick, N.J., 1978).

2. For an interesting examination of the combination of religious and worldy objectives, see Ronald Hoffman, "Charles Carroll of Carrollton: The Formative Years, 1748-1764," Working Papers Series, Cushwa Center for the Study of American Catholicism, Series 12, Number 3 (Fall 1982).

3. Philip Gleason, "John Carroll as Educator," *Review of Politics,* 38 (October 1976), pp. 576-613; Philip Gleason, "From an Indefinite Homogeneity: The Beginnings of Catholic Higher Education in the United States," Church History Seminar, Notre Dame (March 15, 1975).

4. Joseph Chinnici, "Politics and Theology: From Enlightenment Catholicism to the Condemnation of Americanism," Working Paper Series, Cushwa Center for the Study of American Catholicism, Series 9, Number 3 (Spring 1981); Chinnici, "American Catholics and Religious Pluralism, 1775-1820," *Journal of Ecumenical Studies,* 19 (Fall 1979), pp. 727-46.

5. Isaac Hecker to Orestes Brownson, [June 24, 1844], in Joseph F. Gower and Richard M. Leliaert, eds., *The Brownson-Hecker Correspondence* (Notre Dame, 1979), p. 105.

6. Philip Gleason, "The Curriculum of the Old-Time Catholic College: A

Student's View," *Records of the American Catholic Historical Society of Philadelphia,* LXXXVIII (March/December 1977), pp. 102–22.

7. The best survey of American higher education history is Gleason, "American Catholic Higher Education: A Historical Perspective," in Robert Hassenger, ed., *The Shape of Catholic Higher Education* (Chicago, 1967), pp. 15–53.

8. John Tracy Ellis, ed., *Documents of American Catholic History,* II (Chicago, 1967), pp. 465–66.

9. Leo XIII, *Longinqua Oceani,* in Ellis, *Documents,* II, pp. 499–510.

10. Leo XIII, *Longinqua Oceani,* p. 505.

11. Leo XIII, *Longinqua Oceani,* p. 507.

12. John Ireland, "Pastoral Letter on Higher Catholic Education," August 17, 1898, in Ireland Papers (microfilm) University of St. Thomas, St. Paul, Minn.

13. Peter E. Hogan, *The Catholic University of America, 1887–1896: The Rectorship of Thomas J. Conaty* (Washington, D.C., 1949), p. 49.

14. McQuaid to Daniel Hudson, CSC, May 30, 1907, in Hudson Papers, University of Notre Dame. John Whitney Evans argues that a sharp break took place in ministry on the non-Catholic campus after World War I, as Catholic colleges began to expand: "In contrast to the first phase, which was characterized by a strong educational and missionary as well as apologetical fervor, this one presented a sorry picture of students and priests combatting secularism on what had become a hostile campus while also defending their effort before Catholic leaders increasingly suspicious and withdrawn." See his *Apostles of Hope: A History of the Newman Movement, 1883–1971* (Notre Dame, 1985).

15. Ignatius W. Cox, "Ideals in Catholic Education," *Commonweal* (October 21, 1925), p. 582.

16. Quoted in David J. O'Brien, "Peter Guilday: The Catholic Intellectual in the Post-Modernist Church" in Nelson Minnich, ed., *Studies in Church History in Honor of John Tracy Ellis* (Wilmington, Del., 1985), p. 274. See also James Hennessy, S.J., *American Catholics* (New York, 1984).

17. William Halsey, *The Survival of American Innocence* (Notre Dame, 1980).

18. Quoted in Gleason, "In Search of Unity," *Catholic Historical Review,* LXV (April 1979), p. 198. Quotes in the following paragraph are from this article.

19. Gleason, "Historical Perspective," p. 46.

20. William Leahy, S.J., *Adapting to America: Catholics, Jesuits, and Higher Education in the Twentieth Century* (Washington, D.C., 1991), p. 100.

21. Gleason, "Changing and Remaining the Same: A Look at the Record," *Current Issues* (Summer 1989), pp. 4–8.

22. Frank Sheed, *The Church and I* (New York, 1974); John Murray Cuddihy, *No Offense* (New York, 1969).

23. Ellis, "American Catholics and the Intellectual Life," *Thought,* 30 (Autumn, 1955), 353–86; O'Brien, *Renewal,* ch. 2.

24. David Reisman and Christopher Jencks, *The Academic Revolution* (Cambridge, 1968).

25. Theodore M. Hesburgh, "Looking Back at Newman," *America* (March 3, 1962), p. 721.

26. The naming of departments is confusing. Earlier, philosophy dominated the curriculum, but many schools offered courses in religion, usually catechetical or apologetic and somewhat marginal to the curriculum. When theology arrived, it was

initially pushed as a subject of study designed for laypeople and supportive of Catholic Action, the official apostolic work of laypeople under clerical direction. Gradually in the fifties and then dramatically in the sixties, schools upgraded these subjects, placing them on firmer academic ground. Sometimes the department continued to be called religion or religious studies, because theology was still thought proper only in the seminary. By the late sixties, however, the modern understanding of religious studies as an academic discipline studying religion as a phenomenon, distinct from theology, arrived on some campuses. The title was useful where state funding agencies and courts were watchful against proselytization, but it was not always clear whether the title was a secular-sounding cover for theology or represented a formal commitment to a less confessional approach to the subject of religion.

27. Patrick W. Carey, *Theology at Marquette University: A History,* pamphlet (Milwaukee, 1987).

28. Text in Gallin, ed., *American Catholic Higher Education,* pp. 7–13.

4. THE CATHOLIC ACADEMIC REVOLUTION

1. Terence J. Murphy, a young priest and president of St. Thomas College, summarized these considerations for establishing independent boards in a January 1967 speech to the First Friday Club of St. Paul, Minn., reported in the National Catholic Educational Association, College and University Department *Newsletter* (hereafter C&U *Newsletter*) for February 3, 1967. His argument was confirmed during a three-day conversation with Theodore M. Hesburgh, C.S.C., Paul Reinert, S.J., Ann Ida Gannon, Daniel Schlafley, and Edward Stepan at Notre Dame in January 1993.

2. A recent study of 137 colleges and universities by Martin J. Stamm found that 98 percent had boards separate from the religious community. The members were 70 percent laypeople and 30 percent clergy and religious. For this reason I prefer the term independent boards to the more widely used lay boards. *Current Issues* (Summer 1993), pp. 10–17.

3. C&U *Newsletter* (March 6, 1967 and March 1968).

4. Peter O'Reilly, "St. John's I: A Chronicle of Folly," *Continuum,* IV (Summer 1966), pp. 230, 232.

5. *National Catholic Reporter* (February 2, 1966).

6. Norma Krause Herzfeld, "The Problem at Catholic University," *Commonweal* (March 31, 1967).

7. Manning M. Patillo, Jr. and Donald M. McKenzie, *Church-Sponsored Higher Education in the United States* (New York, 1966) p. 204.

8. Rosemary Lauer to Martin Marty in *National Catholic Reporter* (February 9, 1966).

9. *New York Times* (December 11, 1966).

10. John Cogley, "The Future of an Illusion," *Commonweal* (June 2, 1967). For a discussion of sponsorship, see the essays in a special issue of *Current Issues in Catholic Higher Education,* IV (Winter 1984).

11. Gleason, "Historical Perspective," p. 52.

12. Gregory F. Lucey, S.J., "The Meaning and Maintenance of Catholicity as a Distinctive Characteristic of American Catholic Higher Education: A Case Study." Unpublished Ph.D. dissertation, University of Wisconsin, 1978; Donald R. LaMagdeleine, "The Changing American Catholic University." Unpublished Ph.D. dissertation, Loyola University, 1983.

13. Gleason, "American Catholic Higher Education, 1970–1990: The Ideological Context" in George Marsden, ed., *The Secularization of the Academy* (New York, 1992) pp. 234–58.

14. "Bishops and the Catholic College," *Ave Maria* (February 10, 1968).

15. Gallin, *American Catholic Higher Education,* pp. 7–12.

16. *College Newsletter* (March 1973).

17. "University and Catholic: Final Report of the Special Committee on the Christian Character of Marquette University" (December 15, 1969).

18. One almost wants to say new. Of course, the new arrangements were in many ways unique, but the notion of institutions that are both Catholic and self-governing is not unknown in Catholic history or canon law. But in the end, self-governing associations are always accountable to the hierarchy or Papacy. Structurally, only the continuing presence of the religious order and the agreements that define their presence maintain a thread of connection of this kind.

19. "Paul VI to the Jesuits: The Catholic Church and Catholic Universities," *Origins* (August 23, 1974), pp. 175–76.

20. John McGrath, *Catholic Institutions in the United States: Canonical and Civil Law Status* (Washington, 1968). While the date of publication comes after the first moves to separate incorporation, recollections are that the argument was widely known before the book appeared.

21. *Update* (December 1, 1976). The best narrative of these events is Ann Ida Gannon, B.V.M., "Some Aspects of Catholic Higher Education Since Vatican II," *Current Issues*, Summer, 1987, pp. 10–24. See also Alice Gallin, O.S.U., "On the Move: Toward a Definition of the Catholic University," *The Jurist,* 48 (Spring, 1988); James J. Annarelli, *Academic Freedom and Catholic Higher Education* (New York, 1987).

22. For the Curran case see Charles Curran, *Catholic Higher Education, Theology and Academic Freedom* (Notre Dame, 1990); William M. May, ed., *Vatican Authority and American Catholic Dissent: The Curran Case and Its Consequences* (New York, 1987); Larry Witham, *Curran Vs. Catholic University: A Study of Authority and Freedom in Conflict* (Revelend, Md., 1991).

23. Text in *Current Issues* (Winter 1991), pp. 31–42. All the quotations that follow are from this text.

24. *Ibid.* par. 12.

25. Boston *Globe* (September 26, 1990); *Catholic Free Press* (September 28, 1990); *New York Times* (September 26, 1990).

26. Memo from Bishop John Leibrecht to the Archbishops and Bishops of the United States and the Presidents of Colleges and Universities (May 4, 1993), privately circulated.

5. WHAT'S CATHOLIC ABOUT CATHOLIC HIGHER EDUCATION?

1. Theodore M. Hesburgh, C.S.C., "Catholic Education in America," *America* (October 4, 1986), pp. 160–63.

2. Data in this section comes from *Catholic Higher Education: An American Profile,* pamphlet (Washington, D.C., 1993); Joseph Pettit, "Enrollment for Fall, 1988 and Finances and Student Aid for Year Ending June 30, 1988 at U.S. Catholic Colleges and Universities," a report prepared for the ACCU in cooperation with the National Association of Independent Colleges and Universities and Georgetown University (1991).

3. Richard V. Warner, C.S.C. is skeptical that larger Catholic institutions will be able to "preserve and develop their Catholic character without an important, appropriate and determinative role for and by the founding religious congregation." He cites the Notre Dame arrangement of a "bicameral" board of 12 fellows and 50 trustees. The 12 fellows, who include 6 laypeople and 6 religious, are empowered to appoint the lay trustees, amend the by-laws with a two-thirds vote, and protect and promote the Catholic character of the University. It should be added that the Holy Cross religious community has also made a major commitment to having its members and other religious living in university dormitories. See *Current Issues* (Winter 1991), pp. 14–16.

4. *Holy Cross Quarterly* (Spring 1970), pp. 4–10.

5. *National Jesuit News* (December 1991 and November 1992).

6. Charles E. Ford and Edgar L. Roy, Jr., *The Renewal of Catholic Higher Education* (Washington, D.C., 1968), pp. 25–26. See also Gallin, ed., *American Catholic Higher Education*, pp. 71–86.

7. See Alice Gallin, O.S.U., "Sponsorship as Partnership," in *Current Issues* (Winter 1984), pp. 7–11. In 1991 and 1992, the Association of Catholic Colleges and Universities held two successful pilot workshops for teams of trustees from Catholic colleges and universities to provide education and an exchange of views on Catholic issues. Participants, who were to bring this information back to their boards, found the process interesting and, in many cases, altogether new. Similar efforts, along with careful attention to the selection of trustees, would seem imperative.

8. See speech of Paul Reinert, S.J. to College and University Division of the National Catholic Educational Association in 1972 in C&U *Newsletter* (June 1972).

9. J. Patrick Murphy, in a study of five Catholic institutions, found that faculty and staff identified high academic standards, respect and personal care for participants, and outreach to the poor as distinguishing elements of Catholic higher education. They affirmed Catholic identity in these terms, resisted administrative definitions of mission, and endorsed pluralism and academic freedom. *Vision and Values in Catholic Higher Education* (Kansas City, Mo., 1991), pp. 194 ff.

10. Joseph A. O'Hare, "The American Catholic University: Crisis of Identity," in *Readings in Ignatian Higher Education* (Washington, D.C., 1989).

11. "The Jesuits and Catholic Higher Education," *Studies in the Spirituality of Jesuits,* XIII (November 1981), pp. 1–42.

12. Material drawn from personal communication from Father Scanlan (March 5, 1993) and enclosures. Several very small schools have made a similar Catholic option. Thomas Aquinas College in California, Christendom College in Virginia, and Magdalen and Thomas More Colleges in New Hampshire emphasize, in different combinations, orthodox Catholic doctrine, the "Great Books" approach to curriculum, and apostolic formation of students. See an as yet unpublished paper by Mary Jo Weaver, "Self-Consciously Counter-Cultural Alternative Catholic Colleges" (1994).

13. Personal communication from Dr. Pitts (December 1992).

14. Minutes, Purpose and Identity Committee, February 6, 1976; Bernardin, Address at Catholic University of America, November 6, 1985 (privately circulated) and "Catholic Higher Education and the Church's Pastoral Mission," in Gallin, editor, *American Catholic Higher Education,"* pp. 135–152.

15. *Chronicle of Higher Education* (March 26, 1986).

16. "Disciplined Inquiry: A Catholic Reflection on Academic Freedom," in *Current Issues* (Spring 1987), with responses.

17. For a full treatment of this issue see James Heft, S.M., "Academic Freedom and the Catholic University," in John Apczynski, ed., *Theology in the University* (New York, 1987), pp. 207–36.

18. Avery Dulles, S.J., "What is Magisterium?" *Origins* (July 1, 1976).

19. Richard McBrien, "The Pastoral Dimension of Theology Today," *America* (July 28, 1984).

20. See the report "Doctrinal Responsibilities: Procedures for Promoting Cooperation and Resolving Disputes Between Bishops and Theologians," prepared by a joint committee of the Canon Law Society of America and the Catholic Theological Society of America in *Canon Law Society of America Proceedings,* 45 (1983), pp. 261–284.

21. William Shea, "Theologians and Their Catholic Authorities: Reminiscence and Reconnoiter," Presidential Address, College Theology Society, May 31, 1986; Raymond A. Schroth, "Tough Choices on Campus," *Commonweal* (March 28, 1966). See also, from a conservative point of view, Jude P. Dougherty et al., "The Secularization of Western Culture and the Catholic College and University," in *Current Issues* (Summer 1981), pp. 7–23.

22. Timothy Healy, S.J., "The Ignatian Heritage for Today's College," *America* (November 5, 1977).

23. George Higgins, "Forming Prophets of Hope," *Origins* (June 13, 1984).

24. Sr. Kathleen Ashe, "Faculty: Partners in Renewal," *Delta Epsilon Sigma Bulletin,* 23 (May 1978), pp. 39–41.

25. Report of the Council for Partnership in Mission, Gonzaga University (May 29, 1992).

26. Strategic Plan for Georgetown University (August 8, 1992).

27. Robert Lawton, S.J., Address to Faculty, Fall Convocation (October 26, 1993) (typescript).

28. *Ave Maria* (April 16, 1966); on the order's commitment to spiritual formation through pastoral presence, see David Burrell, C.S.C., "Catholic Character of Notre Dame. . . . Remarks for Academic and Faculty Affairs Committee, Board of Trustees, April 30, 1992," kindly made available by Father Burrell.

29. David Lutz, "Can Notre Dame Be Saved?" *First Things* (January 1992), pp. 35–40.

30. Final Report, "Colloquy for the Year 2000," submitted to Board of Trustees (May 7, 1993).

31. Craig Lent, "What is a Great Catholic University: A Comment on the Colloquy for the Year 2000" (April 15, 1992), privately circulated.

32. Report of Task Force on Humanities for Colloquy 2000. I'm grateful to Notre Dame friends for making these documents available to me.

33. Dietrich Reinhart, O.S.B., "Inaugural Address," pamphlet (September 13, 1991).

6. FROM SECULARIZATION TO AMERICANISM

1. "The Catholic Character of the Catholic University," *Origins* (August 6, 1974).

2. William Leahy, S.J., *Adapting to America: Catholics, Jesuits, and Higher Education in the Twentieth Century* (Washington, D.C., 1991), p. 100.

3. Several of these will be cited ahead. For Woodward, see "Catholic Higher Education: What Happened?" in *Commonweal* (April 4, 1993), pp. 15–18. Steinfels presented his views in a Fordham commencement address in June 1992, which has been privately circulated.

4. *New York Times* (May 1, 1991).

5. Gleason's best summary of this argument is in "The American Background of *Ex Corde Ecclesiae*: A Historical Perspective," in *Catholic Universities in Church and Society,* cited above, pp. 1–19, and "American Catholic Higher Education, 1940–1980: The Ideological Context," in George Marsden, ed., *The Secularization of the Academy* (New York, 1992), pp. 234–258. But see also the other Gleason essays cited in chapter 2.

6. C&U *Newsletter* (December 1968).

7. See "Notre Dame's Catholic Character," in *Commonweal* (April 19, 1974), pp. 155–172. I have a copy of the report on "Priorities and Commitments for Excellence," which appeared a few years later.

8. "Catholic Institutions of Higher Learning: Dutiful Yet Free in Church and State," *Current Issues* (Summer 1988), pp. 19–21. Materials on the negotiations and consultation leading to this report are in the papers of the College and University Department of the National Catholic Educational Association at Catholic University.

9. James Tunstead Burtchaell, "The Decline and Fall of the Christian College," *First Things*, I (April 1991), pp. 16–29 and (May 1991), 30–38.

10. Vanderbilt is only one example of this process. One 1890 study showed that 22 of 24 state universities held chapel services in university facilities, and as late as 1939 a majority of state schools took financial responsibility for such services. See Marsden, "The Soul of the American University," *First Things*, I (January 1990), pp. 34–47, and his edited collection of essays cited above.

11. See the Buckley articles cited in Chapter 2. The quotations here come largely from *America* (May 19, 1993).

12. Alice Gallin, O.S.U., "American Church-Related Higher Education: Comparison and Contrast," Paper delivered at Convention of American Historical Association, December 29, 1992.

13. Henry C. Johnson, Jr., "Down from the Mountain: Secularization and the Higher Learning in America," *Review of Politics*, 54 (Fall 1992), pp. 551–588.

14. James Turner, "The Catholic University in Modern Academe: Challenge and Dilemma," paper presented at a conference on "The Storm over the University" at the University of Notre Dame (October 13, 1992).

15. See for example Joseph Komonchak, "Recovering the Great Tradition: In Memoriam Henri deLubac," *Commonweal* (January 31, 1992), pp. 14–17.

16. Robert Imbelli, "Vatican II: Twenty Years Later," *Commonweal* (October 8, 1992), pp. 522–526.

17. William Shea, "Is there a Borderline Between Church and Culture?" Kileen Lecture, St. Norbert's College (September 27, 1990), p. 16. A brief version of this

paper is published as "Catholic Higher Education and the Enlightenment: On Borderlands and Roots" *Horizons*, 20 (Spring 1993), pp. 99–105.

18. John Haughey, S. J., "Theology and the Mission of the Jesuit College and University," *Conversations* (Spring, 1994), pp. 5–21.

19. William M. Shea, "Dual Loyalties in Catholic Theology," *Commonweal* (January 31, 1992), pp. 9–15.

20. Response in *Commonweal* (April 24, 1992), pp. 21–23.

21. Shea, Response in same issue of *Commonweal*.

22. "Religious Pluralism in the State University: Lessons for a Theologian," *Current Issues* (Winter, 1987), pp. 13–17.

23. At times it seems like the whole dispute may revolve around the number of Catholics who live nearby. In Japan, for example, there is simply no question of hiring only Catholics or admitting only Catholic students, or of respecting the diverse values of those who come. Seattle University is a Jesuit school in a part of the country where Catholics are a small minority. President William Sullivan told his faculty that they are trying to bring to life "the Catholic and Jesuit tradition of humanist Christianity" not in isolation but "in the closest possible contact with the culture in which it will be inserted." If the world is a diverse place, as it seems to be, and if the insertion is to be done by graduating students, then Sullivan and Shea suggest that faith and reason should enter into conversation precisely amidst that diversity. Sullivan, "Christian Anthropology and the University: Fall Convocation Address," September 19, 1990.

24. Shea, "Beyond Tolerance: Pluralism and Catholic Higher Education," *Current Issues* (Winter 1989), p. 41, and "Borderline," p. 28.

25. Raymond Schroth, *National Catholic Reporter* (October 3, 1986).

26. Bishop James Malone, "The Catholic University and the Catholic Community" in *Origins* (June 15, 1986), p. 118.

27. Lisa Sowle Cahill, quoted in *New York Times*, May 1, 1991.

7. A CASE STUDY

1. Louis Dupre, "On Being a Christian Teacher of the Humanities," *Christian Century* (April 29, 1992), pp. 452–455.

8. ABORTION

1. This paper was originally delivered as the inaugural lecture as Loyola Professor of Roman Catholic Studies (April 27, 1992).

2. A packet of documentation on such cases has been made available to me by the Association of Catholic Colleges and Universities. See also Lisa Holewa, "Abortion debate issue grips Catholic campuses," *National Catholic Reporter* (May 10, 1991). The most widely publicized, and disturbing, case is at Georgetown University. For an account of events and the text of President Leo J. O'Donovan's open letter explaining that university's decision to recognize a pro-choice discussion group, see *Georgetown*, XXIV (Winter 1992), pp. 11–16. For Cardinal James

Hickey of Washington's response, see the *Washington Standard* (March 5, 1992) and *Origins* (March 22, 1992), pp. 691–692. The *New York Times* for April 25 carried news that Georgetown had reversed its decision and withdrawn space and the $150 funds from "G.U. Choice."

3. Jesuit Association of Student Personnel Administrators, "A Working Paper on Registration of Controversial Student Organizations on Jesuit College Campuses" (August 1991). The paper dealt particularly with gay and lesbian groups and noted that pro-choice groups posed a more difficult moral question. The authors argue that all decisions should focus upon personal concern for students and respect for their views. It is a sign of the Catholic times that this balanced and eminently reasonable paper has aroused Roman anxieties, requiring Jesuit authorities to offer explanations. Later, at a conference sponsored by Foundations and Donors Interested in Catholic Activities, Kevin Duffy, vice president for student affairs at Boston College and a co-author of the paper, reported that people were very nervous about working on it and did not want their names publicly attached to it. There was, he claimed, "tremendous fear" about how they would be treated on their own campus or, in the case of Jesuits, within their Jesuit community.

4. I would not want to suggest that there has been no open discussion of abortion on Catholic campuses. Indeed, there have in fact been some impressive debates, with participation by Catholic dissenters and pro-choice leaders. See, for example, "The Catholic Legacy and Abortion: A Debate," with papers by Daniel C. Maguire and James Tunstead Burtchaell, the papers and exchange produced by a debate at Notre Dame, February 9, 1987, in *Commonweal* (November 20, 1987), pp. 657–680. In 1992, when Boston College students invited the bishops' spokesperson on abortion, Helen Alvarez, to campus, she suggested that they ask Frances Kissling of Catholics for a Free Choice to join her, a striking witness to the need to sustain the pro-life argument amid and not apart from the *de facto* pluralism in society and in the church. I have the impression, interestingly enough, that many of these occasions arose from student initiatives, as they have at Holy Cross. Less visible has been the presence of support and discussion groups, often organized by campus ministries, which have provided forums for discussion and mutual support for supposed dissenters that eases the pressure for formation of controversial organizations.

5. Lawrence Tribe, *A Clash of Absolutes* (Cambridge, 1989).

6. Susan Faludi, *Backlash: The Undeclared War Against American Women* (New York, 1991), chap. 14.

7. Data is taken from *Abortion and Women's Health*, produced by the Alan Gutmacher Institute (New York, 1990) and from the Surgeon General's Report, noted below.

8. Stanley K. Henshaw, "The Accessibility of Abortion Services in the United States," *Family Planning Perspectives*, XXIII (November/December 1991), pp. 246–252.

9. George Gallup, Jr., and Jim Castelli, *The People's Religion: American Faith in the '90s* (Macmillan, 1989), pp. 169–175.

10. See, for example, "In Bitter Abortion Debate, Opponents Learn to Reach for Common Ground," *New York Times* (February 17, 1992).

11. Meg Broadhead of Clark University, assisted by Diane Bell and several other people at Holy Cross, organized a public forum here in 1992 on this subject.

12. Sidney Callahan, "Abortion and the Sexual Agenda: A Case for Pro-Life Feminism," *Commonweal* (April 25, 1986), pp. 232–238; Daniel C. Maguire, "The Catholic Legacy and Abortion: A Debate," *Commonweal* (November 20, 1987), pp. 657–662; Mary C. Segers, "Abortion and the Culture: Toward a Feminist Perspective," in Sidney Callahan and Daniel Callahan, eds., *Abortion: Understanding Differences* (New York, 1984), pp. 203–224.

13. C. Everett Koop to President Reagan, January 9, 1989; "The Surgeon-General's Report: The Public Health Effects of Abortion," documents released under the Freedom of Information Act and later by Representative Ted Weiss, made available courtesy of Paul and Debbie Walker.

14. Mary Ann Glendon, *Abortion and Divorce in Western Europe and the United States* (Cambridge, 1985); Glendon, "Life After Roe: Widening the Discussion," *Church*, 5 (Winter 1989), pp. 5–9; Elise F. Jones et al., "Teenage Pregnancy in Developing Countries," *Family Planning Perspectives*, 17 (March/April 1985), pp. 53–62.

15. Daniel Callahan, "An Ethical Challenge to Prochoice Advocates," *Commonweal* (November 23, 1990), pp. 681–687; Interview with Frances Kissling in *National Catholic Reporter* (February 8, 1991), p. 17.

16. Kristin Luker, "Abortion and the Meaning of Life," in Sidney Callahan and Daniel Callahan, eds., *Abortion: Understanding Differences* (New York, 1984), pp. 25–46 and her *Abortion and the Politics of Motherhood* (Berkeley, 1984).

17. For an example of constructive, if frustrating, conversation seeking a compelling middle ground, see Sidney Callahan and Daniel Callahan, eds., *Abortion: Understanding Differences*, especially the essays of Mary C. Segers, "Abortion and Culture: Toward a Feminist Perspective," pp. 229–252 and Daniel Callahan, "The Abortion Debate: Is Progress Possible?" pp. 309–324.

18. "The Challenge of Peace: God's Promise and Our Response" (Washington, D.C., 1983), p. 42.

19. The contrast is highlighted by Mary C. Segers, "A Consistent Life Ethic: A Feminist Perspective on the Pro-Peace and Pro-Life Activities of the American Catholic Bishops," in Jean Bethke Elshtain and Sheila Tobias, eds., *Women, Militarism and War* (Savage, Md., 1990), pp. 61–84 (reference courtesy of Professor Ann Tickner); Christine E. Gudorf, "To Make a Seamless Garment, Use a Single Piece of Cloth," in Patricia Beattie Jung and Thomas A. Shannon, eds., *Abortion and Catholicism* (New York, 1988), pp. 279–295.

20. It may be that early educational efforts had some effect in increasing opposition to abortion and that things have now begun to swing back. In 1968 an unpublished poll of New York Catholics, commissioned by the bishops, showed that 75 percent of the state's Catholics favored access to abortion in the limit cases; even among those who described themselves as involved in the church, 91 percent of whom knew that the bishops opposed changing New York's anti-abortion law, 61 percent nevertheless favored the change. As one bishop noted, people accepted church teaching on the moral issue, but resented any effort "to impose our will on the electorate." David O'Brien, *Faith and Friendship: Catholicism in the Diocese of Syracuse, 1886–1986* (Syracuse, 1986), p. 450.

21. Gallup and Castelli, *People's Religion*, pp. 160–170; Andrew Greeley, *The Catholic Myth* (New York, 1988), p. 177. Gallup and Castelli believe that the 20 percent Hispanic population, 5–1 against abortion, masks deeper changes; 64

percent of non-Hispanic Catholics agree that the choice of abortion should be left entirely to the woman and her doctor, with only 32 percent disagreeing: "Catholics in Survey Endorse Abortion," *New York Times* (November 11, 1979). See also James R. Kelly, "Abortion: What Americans Really Think, and the Catholic Challenge," *America* (November 2, 1991), pp. 310–316.

22. See John T. Noonan, Jr., "An Almost Absolute Value in History" in John T. Noonan, Jr., ed., *The Morality of Abortion: Legal and Historical Perspectives* (Cambridge, 1970), pp. 1–59. For a full range of Catholic opinions, see Jung and Shannon, *Abortion and Catholicism*, cited above.

23. *National Catholic Reporter* (February 2, 1992).

24. For two examples see Barbara Ferraro, Patricia Hussey with Jane O'Reilly, *No Turning Back: Two Nuns' Battle with the Vatican over Women's Right to Choose* (New York 1990); and Madonna Kolbenschlag, ed., *Authority, Community and Conflict* (Kansas City, 1986), which deals with the treatment of sisters in government offices. Polls show again and again that overwhelming majorities of Catholics dislike the way in which the bishops treat Catholic politicians, who for one reason or another take the position best stated by Governor Mario Cuomo, distinguishing private beliefs from public responsibility. See for example "Polls say Catholics reject Bishops' abortion politicking," *National Catholic Reporter* (November 30, 1990).

25. For one dramatic example, see the lengthy interview with Frances Kissling, executive director of Catholics for a Free Choice in the *National Catholic Reporter* (February 8, 1991).

26. Joseph Cardinal Bernardin, *Consistent Ethic of Life* (Kansas City, 1988).

27. The Political Action Committee JUSTLIFE, formed in 1986, has introduced eight model bills for post-Webster state legislatures. They include informed consent, viability testing, and prohibition of the use of public funds and facilities save in the limit cases, but also coordination of services for pregnant women, parental leave, inclusion of unborn children in AFDC and medicaid, and adoption subsidies. See James R. Kelly, "A Political Challenge to the Prolife Movement," *Commonweal* (November 23, 1990), pp. 692–696.

28. Charles E. Curran, *Catholic Higher Education, Theology and Academic Freedom* (Notre Dame, 1990).

29. The university, "espousing its own set of human values" and "guiding its institutional actions in light of the moral principles it espouses" (Boston College), will deny recognition to organizations that "conflict with a Catholic doctrine or moral issue" (Dayton) and will recognize only organizations "consistent with the University's mission and its Catholic, Jesuit character" (Santa Clara). In the case of Loyola of Chicago's Statement on Student Organization: "Loyola's policy is to encourage discussion of moral issues as part of the educational process. Organized advocacy of a position violating the University's Catholic tradition is not endorsed or funded by the University." Hickey said of Georgetown's group: "This discussion group does not share the clear institutional commitment of Georgetown University to the church's teaching with respect for the humanity of the unborn child."

30. John Paul II, "Apostolic Constitution of the Supreme Pontiff," *Current Issues in Catholic Higher Education*, XI (Winter 1991), p. 33.

31. This subject is discussed in the 1989 report of the Ad Hoc Commission on the Mission of the College, where the work of William Shea is cited. See more recently

Shea's "Dual Loyalties in Catholic Theology," *Commonweal* (January 31, 1992) and criticism and responses in subsequent issues, especially April 24, 1992.

32. Robert Carlson, Letter to the Editor, *New York Times* (January 14, 1992).

33. What I have written here could be repeated on the subject of homosexuality. In December, 1992, Cardinal Pio Laghi of the Vatican Secretariat on Catholic Education responded to Seattle Archbishop Thomas Murphy on the results of his inquiries with Jesuit General Kolvenbach and Seattle University President William Sullivan, S.J. regarding the university's alleged recognition of a "gay rights" group. Such recognition was not "consistent with the identity of the institution," Cardinal Laghi wrote. "In a Catholic University support can be given to Catholic teaching on homosexuality and to Catholic pastoral practice to help homosexual persons." The university's recognition of the group was ambiguous and did not make the Church's position clear. This judgment was passed to Sullivan and other Jesuit Presidents by their superiors. (From materials made privately available.)

9. CATHOLICS AS INTELLECTUALS

1. Newman to George Fottrell, December 10, 1873, in Charles S. Dessain and Thomas Gornell, S.J., eds., *The Letters and Diaries of John Henry Newman*, 26 (Oxford, 1974), p. 394.

2. These quotes are taken from "The Faculty and the Formative Educational Role," in *Current Issues* (Summer 1992), pp. 21–25. The overall argument is made in Monan's Toulouse paper, "The University in the American Experience" (typescript), p. 17.

3. Ronald Anderson, S.J. and Francis X. Clooney, S.J., "Report on the Meeting on Jesuit Scholarship in the Post-Modern Age," June 2 and 3, 1991 (typescript).

4. W. E. B. DuBois, *The Souls of Black Folk* (New York, 1953), pp. 16–17.

5. *New York Review of Books* (June 14, 1984).

6. Nathan Hatch, "The Christian Movement and the Demand for a Theology of the People," *Journal of American History*, 22 (December 1988), p. 547.

7. *Origins* (January 1989), pp. 553–556.

8. Michael J. Boughton, S.J. and Maureen Fuechtmann, unpublished paper presented to AJCU Campus Ministry meeting (September 28, 1987).

9. An early example in C&U *Newsletter* (March 1967). See also *The Hesburgh Papers* (Kansas City, 1979), p. 39.

10. *Critic* (October-November 1961).

11. This report, prepared by Richard Breslin and dated September 30, 1977, is in the papers of the College and University Department of the National Catholic Educational Association, located in the archives of the Catholic University of America.

12. Gleason, "American Background of *Ex Corde Ecclesiae*," p. 9.

13. *National Catholic Reporter* (December 10, 1993).

14. Ray L. Hart, "Religious and Theological Studies in American Higher Education: A Pilot Study," *Journal of the American Academy of Religion*, 54 (Winter 1991), pp. 715–827.

15. "The Soul of the University," *First Things*, 1, p. 44.

16. "Is Theology Academic?" *Sh'ma*, 22 (May 1, 1992), pp. 102-104.

17. See for example Matthew Lamb in *America* (March 26, 1990). I also was privileged to sit in on a meeting of chairs of departments of theology offering graduate degrees held at Boston College, February 12-13, 1993.

18. See the forthcoming essay of John Haughey, S.J., "Theology in Jesuit Colleges and Universities," in *Conversations*, cited above. Also Robert J. Egan, "Who's Doing Catholic Theology?" *America* (March 13, 1992).

19. Hart, "Religious and Theological Studies," pp. 811-813.

20. Turner, "The Catholic University in Modern Academe," p. 19.

21. Michael Lacey, "The Backwardness of American Catholic Intellectual Life," Address to Catholic Theological Society of America (June 12, 1991) (typescript).

22. Kolvenbach, Address at Weston School of Theology (October 8, 1988) (typescript).

23. John Coleman, "A Company of Critics: Jesuits and the Intellectual Life," *Studies in the Spirituality of Jesuits*, 21 (January,1992).

24. "The Jesuit Mission in University Education", p. 36.

25. Coleman, "Company of Critics," p. 41.

26. Joseph Appleyard, S.J. "The Languages We Use: Talking About Religious Experience," *Studies in the Spirituality of Jesuits*, 19 (March, 1987).

27. *Boston College Magazine* (Spring, 1993), pp. 7-9.

28. James Hennessy, S.J., "Catholic Scholarship: Have We Made a Hospitable Home," *Current Issues* (Winter, 1986).

29. These quotes are taken from revised drafts of Catholic Studies proposal kindly made available by John Breslin, S. J.

30. James R. Kelly, "Collegium and the Futures of Catholic Higher Education," *America* (September 15, 1993), pp. 15-18. I sit on the board of this group and participated in its first summer institute.

31. Donald J. Kirby, S.J. et al., *Ambitious Dreams: The Values Program at LeMoyne College* (Kansas City, 1990).

32. Richard Hutchison, "Are Church-Related Colleges Also Christian Colleges?" *Christian Century* (September 28, 1988), pp. 832-41.

33. I was allowed to examine many of the materials of this group at their Washington office, I receive their monthly newsletter, and I learned more about them in a meeting with the president of Gordon College in Hamilton, Mass.

34. Materials made available by Nathan Hatch and Michael Hamilton.

35. "Strengthening Protestant Evangelical Scholarship: Developing a Comprehensive Strategy; A Report to the Pew Charitable Trust" (October 1988).

36. "Rationale for a Liberal Arts Core at Mount Saint Mary's College" (typescript), made available by Professor William Portier.

37. Lee Hardy, "Christian Education and the Postmodern Reconfiguration of Public Space," Review Essay on Stanley Hauerwas and John H. Westerhoff, *Schooling Christians: Holy Experiments in American Education* (Grand Rapids, 1992) pp. 34-37.

38. Mark Schwehn, "The Academic Vocation: 'Specialists without Spirit, Sensualists without Heart,'" *Cross Currents* (Summer 1992), pp. 185-199; *Exiles from Eden: Religion and the Academic Vocation* (New York, 1992).

10. DISCIPLES AND CITIZENS

1. Pedro Arrupe, S.J., *Men for Others* (pamphlet), (Washington, D.C., 1974).

2. Cesar Jerez Garcia, Commencement Address, privately circulated.

3. *Documents of the Thirty-Second General Congregation of the Society of Jesus* (Washington, D.C., 1974).

4. Pope John XXIII, *Pacem in Terris*, para. 153, in David O'Brien and Thomas Shannon, eds., *Renewing the Earth*, pp. 161–162.

5. U.S. Catholic Bishops, *To Teach as Jesus Did* (Washington, D.C, 1976), para. 10.

6. *Catholic Higher Education and the Pastoral Mission of the Church* (Washington, D.C.: United States Catholic Conference, 1980).

7. "Pastoral Constitution on the Church and the Modern World," in Abbott, *Documents*, p. 229.

8. Pope John Paul II, Speech at Hiroshima (February 25, 1981).

9. Jon Sobrino, "The University's Christian Inspiration" (typescript). For a more recent direct application of this challenge to North American higher education, see Dean Brackly, S.J., "The Christian University and Liberation," in *Discovery: Jesuit International Ministries* (December 1992).

10. Avery Dulles, "Faith, Justice and Jesuit Mission" in *Faith/Justice Mission in Higher Education: Theological and Educational Dimensions* (pamphlet) (Washington, D.C., 1990), pp. 19–25.

11. For a review of such programs, see *Current Issues* (Winter 1981).

12. Materials made available by Professor Nyden, February 2, 1993.

13. Loretta Carey, "Report on the Development of Peace Education in U.S. Catholic Colleges and Universities," privately circulated. See also David Johnson, ed., *Justice and Peace Education* (Maryknoll, N.Y., 1975).

14. I have offered comments on education for justice in "The Jesuits and Higher Education," *Studies in the Spirituality of Jesuits,* XIII (November 1981), pp. 1–41, and in an unpublished follow-up essay, "Where Do We Go From Here?" which is available on request.

15. "Justice in the World," para. 51, in O'Brien and Shannon, *Renewing the Earth*, p. 391.

16. *Public Catholicism*, chap. 10.

17. I have discussed the increasingly evangelical character of American Catholicism in an article "Religion and Literacy: An American Historical Perspective," in the *Proceedings* of the College Theology Society for 1982.

18. *The Context of Our Ministries* (Jesuit Conference, 1981) p. 23.

19. Thomas Landy, S.J., "Myths that Shape Us: Jesuit Beliefs About the Value of Institutions," forthcoming in *Studies in the Spirituality of Jesuits.*

20. J. Bryan Hehir, "A Public Church," *Origins,* May 31, 1984, and Speech at Washington National Cathedral, October 3, 1983 (typescript).

21. Derek Bok, "The Social Responsibilities of American Universities," June 6, 1991 (typescript).

22. John Coleman, S. J. "The Two Pedagogies: Discipleship and Citizenship" in Mary C. Boys, ed., *Education for Citizenship and Discipleship* (New York, 1985), pp. 35–78. See also "The Catholic as Citizen," *Commonweal,* September 9, 1983, pp. 457–422.

23. Laurence R. Veysey, *The Emergence of the American University* (Chicago, 1965).

24. David Reisman and Christopher Jencks, *The Academic Revolution* (Garden City, N.Y., 1968).

25. William Leahy, S.J., *Adapting to America: Catholics, Jesuits and Higher Education in the Twentieth Century* (Washington, D.C., 1991), pp. 156–157.

26. Lacey, "Backwardness."

27. Mark Schwehn, *Exiles*, p. 125.

Index